C000225694

GREAT
CARRIER
AIRCRAFT

GREAT CARRIER AIRCRAFT

Blitz Editions

Published by Blitz Editions
an imprint of Bookmart Ltd
Registered Number 2372865
Trading as Bookmart Ltd
Desford Road
Enderby
Leicester LE9 5AD

ISBN: 1-85605-343-1

Material previously published in 1993 as part of the encyclopedia set *Airplane* (Orbis Publishing)

This edition published in 1996

Designed by Brown Packaging Ltd,
255-257 Liverpool Road, London N1 1LX

Printed in Slovakia
60083

CONTENTS

Fairey Swordfish: Taranto Tinfisher

Archaic in appearance even when it first flew, the venerable Swordfish survived as an anachronism throughout World War II, outlived its replacement and destroyed a greater tonnage of enemy shipping than any other Allied torpedo bomber. It was best known for the courageous attack on the Italian fleet at Taranto.

The origins of the Swordfish lay in the Fairey Aviation Company's privately-sponsored tender to Air Ministry Specification S.9/30, which called for a torpedo-carrying fleet spotter in the early 1930s. The TSR I prototype, powered by a 474-kW (635-hp) Bristol Pegasus IIM nine-cylinder air-cooled radial engine, was flown on 21 March 1933 but was soon shown to be underpowered and directionally unstable, being destroyed after failure to recover from a spin some six months later.

A revised Specification, S.15/33, was drafted and Fairey produced the TSR II with lengthened fuselage, revised tail unit and an uprated Pegasus IIIM3 developing 578 kW (775 hp). Its structure was largely of fabric-covered metal with split-axle wheel landing gear capable of replacement by twin single-step Fairey floats. With a maximum sea-level speed of 235 km/h (146 mph) and first flown on 17 April 1934, this aircraft exceeded the specified performance demands and three prototype development aircraft, named Swordfish, were ordered to meet Specification S.38/34; the third aircraft was completed as a floatplane, making its first flight on 10 November 1934.

The first production order for 86 aircraft was placed in 1935 and initial deliveries were made the following February to No. 823 Squadron, which embarked in HMS *Glorious* later that year, replacing Shark Mk IIs. The standard three-seat production aircraft had a maximum speed of 222 km/h (138 mph) and was easily capable of lifting a standard 457-mm (18-in) 731-kg (1,610-lb) torpedo from the decks of all British carriers with full load, its range in this configuration being 879 km (546 miles).

Further orders continued with Fairey until, by the outbreak of war in 1939, a total of 689 Swordfish aircraft had been completed or were on order. Mk I floatplanes were serving with Nos 701, 702 and 705 Catapult Flights of the Fleet Air Arm, being embarked in most of the Royal Navy's battleships, battle-cruisers and cruisers in commission, as well as serving with wheel landing gear in 13 squadrons, of which eight were at sea in the carriers HMS *Ark Royal, Argus, Courageous, Eagle, Furious, Glorious* and *Hermes*.

Swordfish were in action from the earliest days of the war and it was a floatplane flown by Lieutenant Commander W.M.L. Brown from HMS *Warspite* during the Battle of Narvik on 13 April 1940 that was used to direct the fire of the battleship's guns, resulting in the destruction of seven German destroyers, one of which was finished off by a bomb from Brown's aircraft; he also sank with bombs the German submarine *U-64* in Herjangsfjord.

In 1940, as production of the Fairey Fulmar fleet fighter increased at Fairey's Hayes factory, responsibility for the Swordfish was taken over entirely by Blackburn Aircraft Limited at Sherburn-in-Elmet, Yorkshire, the first aircraft being completed on 29 December. After 300 Mk Is had been delivered in nine months, Blackburn production switched to the Mk II with strengthened lower wing, with metal skin to permit the carriage of eight rocket projectiles. The provision for interchangeability of wheel and float landing gear was discarded after

Originally referred to as the Fairey TSR 2, the prototype Swordfish, K4190, was designed and built to Specification S.15/33 and carried the Fairey works no. F2038 in small characters aft of the service serial number on the rear fuselage.

A formation of early Swordfish Mk Is in November 1938 from the second and third production batches; these aircraft had provision for interchangeable wheel and float undercarriage. The aircraft shown here were clearly squadron aircraft, although probably not embarked in a carrier (note absence of fuselage chevron).

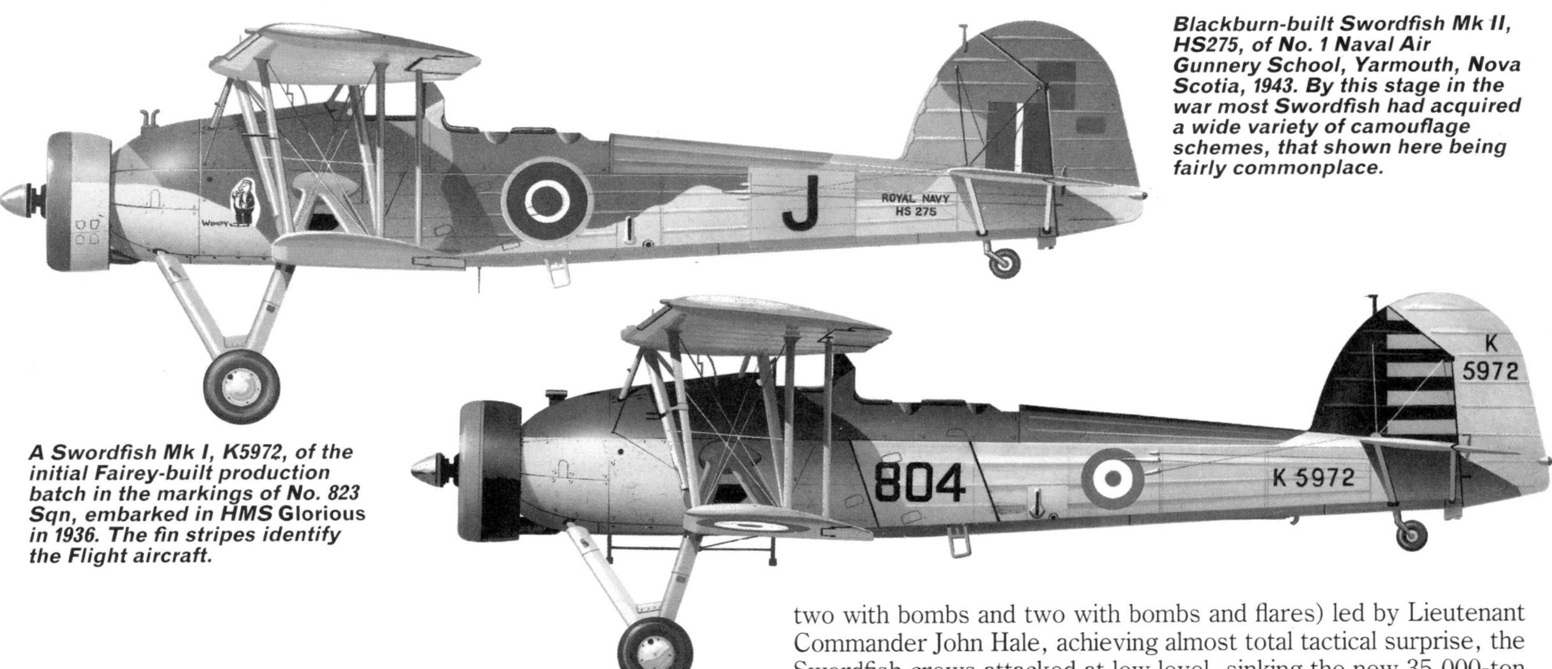

Blackburn-built Swordfish Mk II, HS275, of No. 1 Naval Air Gunnery School, Yarmouth, Nova Scotia, 1943. By this stage in the war most Swordfish had acquired a wide variety of camouflage schemes, that shown here being fairly commonplace.

A Swordfish Mk I, K5972, of the initial Fairey-built production batch in the markings of No. 823 Sqn, embarked in HMS* Glorious *in 1936. The fin stripes identify the Flight aircraft.

termination of the Mk I production.

Mk Is continued in service throughout 1940, and once again it was Lieutenant Commander Brown who provided excellent spotting services for HMS *Warspite*'s main armament in the 'Action off Calabria' against the Italian fleet on 9 July.

Taranto attack

Later that year, however, the brilliantly-executed attack on the Italian fleet in Taranto harbour on 11 November constituted the pinnacle on which the Swordfish's fame was forever to stand. Following a remarkable feat of low-level reconnaissance by a Maryland crew which disclosed a concentration of Italian naval vessels in the port, it was decided to launch a night strike by the Swordfish of Nos 813, 815, 819 and 824 Squadrons from HMS *Illustrious* (Rear Admiral Lumley Lyster, himself an experienced naval pilot who had served at Taranto during World War I). Led by Lieutenant Commander Kenneth Williamson, the first wave of 12 aircraft (six with torpedoes, four with bombs and two with bombs and flares) was launched 10 minutes before a second wave of nine aircraft (five with torpedoes, two with bombs and two with bombs and flares) led by Lieutenant Commander John Hale, achieving almost total tactical surprise, the Swordfish crews attacked at low level, sinking the new 35,000-ton battleship *Littorio* at her moorings, and crippling the two older battleships *Conte di Cavour* and *Caio Duilio*, as well as a heavy cruiser and a destroyer. At a single stroke Italy's naval power in the Mediterranean was reduced by a half, at a cost of two Swordfish (Williamson himself being shot down and taken prisoner). A postscript to this attack lay in the fact that the Japanese naval attaché in Rome was recalled to Tokyo and became the architect of the Japanese attack on Pearl Harbor one year later.

Thereafter, and for many months to come, Fleet Air Arm Swordfish, based on Malta, became the scourge of Axis shipping in the Mediterranean, between them sinking more than a million and a half tons of German and Italian ships during 1941-3. Among their other widely varying tasks in that theatre were minelaying, fleet reconnaissance, gunnery spotting, coastal bombing attacks and even agent-dropping. One Swordfish is recorded as having flown 12 minelaying sorties in a single 24-hour period.

A Swordfish Mk II of the main Blackburn-built production batch. Carrying a smoke float under the starboard wing, this aircraft was typical of the many carrier-based 'Stringbags'.

Super wartime photo of a Swordfish Mk I (P4084) with float undercarriage being launched from a slipway. These aircraft were widely used aboard Royal Navy ships during World War II for reconnaissance and gunnery spotting duties.

The most famous of all Swordfish pilots now joins the story. Lieutenant Commander Eugene Esmonde, a peacetime Imperial Airways pilot from Ireland, and who now commanded a Swordfish squadron aboard HMS *Victorious*, led a torpedo attack by nine aircraft on the German battleship *Bismarck* at large in the Atlantic on 26 May 1941 as she made her way towards Brest. The attack resulted in at least one vital hit, which crippled the vessel's steering mechanism, thereby allowing the British fleet to catch and sink her. Esmonde was awarded the DSO for his part in the operation, and he now joined HMS *Ark Royal* in the Mediterranean; however, when the carrier was torpedoed he managed to fly off all his Swordfish and make for Gibraltar before the ship sank.

By the end of the year Esmonde was stationed in Kent, commanding No. 825 Squadron, deployed to counter any attempt by the German warships *Scharnhorst* and *Gneisenau* to break out of Brest and escape up the English Channel to Germany. On 12 February 1942 the worst British fears were realised when the German ships evaded all patrols and reached the eastern end of the Channel before being spotted. Esmonde's six Swordfish were thus the only aircraft readily available for an initial strike. Flying from Manston, the Swordfish crews missed their fighter rendezvous but pressed home their attack in the face of overwhelming enemy fighter and flak defences. Esmonde, in a Swordfish Mk II (W5984), was himself one of the first to be shot down by a Focke-Wulf Fw 190, followed by all five of his fellow pilots; none of their torpedoes found its mark. Of the 18 crew members only five survived to be rescued from the sea and all received the DSO or CGM. Esmonde was awarded a posthumous Victoria Cross.

Meanwhile efforts had been made to speed a replacement for the now-famous old 'Stringbag' biplane. The Fairey Albacore had been in production for some months but never lived up to its modest expectations (800 were produced, but manufacture stopped in 1943, while that of the Swordfish continued for a further year). The Fairey Barracuda (a Merlin-powered monoplane) for all its grotesque appearance might have had a distinguished career had it not been severely delayed after the abandoning of its original Rolls-Royce Exe engine.

Later Blackfish

As it was, Blackburn continued to produce Swordfish Mk IIs (known locally as 'Blackfish') until 1944, completing the last of 1,080 examples on 22 February that year. Production then switched to the Mk III, which was fitted with a large ASV scanner between the landing gear legs, thereby preventing carriage of the torpedo; when employed on anti-shipping torpedo strikes it was normal practice for one Mk III to assume the search role, while Mk IIs in the strike unit carried bombs and torpedoes. Swordfish were widely used aboard the relatively small escort carriers which were hurriedly introduced for convoy duties, particularly in the North Atlantic in the mid-war years, their normal complement of six Swordfish and six Grumman Martlet fighters being permanently ranged on their steeply pitching decks at the mercy of the elements.

The final version was the Mk IV, retrospectively modified Mk IIs and Mk IIIs with a rudimentary cockpit enclosure, and this version continued in service until the end of the war in Europe. A small number of Swordfish was sent to Canada for operational and training purposes, some serving with No. 1 Naval Air Gunnery School at Yarmouth, Nova Scotia.

The last Mk III (NS204) was completed at Sherburn on 18 August 1944, and it was a Swordfish that flew the Fleet Air Arm's last operational sortie by a biplane on 28 June 1945. By 1967 only six complete Swordfish, of the 2,396 production aircraft built, were known to survive: of these, one (LS326, once registered G-AJVH) has remained in flying condition and still makes frequent visits to air displays throughout Britain with the Royal Navy's Historic Flight, based at RNAS Yeovilton in Somerset.

Fairey Swordfish II cutaway drawing key:

1 Rudder structure
2 Rudder upper hinge
3 Diagonal brace
4 External bracing wires
5 Rudder hinge
6 Elevator control horn
7 Tail navigation light
8 Elevator structure
9 Fixed tab
10 Elevator balance
11 Elevator hinge
12 Starboard tailplane
13 Tailplane struts
14 Lashing down shackle
15 Trestling foot
16 Rear wedge
17 Rudder lower hinge
18 Tailplane adjustment screw
19 Elevator control cable
20 External bracing wires
21 Elevator fixed tab
22 Tailfin structure
23 Bracing wire attachment
24 Aerial stub
25 Bracing wires
26 Port elevator
27 Port tailplane
28 Tailplane support struts
29 Dinghy external release cord
30 Tailwheel oleo shock absorber
31 Non-retractable Dunlop tailwheel
32 Fuselage framework
33 Arrester hook housing
34 Control cable fairleads
35 Dorsal decking
36 Rod aerial
37 Lewis gun stowage trough
38 Aerial
39 Flexible 0.303-in (7.7-mm) Lewis machine gun
40 Fairey high-speed flexible gun mounting
41 Type O-3 compass mounting points
42 Aft cockpit coaming
43 Aft cockpit
44 Lewis drum magazine stowage
45 Radio installation
46 Ballast weights
47 Arrester hook pivot
48 Fuselage lower longeron
49 Arrester hook (part extended)
50 Aileron hinge
51 Fixed tab
52 Starboard upper aileron
53 Rear spar
54 Wing ribs
55 Starboard formation light
56 Starboard navigation light
57 Aileron connect strut
58 Interplane struts
59 Bracing wires
60 Starboard lower aileron
61 Aileron hinge
62 Aileron balance
63 Rear spar
64 Wing ribs
65 Aileron outer hinge
66 Deck-handling/lashing grips
67 Front spar
68 Interplane strut attachments
69 Wing internal diagonal bracing wires
70 Flying wires
71 Wing skinning
72 Additional support wire (fitted when underwing stores carried)
73 Wing fold hinge
74 Inboard interplane struts
75 Stub plane end rib
76 Wing locking handle
77 Stub plane structure
78 Intake slot
79 Side window
80 Catapult spool
81 Drag struts
82 Cockpit sloping floor

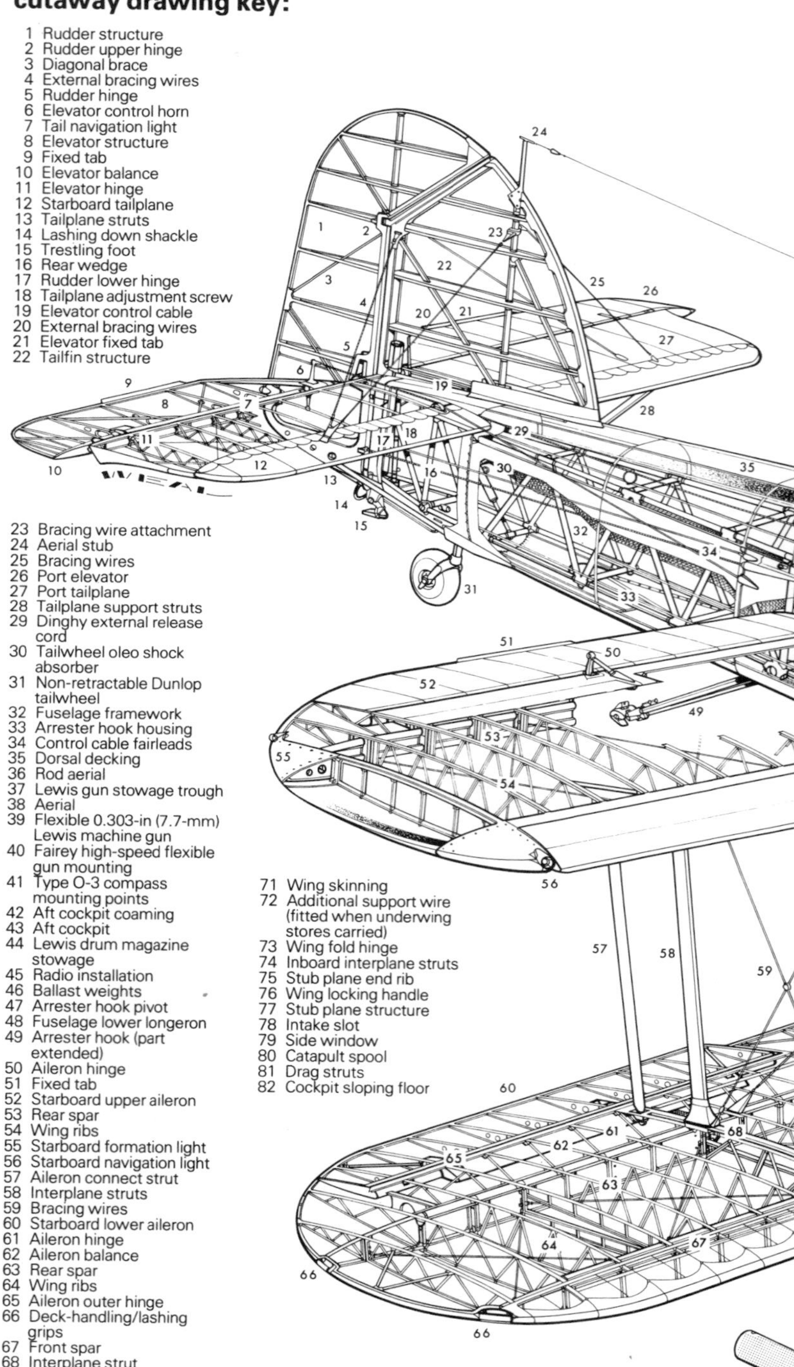

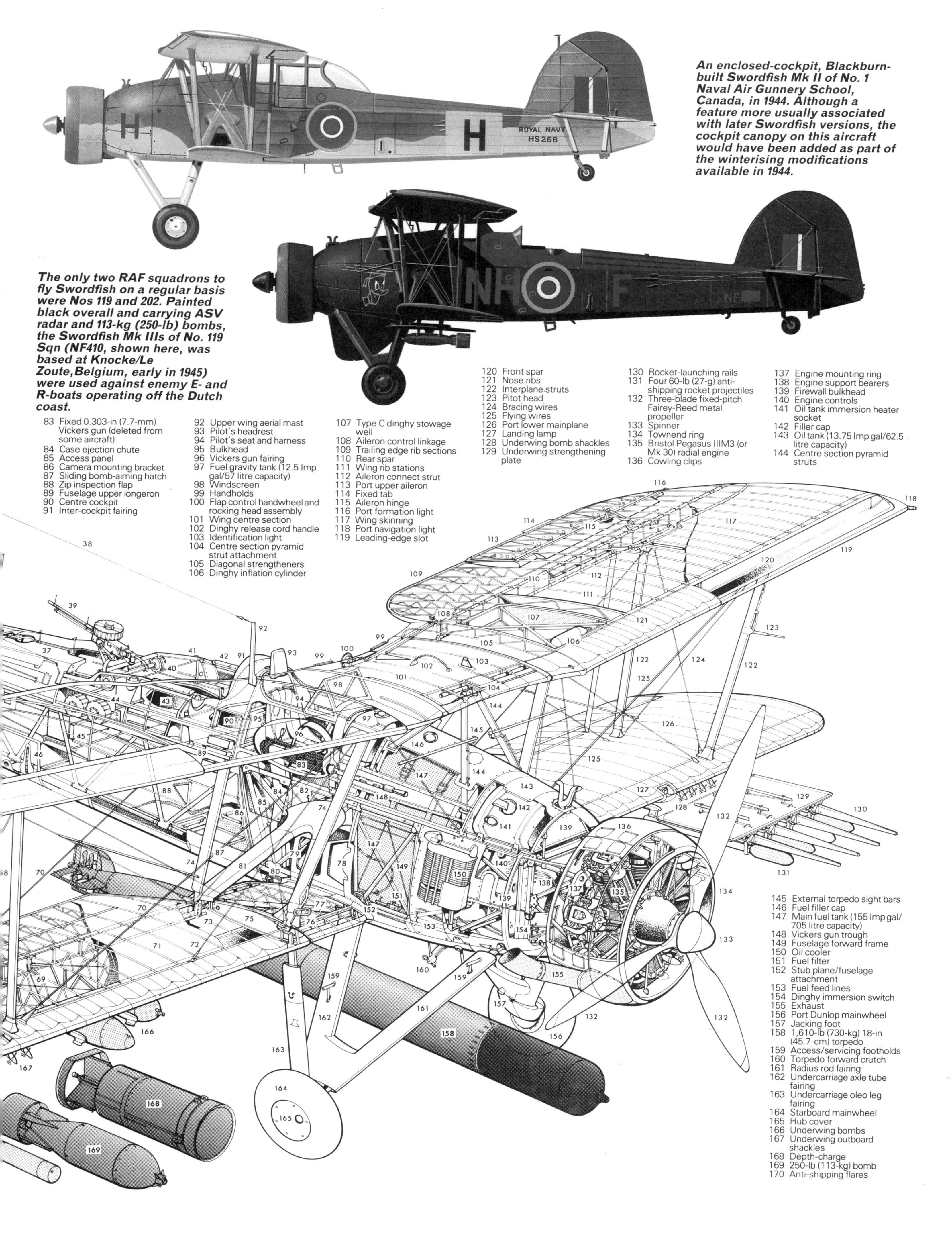

An enclosed-cockpit, Blackburn-built Swordfish Mk II of No. 1 Naval Air Gunnery School, Canada, in 1944. Although a feature more usually associated with later Swordfish versions, the cockpit canopy on this aircraft would have been added as part of the winterising modifications available in 1944.

The only two RAF squadrons to fly Swordfish on a regular basis were Nos 119 and 202. Painted black overall and carrying ASV radar and 113-kg (250-lb) bombs, the Swordfish Mk IIIs of No. 119 Sqn (NF410, shown here, was based at Knocke/Le Zoute, Belgium, early in 1945) were used against enemy E- and R-boats operating off the Dutch coast.

Fairey Swordfish

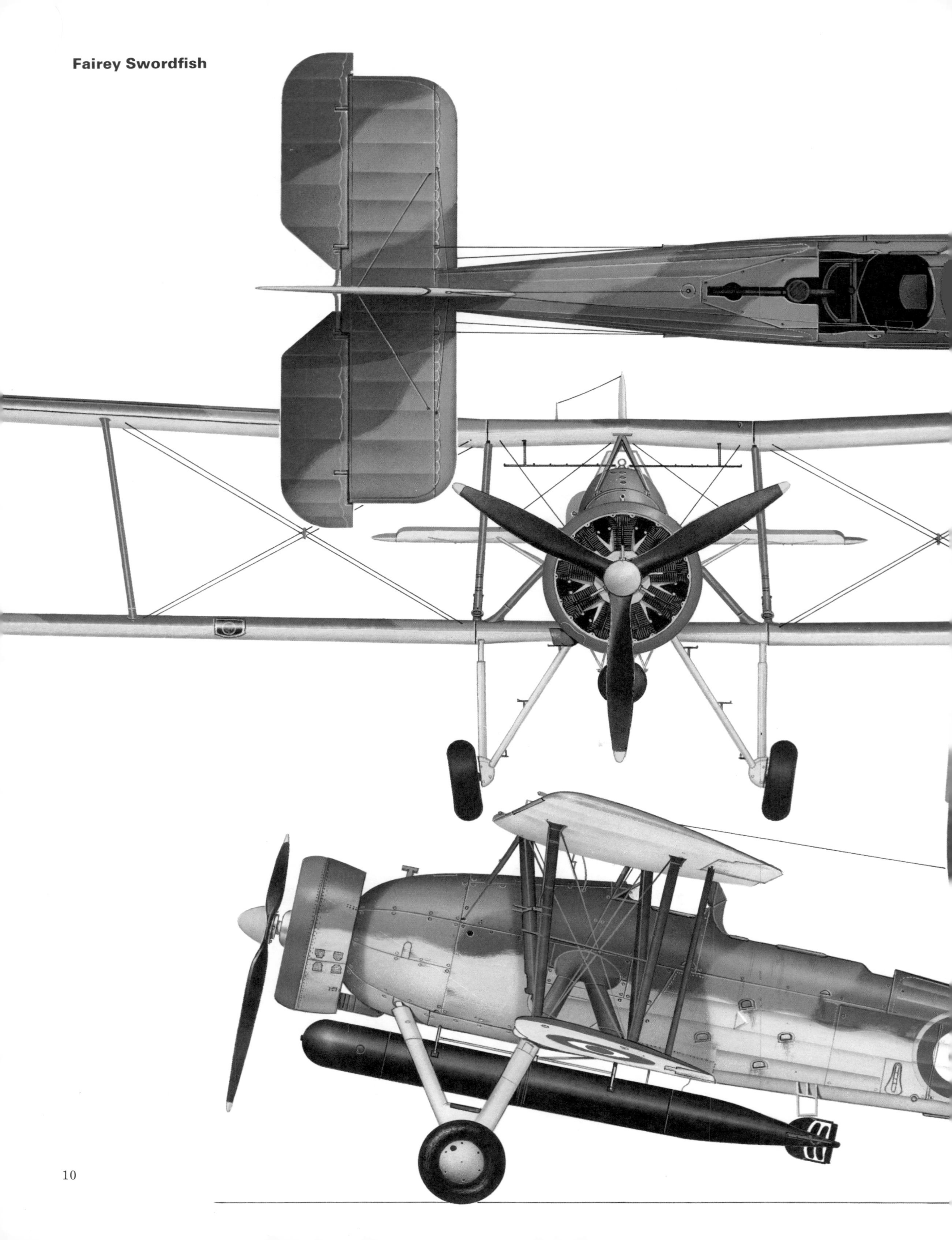

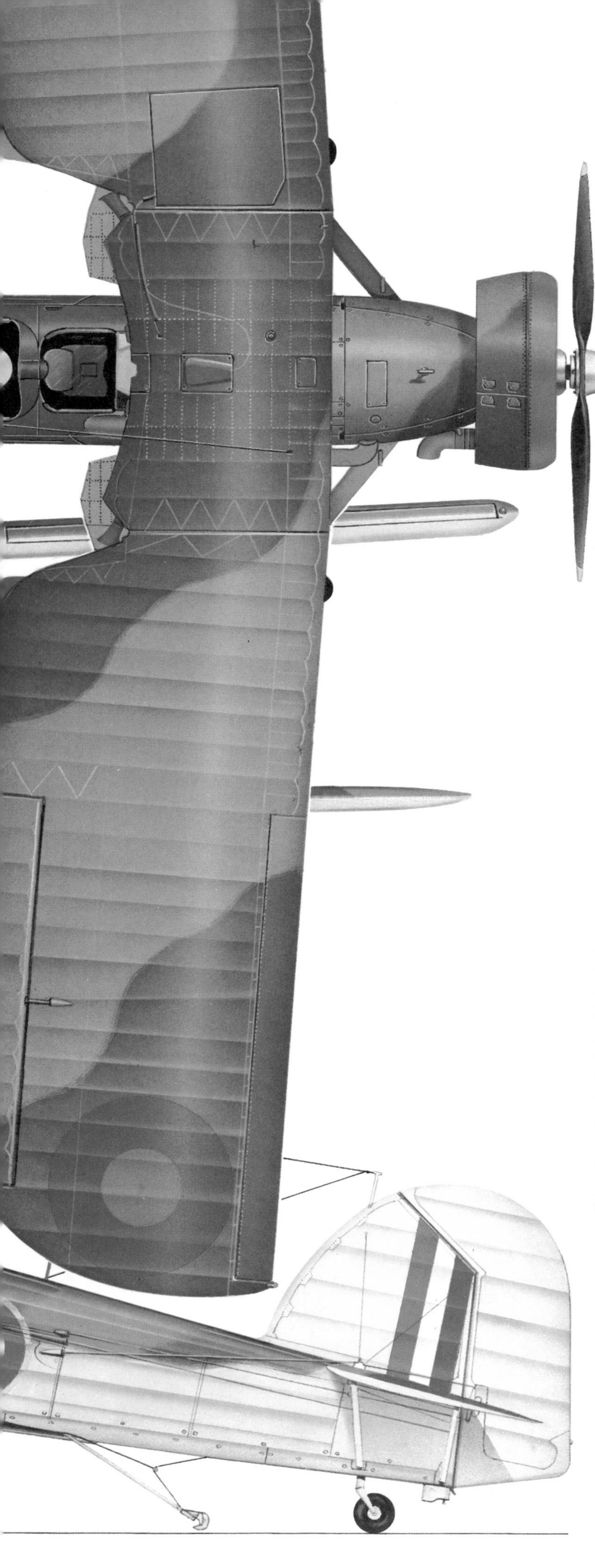

Although fairly anonymous in being bare of serial number, Royal Navy ship and squadron markings, this Swordfish is shown in a colour scheme typical of around 1940-1 (the period of the Battle of Taranto) and is carrying a standard naval 457-mm (18-in) torpedo. The horizontal bar suspended from the top wing centre section, visible in the front view, is the aim-off sight, used for attacks on ships, and the emergency dinghy stowage was located in the top wing immediately outboard of the wing-fold; the rear Lewis gun is shown in the stowed position.

Specification

Fairey Swordfish Mk II

Type: two/three-seat deck-landing or float-equipped torpedo-carrying naval aircraft

Powerplant: one 560-kW (750-hp) Bristol Pegasus 30 radial piston engine

Performance: maximum speed 222 km/h (138 mph); climb to 1525 m (5,000 ft) in 10 minutes 0 seconds; service ceiling 3260 m (10,700 ft); range without weapons 1658 km (1,030 miles), with torpedo 885 km (550 miles)

Weights: empty 2359 kg (5,200 lb); maximum take-off 4196 kg (9,250 lb)

Dimensions: span 13.92 m (45 ft 6 in); length 11.12 m (36 ft 4 in); height 3.93 m (12 ft 10 in); wing area 56.39 m^2 (607 sq ft)

Armament: one fixed forward-firing 7.7-mm (0.303-in) Vickers machine-gun and one flexible 7.7-mm (0.303-in) Vickers 'K' or Browning machine-gun in rear cockpit, plus provision for one 457-mm (18-in) 731-kg (1,610-lb) torpedo, or 681-kg (1,500-lb) mine or bombs under the fuselage, or up to eight 76.2-mm (3-in) 27-kg (60-lb) rockets or four 113-kg (250-lb) bombs under wings

Fairey Swordfish variants

Fairey TSR I: one prototype to Specification S.9/30; Pegasus IIM of 474 kW (635 hp); crashed from spin and destroyed
Fairey TSR II: one prototype (K4190) to Specification S.15/33; Pegasus IIIM3 of 578 kW (775 hp); first flight 17 April 1934
Fairey Swordfish Mk I: to Specification S.38/34, and powered by Pegasus IIIM3 of 515 kW (690 hp) (three prototypes, K5660-K5662, K5662 being completed as floatplane)
Fairey Swordfish Mk I: Fairey production 1935-40, with Pegasus IIIM3; all convertible to floatplanes; K,L and P serials (689 built)
Fairey Swordfish Mk I: Blackburn production 1940-1; aircraft as Fairey-built Mk Is; V serials (300 built)
Fairey Swordfish Mk II: Blackburn production 1941-4, with Pegasus 30 of 560 kW (750 hp); wheel landing gear only and metal-covered lower wings; W, DK, HS, LS, NE and NF serials (1,080 built, some later converted to Swordfish Mk IV with enclosed cockpit)
Fairey Swordfish Mk III: Blackburn production 1944, with Pegasus 30; wheel landing gear only; ASV radar (most aircraft with provision for rocket projectiles); FF, NF, NR and NS serials (327 built, many converted to Swordfish Mk IV with enclosed cockpit)
Fairey Swordfish Mk IV: conversions from Mks II and III with enclosed cockpit

Grumman F9F

The Grumman F9F family was one of the leading examples of post-war fighter design. A confluence of circumstance provided both the engine and the aerodynamic know-how to build first the Panther and then the Cougar, which both proved their worth over Korea and beyond.

Thanks to the availability of an outstanding British engine, the Grumman F9F was created with speed and assurance, and it fully met the US Navy's extremely demanding requirements for long-range carrier operation at a time when no jet carrier experience existed outside the UK. Yet, while the British naval staff fumbled and hesitated, so that not a single Fleet Air Arm jet went to Korea, the F9F flew 78,000 combat missions in that conflict. The family was continuously extended by improved versions, until no fewer than 3,188 had been delivered.

Curiously, the family was launched by the May 1945 decision of the US Navy Fighter Branch in the Bureau of Aeronautics to draw up a requirement for a radar-equipped all-weather and night fighter to operate from carriers. Grumman Aircraft Engineering Corporation, of Bethpage, Long Island, NY, was one of the four finalists announced on 3 April 1946. Eight days later Grumman received a contract for its G-75 submission as the XF9F-1, but the proposal remained in a state of flux. Side-by-side seats changed to tandem, and after agonising doubts the powerplant chosen was the Westinghouse 19B (J30) small axial turbojet, four in the thickened wing roots. But Grumman had already seen the difficulties of fitting its big F7F Tigercat on to carriers, and the big (16.92-m/55-ft 6-in span) jet was likely to prove even more of a handful. Grumman saw a future of problems, delays, small production and the loss of its proud position as the leading supplier of fighters to the US Navy.

After plain talking through the summer, the company and US Navy horse-traded the XF9F-1 for a simpler day-fighter, the XF9F-2. Grumman prepared a series of totally new projects designated G-79, and in August 1946 the US Navy picked the G-79D, to be powered by a single large centrifugal turbojet fed by wing-root inlets. Later this design got a short jetpipe with the nozzle about halfway between the wing and tail, in some ways reminiscent of the Mikoyan-Gurevich MiG-15 which was being designed at the same time. Moreover the engines were the same, because by August 1946 the US Navy had become very interested in the Rolls-Royce Nene which gave 22.24 kN (5,000 lb) thrust for a weight of only 771 kg (1,700 lb).

John Herriott quickly brought two Nenes from the Barnoldswick works to the Philadelphia Navy Yard, where in December 1946 they sailed through the very severe type test schedule with ease. The US Navy was elated; no jet had ever succeeded in passing the test. An option on a Nene licence had been acquired by Phil Taylor, former chief engineer of Curtiss-Wright, and he collected almost $1 million on turning over the rights to the US Navy engine contractor, Pratt & Whitney. Though many of the dour and cautious executives at the Hartford company were suspicious of the import from the UK, they saw good business, and quickly the Nene became known in the USA as 'the Needle Engine', spurring American design teams to beat it. Allison responded and worked hard at their own Whittle-derived J33, pushing up its thrust from 17.79 to 20.46 kN (4,000 to 4,600 lb). Pratt & Whitney redesigned the details of the Nene to turn it into the Americanised J42, initially matched to the XF9F-2.

To preserve competition the US Navy finally settled on J42 power for the first and third XF9F-2s and J33 power for the second aircraft. BuAer numbers were 122475 to 122477, so the Allison prototype, later designated XF9F-3, was 122476. In most essentials the XF9F was straightforward. The fuselage was extremely large, giving plenty of room for a sealed plenum chamber around the 1.26-m (49.5-in) diameter engine and also providing room for two enormous fuel tanks which provided roughly twice as much fuel as in the Nene-engined Sea Hawk that had yet to be developed at Armstrong Whitworth from the Hawker P.1040. Downstream of the diagonal inlet ducts the inboard wing turned into a giant fillet, with split flaps going round under the fuselage. Ahead of them, under the pressurised cockpit with its early ejection seat, were perforated speed brakes driven to 75°. The centre-section, with inward-retracting main gears, was very short. The long unswept outer panels had a thick-

In the 1960s and early 1970s the Grumman TF-9J (formerly the F9F-8T) fulfilled the role that subsequently became the responsibility of the McDonnell Douglas TA-4 Skyhawk and now the same company's T-45 Goshawk, namely that of naval pilot carrier training. The TF-9J was a most popular aircraft, used in large numbers, as 400 were built. Note the broad flaps partially depressed, with sections visible under the fuselage, a pointer to the type's good handling characteristics.

Long since decommissioned, VF-781 was one of the US Navy fighter squadrons which fought in Korea, this standard F9F-2 being one of its aircraft. There may not appear to be much room in the fuselage except for the large cockpit and centrifugal engine, but in fact fuselage fuel was roughly double that of the similarly powered Sea Hawk.

Not only the chrome-yellow paint but also the row of special communications (VHF/UHF) blade aerials under the nose identify this Panther as an F9F-2 rebuilt as an F9F-2KD target drone. This particular machine served with a missile research unit, possibly at the Naval Ordnance Test Station at China Lake.

ness/chord ratio of 12 per cent, powered 19° droop leading edges, plain slotted flaps and hydraulically boosted ailerons. On each tip was a fixed tank of 454-litre (120-US gal) capacity. The nose could be pulled on dollies for access to the radio and armament of four 20-mm M3 cannon, while the complete rear fuselage could likewise be dollied out to permit an engine change. When the landing gear was selected down, a hydraulic tail-bumper (skid) extended under the jet nozzle while the long sting-type hook was extended horizontally from its box under the jetpipe until when fully out it could fall down to trail on its pivots.

By mid-1947 Pratt & Whitney were still rapidly organising J42 production, but Grumman received two Nenes in July and one of these was installed in the first XF9F-2. This machine, unpainted and with a panther painted on its probe-equipped nose, was rolled out without guns or tiptanks in mid-November 1947, and made a 'hop' during taxiing trials on 21 November. Three days later engineering test pilot Corwin H. 'Corky' Meyer made an excellent first flight. Because of doubts about braking capacity he made the first landing on the incomplete, but very long, first runway at Idlewild, the vast new airport then being built for New York. Having stopped in a short distance in the barren wastes of the new airport, Meyer then opened up the Nene and returned to Bethpage.

Trials and tribulations

The modifications needed were mostly small, though there was persistent difficulty with snaking (small oscillation of the nose to left and right) which was never eliminated even in the later production machines. The tiptanks, tested from February 1948, actually enhanced the rate of roll instead of reducing it, though roll was never very good and with hydraulic boost inoperative the stick forces were excessive. The second prototype, with one of the first J42 engines, flew in March 1948, and the first of the Allison-engined F9F-3s followed on 16 August 1948. Preliminary US Navy trials at Patuxent River began in October 1948, these being interrupted by the loss of the first aircraft but resumed in November with the first production machine, which was painted midnight blue. The basic soundness of the Panther was marred by many difficulties with both the J42 and J33 engines, by poor stability and control in many regimes, and by the fast landing which on at least two occasions resulted in the hook pulling the tail off. Later a shiny unpainted aircraft was mated to a midnight-blue rear fuselage and tail, the combination inevitably gaining fame as *The Blue-Tail Fly*.

Final carrier trials took place aboard the USS *Franklin D. Roosevelt* in March 1949, and deliveries of the F9F-2 to US Navy fighter squadron VF-51 began on 8 May. In July 1950 this was the first naval jet unit to go into action, over Korea. Allison supplied J33-8 engines for 54 of a planned 71 F9F-3s, but these engines suffered repeated bearing failures and from February 1950 the aircraft were re-engined with the J42, becoming F9F-2s. Total production of the F9F-2, in successive blocks introducing minor improvements, amounted to 567, not including the 54 converted F9F-3s. The vertical tail was slightly enlarged, baffles added in the fuselage tanks to reduce sloshing of the fuel, and in the penultimate block underwing racks were added for two 454-kg (1,000-lb) bombs and six 127-mm (5-in) HVARs (high-velocity aircraft rockets), which were needed for Korea. The attack aircraft was designated F9F-2B, but eventually almost all were retrofitted for attack weapons and the 'B' suffix was deleted.

One of the first air-to-air photographs ever taken of a Panther with tip tanks, this picture shows the first prototype on test off Long Island in February 1948. The perforated airbrakes are open to assist test pilot Meyer to hold station on the piston-engined photo aircraft. Both prototypes had the black panther motif.

The fifth production Panther, BuAer no. 122564 was originally fitted with the Allison J33-A-8 engine and designated F9F-3 as illustrated. But recurring failures led to 54 F9F-3s being converted to F9F-2 standard.

The F9F-5P was an extremely successful unarmed photo-reconnaissance Panther which led to the swept-wing F9F-6P and F9F-8P Cougars. In this view the camera bay can be seen clearly, as well as the large fence added outboard of the inlets on the J48-P-5 to reduce stalling speed (albeit with loss in warning) in the landing configuration.

Allison proposed to substitute a new and very powerful engine, the J33-A-16 with major redesign and water injection to give wet take-off thrust of 30.91 kN (6,950 lb). The first 73 F9F-4s with this American engine were included in the 1949 budget, but though one aircraft (converted F9F-2 no. 123084) did fly with the J33-A-16 engine as the XF9F-4, it was the only one with this problem-ridden engine. Allison kept eliminating the snags, and eventually got into production in the era of the swept-wing Cougar. Meanwhile, their competition spurred Pratt & Whitney to keep improving the J42, and the obvious thing to do was go along with Rolls-Royce. Though there was no British market for the Nene apart from a small run of naval Attackers and Sea Hawks, Rolls-Royce continued development of this world-beating engine to give much greater thrust as the Tay. This was put to no use whatever in the UK, though it was reliable and gave far more thrust than anything else available in the late 1940s, but it was eagerly snapped up by Rolls-Royce licensees including Pratt & Whitney, which Americanised it as the J48. (Pratt & Whitney even developed a big afterburner for it, but this was not used on F9Fs.)

This fine engine was further boosted by water/alcohol injection from a 95-litre (25-US gal) tank at the base of the fin, and provided a welcome boost in all-round performance and agility. The resulting Panther, the F9F-5, was the most important of the straight-wing versions. The XF9F-5 prototype (123085) flew as early as 21

This Panther, BuAer no. 123713, was the last aircraft in one of the big blocks of the initial production model, the F9F-2. It is a standard aircraft seen over South Korea in 1951 in service with US Navy squadron VF-721. Together with the F2H, the straight-wing F9F carried the Navy day fighter burden in that war.

Grumman F9F-8 (F-9J) Cougar cutaway drawing key

1 Flight refuelling probe
2 Deck barricade deflector
3 Cannon muzzles
4 Gun ranging radar antenna (AN/APG-30A)
5 D/F loop aerial
6 D/F transmitter/receiver
7 Battery
8 Voltage regulators
9 Cannon barrels
10 UHF homing adapter antenna
11 Antenna housing
12 Cannon recoil spring
13 M-3 20-mm cannon (four)
14 Nose cone withdrawal rail
15 Inboard gun ammunition tanks (190 rpg)
16 Ammunition feed chutes
17 Outboard gun ammunition tanks (190 rpg)
18 Armoured cockpit front pressure bulkhead
19 Nose undercarriage leg strut
20 Shimmy damper
21 Nosewheel
22 Torque scissor links
23 Nosewheel doors
24 VHF aerial on starboard nosewheel door
25 Alternators
26 Nosewheel bay
27 Cockpit floor level
28 Rudder pedals
29 Ejection seat footrests
30 Control column
31 Instrument panel
32 Instrument panel shroud
33 Bullet proof windscreen
34 Radar gunsight (Aero 5D-1)
35 Starboard side console panel
36 Pilot's ejection seat
37 Engine throttle control
38 Retractable boarding step
39 Perforated ventral airbrake (port and starboard)
40 Airbrake hydraulic jack
41 Kick-in boarding steps
42 Boundary layer splitter plate
43 Port air intake
44 Cockpit port side console panel
45 Pressurization and air conditioning valves
46 Cockpit rear pressure bulkhead
47 Safety harness
48 Face blind firing handle
49 Sliding canopy rail
50 Cockpit canopy cover
51 Ejection seat launch rails
52 Pilot's back armour
53 Canopy external latch
54 Oxygen bottle
55 Equipment bay access door
56 Forward fuselage fuel tank
57 Fuselage frame and stringer construction
58 Main longeron
59 Canopy aft glazing
60 Sliding canopy jack
61 Wing-fold spar hinge joint
62 Wing-fold hydraulic jack
63 Fuel filler cap
64 Starboard wing fence
65 Wing main fuel tanks (total internal capacity 1,063 US gal/4024 litres)
66 Leading edge integral fuel tank
67 Starboard navigation light
68 Wing tip fairing
69 Starboard wing folded position
70 Fixed portion of trailing edge
71 Lateral control spoilers divided lengthwise between 'flaperons' (forward) and 'flaperettes' (aft)
72 Starboard flap
73 Spoiler hinge control links
74 Spoiler hydraulic jack
75 Rear spar hinge joint
76 Fuselage skin plating
77 Wing spar/fuselage main frame
78 Fuel system piping
79 Fuel filler caps
80 Fuselage rear fuel tank
81 Control cable ducts
82 Rear spar/fuselage main frame
83 Engine accessory compartment
84 Compressor intake screen
85 Supplementary air intake doors (open)
86 Pratt & Whitney J48-P-8A centrifugal-flow turbojet
87 Rear fuselage break point (engine removal)
88 Engine mounting main frame
89 Engine flame cans
90 Secondary air intake door, open
91 Fireproof bulkhead
92 Jet pipe heat shroud
93 Water injection tank
94 Water filler cap
95 Fuselage/fin root frame construction
96 Fin attachment joint
97 Tailfin construction
98 Starboard tailplane
99 Starboard elevator
100 Fin tip VHF aerial
101 Rudder construction
102 Rudder mass balance
103 Fin/tailplane fairing
104 Tail navigation lights
105 Lower rudder segment trim tab
106 Elevator trim tab
107 Port elevator
108 Elevator horn balance
109 Port tailplane construction
110 Trimming tailplane hinge joint

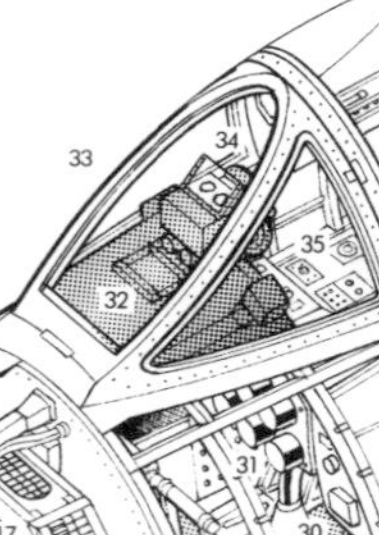

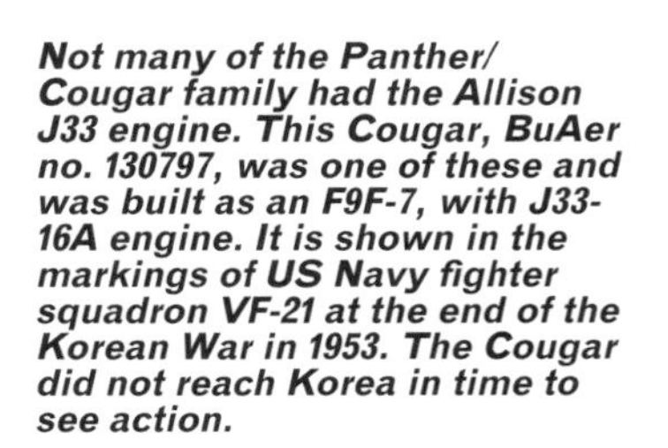

Not many of the Panther/ Cougar family had the Allison J33 engine. This Cougar, BuAer no. 130797, was one of these and was built as an F9F-7, with J33-16A engine. It is shown in the markings of US Navy fighter squadron VF-21 at the end of the Korean War in 1953. The Cougar did not reach Korea in time to see action.

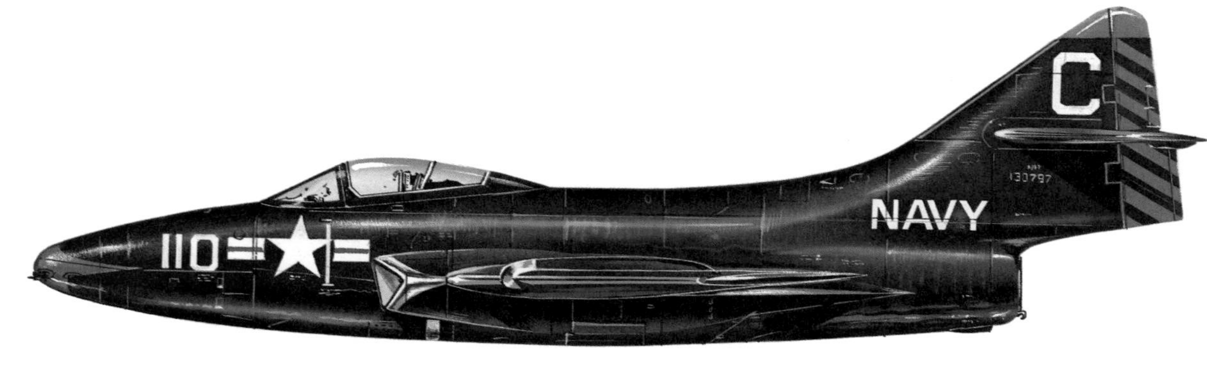

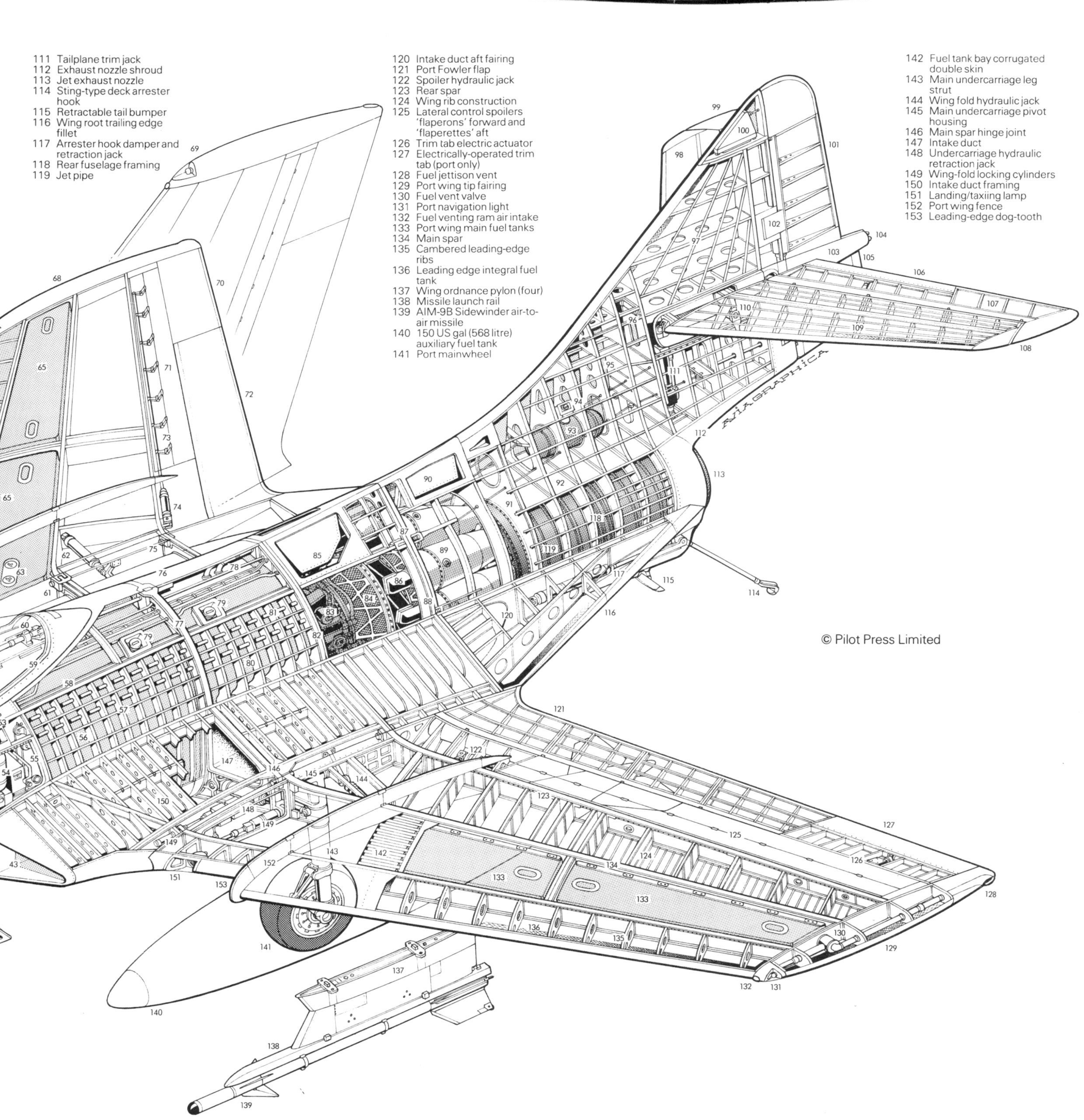

111 Tailplane trim jack
112 Exhaust nozzle shroud
113 Jet exhaust nozzle
114 Sting-type deck arrester hook
115 Retractable tail bumper
116 Wing root trailing edge fillet
117 Arrester hook damper and retraction jack
118 Rear fuselage framing
119 Jet pipe
120 Intake duct aft fairing
121 Port Fowler flap
122 Spoiler hydraulic jack
123 Rear spar
124 Wing rib construction
125 Lateral control spoilers 'flaperons' forward and 'flaperettes' aft
126 Trim tab electric actuator
127 Electrically-operated trim tab (port only)
128 Fuel jettison vent
129 Port wing tip fairing
130 Fuel vent valve
131 Port navigation light
132 Fuel venting ram air intake
133 Port wing main fuel tanks
134 Main spar
135 Cambered leading-edge ribs
136 Leading edge integral fuel tank
137 Wing ordnance pylon (four)
138 Missile launch rail
139 AIM-9B Sidewinder air-to-air missile
140 150 US gal (568 litre) auxiliary fuel tank
141 Port mainwheel
142 Fuel tank bay corrugated double skin
143 Main undercarriage leg strut
144 Wing fold hydraulic jack
145 Main undercarriage pivot housing
146 Main spar hinge joint
147 Intake duct
148 Undercarriage hydraulic retraction jack
149 Wing-fold locking cylinders
150 Intake duct framing
151 Landing/taxiing lamp
152 Port wing fence
153 Leading-edge dog-tooth

Very much the best of all F9F fighter versions, the F9F-8 (this is BuAer no. 141140) had all the aerodynamic changes needed to make full use of the power of the tough J48-P-8A engine, perhaps the last to have descended directly from Whittle. It has all six pylons, for tanks and four Sidewinders.

This photograph emphasises the broad and stubby wing of the final production model, the F9F-8, with a giant fillet at the trailing edge. This aircraft is an unarmed F9F-8P photo-reconnaissance machine with tandem camera installations in a lengthened nose more capacious than that of the previous F9F-5P.

December 1949, and it introduced a longer fuselage ahead of the wing spar to increase internal fuel to 2888 litres (763 US gal) and a corresponding further increase in the height of the vertical tail. Development went well, though stall fences had to be added, but production had to await termination of F9F-2 contracts in August 1951. By this time over 300 Panthers were in Korea, on board US Navy carriers and on US Marine airstrips, and though it was to remain an infrequent event the commander of VF-111 'Sundowners' had shot down a MiG-15 on 9 November 1950. The Korean War continued to demand massive (by so-called peacetime standards) orders, and 595 of the new F9F-5 model were delivered, as well as 109 aircraft ordered as Allison-engined F9F-4s. In addition there were 36 unarmed F9F-5P photo-reconnaissance Panthers, with G-3 autopilot, making a total of this series of 740.

From Panther to Cougar

Panthers continued in service until 1958, by which time many of the earlier machines had been converted as F9F-2KD and F9F-5KD drone targets, or F9F-2D and F9F-5D drone control aircraft, used in such missile programmes as Sidewinder, Sparrow, Regulus I and II, Rigel, Oriole and Triton. Captain 'Winkle' Brown from the Royal Navy used an F9F-5 to make the first tests on simulated angled decks, and later (1952) the breathtaking shots with the UK's new steam catapult from HMS *Perseus* while anchored at Philadelphia. Several aircraft were fitted with British inflight-refuelling probes, convincing the US Navy and US Marines that this was the way to go, and one F9F-4 (125156) in 1954 became the first aircraft to be fitted with blown flaps, then called the Attinello flap. Hundreds were refurbished as advanced trainers, and one batch of F9F-2s was reconditioned in 1966 as fighters for the Argentinian navy. From 1962 the designation was F-9, the drones being the DF-9B (F9F-2) and DF-9E.

Leroy Grumman, executive vice-president Bill Schwendler, and the men most directly concerned with F9F development, Dick Hutton and Robert Hall, had by no means been unaware of German swept-wing research, and had begun swept-wing F9F studies in December 1945. Perhaps wisely, they stuck to straight wings for carrier operation, even though the US Navy had requested data for a swept version at the time of the first F9F contract in September 1946. But by 1948 the US Navy had contracted for the all-swept McDonnell F3H Demon and tailless-delta Douglas F4D, both for carrier operation, and Grumman became restless. In March 1950 the company made a formal proposal for a swept-wing Panther, the G-93, and with the threat of the MiG-15 in action there could hardly be a refusal. In fact Grumman looked hard at completely new designs, and (leaving aside the swing-wing XF10F Jaguar) later built the beautiful F9F-9 Tiger which had nothing in common with the F9F family but the designation. Eventually it was judged that a swept Panther was the best bet for speedy results and a continued successful programme, even though the Whittle-derived centrifugal engines were beginning to be a little *passé* and the basic F9F was also becoming somewhat dated.

Grumman got a contract on 2 March 1951 for three prototypes, not unnaturally designated XF9F-6, with BuAer numbers 126670 to 126672. The first, with a giant striped nose probe, was flown on 20 September 1951 and was sufficiently different from the straight-wing fighter to merit its new name, Cougar. In fact, not much apart from the forward fuselage was retained, and the tunnel programme was actually greater than that for the original G-79 design.

A successful progression

The wing had a ruling sweepback of 35° and considerably greater chord than before, resulting in an area increase of more than 40 per cent. The main spar frames in the fuselage had to be moved forward until they were touching the cockpit rear pressure bulkhead. The leading edge was fitted with full-span slats extending inboard as far as the large forwards extension accommodating the redesigned inlet ducts. The trailing edge was fitted with full-span slotted flaps, lateral control being by outboard spoilers which in fact worked better than the previous rather unsatisfactory ailerons. There were no tiptanks. Inboard, the trailing-edge fillet on the fixed centre-section was

Taken in August 1958, this striking vertical photograph – possibly taken by an F9F-8P – shows four F9F-8B Cougars of Navy fighter squadron VF-81 over the Atlantic. The wing root fillets look grotesquely large in this final version of the US Navy's most important carrier-based fighter of the 15 years following World War II.

The subject of this profile was an F9F-8 Cougar, identifiable by the large nose blister and redesigned wing. All Cougars had the modified vertical tail, but the extended chord of the lower rudder was introduced in the course of production. Today's 'Jolly Rogers' Navy fighter squadron is of course VF-84.

Several paint schemes were used for the remotely piloted Panther and Cougar conversions, this QF-9J of the 1969-70 period having a more unusual one. This particular aircraft was built as the second in the final block of F9F-8s and became an F9F-8B for four years before conversion to QF-9J standard.

greatly increased in size. The tail was made thinner yet stronger, with a swept tailplane carrying narrow-chord powered elevators. The engine was the J48-8, with water/alcohol injection for a take-off rating of 32.25 kN (7,250 lb).

A growing test team worked under pressure to rectify faults and improve the F9F-6, adding camber to the outer leading edge, larger inboard fences and modified spoilers extending from the fence to the tip. The most important change of all was the adoption of a powered 'all-flying' horizontal tail very much like that then being provided for the F-86E. The US Navy had already issued letters of intent to continue with the F9F-6, and the first production Cougar (126257) came off the Bethpage line in early February 1952. By November of the same year the last straight-wing Panther was delivered and VF-32 was already working up with the new Cougar, which offered considerably enhanced performance. Armament was unchanged, though a radar-ranging gunsight was fitted, causing a small bulge under the nose. This was later retrofitted to many Panthers.

Altogether 646 F9F-6 Cougars were built, plus 60 unarmed F9F-6Ps with the same K-17 and Trimetrogon vertical/oblique fan camera installation as used for the F9F-5P. By this time Allison was at last out of the wood with the J33-16A engine of 28.24-kN (6,350-lb) rating, and this powered 168 examples of the F9F-7 otherwise almost identical with the F9F-6. Cougars were just getting to Korea in substantial numbers when the conflict was arrested by an armistice.

Grumman is not a company to rest on its laurels, and as early as 1951 had identified several ways in which the Cougar could be further developed without changing the engine. By late 1952 the G-99 design had been completed and in due course this replaced the F9F-6 and F9F-7 on the production line as the F9F-8, the first (there was no prototype) being BuAer 131063 flown on 18 December 1953. Basically the design was stretched axially, so that the centre fuselage and wing chord were all longer. Span was actually reduced, but chord was increased by no less than 22 per cent, which by itself substantially raised critical Mach number without making the wing any thinner. The leading edge was fixed but the droop was considerably increased, and the outer leading edge was further extended with a dogtooth discontinuity. This enabled 95 litres (25 US gal) of fuel to be added in each wing, while the longer fuselage added a further 252 litres (66.6 US gal). The wing root fillet became grotesquely large, extending to the tail, and the lower rudder was increased in chord. There were many minor changes including a reprofiled canopy to improve rear view. In January 1954 the first F9F-8 exceeded Mach 1 in a shallow dive, one of very few aircraft with centrifugal engines to do so.

Production amounted to 662, many of which were converted to F9F-8B standard with Bullpup radio-command datalink. Another modification was wiring and launch rails for up to four early AAM-N-7 Sidewinder missiles. The corresponding F9F-8P reconnaissance aircraft had in effect twice the capability of earlier photo versions, with a forward oblique camera plus two tandem Trimetrogon fans with large rectangular windows on each side and vertically below. The nose was further extended and drooped, and all 110 of this type had a refuelling probe.

The final new-build version was the F9F-8T dual trainer. This was a major programme, the forward fuselage being 0.86 m (34 in) longer yet having nothing in common with that of the F9F-8P. The Cougar trainer was one of the first aircraft with a properly planned tandem dual cockpit with the intructor significantly higher than the pupil, eliminating the need for a periscope. Unlike the fighters, which had a sliding canopy, the F9F-8T had a long clamshell hood hinged up from the rear. The first flew on 4 April 1956 as the YF9F-8T (141667), and following extremely encouraging trials a further 400 trainers were delivered, the last (147429) in late 1959.

Total production of F9Fs thus amounted to a useful 3,414. After 1962 the F9F-8T became the TF-9J, re-equipped with Martin-Baker A5A seats, while the F9F-8B with Martin-Baker Z5 seats became the AF-9J. Other designations included the F-9F (F9F-6), DF-9F (F9F-6D drone director), QF-9F (F9F-6K target drone), QF-9G (different guidance), F-9H (F9F-7), F-9J (F9F-8), RF-9J (F9F-8P) and QF-9J RPV, which had no pre-1962 designation because it did not then exist. TF-9Js were not officially retired until February 1974, and many were still flying later than that.

As the Panther gave way to the Cougar in front-line service, a small batch of early F9F-2 Panthers was purchased by Argentina for use by that country's naval air arm. Subsequently a small batch of Cougars was bought. The bulge under the nose shows that a radar-ranging sight was fitted.

Grumman F9F variants

XF9F-1: four-engine night-fighter project
XF9F-2: two prototypes with Nene and J42
F9F-2: production fighter with J42-P-8 (total 567)
F9F-2B: temporary designation after fitting external weapons pylons
F9F-2KD: target drone conversions
XF9F-3: prototype with J33-A-8 engine
F9F-3: production aircraft with J33-A-8 (total 54 all later converted to F9F-2 standard)
XF9F-4: F9F-2 re-engined with J33-A-16 engine
F9F-4: ordered with J33-A-16 but completed as F9F-5 (total 109)
XF9F-5: F9F-2 re-engined with J48-P-2
F9F-5: production fighter with J48-P-4, 6A or 8, many airframe modifications and revised equipment (total 595)
F9F-5P: unarmed photo aircraft (total 36)
F9F-5KD: target drone conversions of F9F-5 and F9F-5P
XF9F-6: three prototypes with J48 engines and swept wings and tail
F9F-6: production aircraft with J48-P-8A engine (total 646)
F9F-6D: target-drone director conversions
F9F-6K: target drone conversions
F9F-6P: unarmed photo aircraft (total 60)
F9F-6PD: drone director conversions of F9F-6P
F9F-7: production with J33-A-16A engine (total 168)
F9F-8: completely revised fighter (total 662)
F9F-8B: conversions to launch Bullpup missile
F9F-8P: unarmed photo aircraft (total 110)
YF9F-8T: trainer prototype
F9F-8T: tandem trainer (total 400)

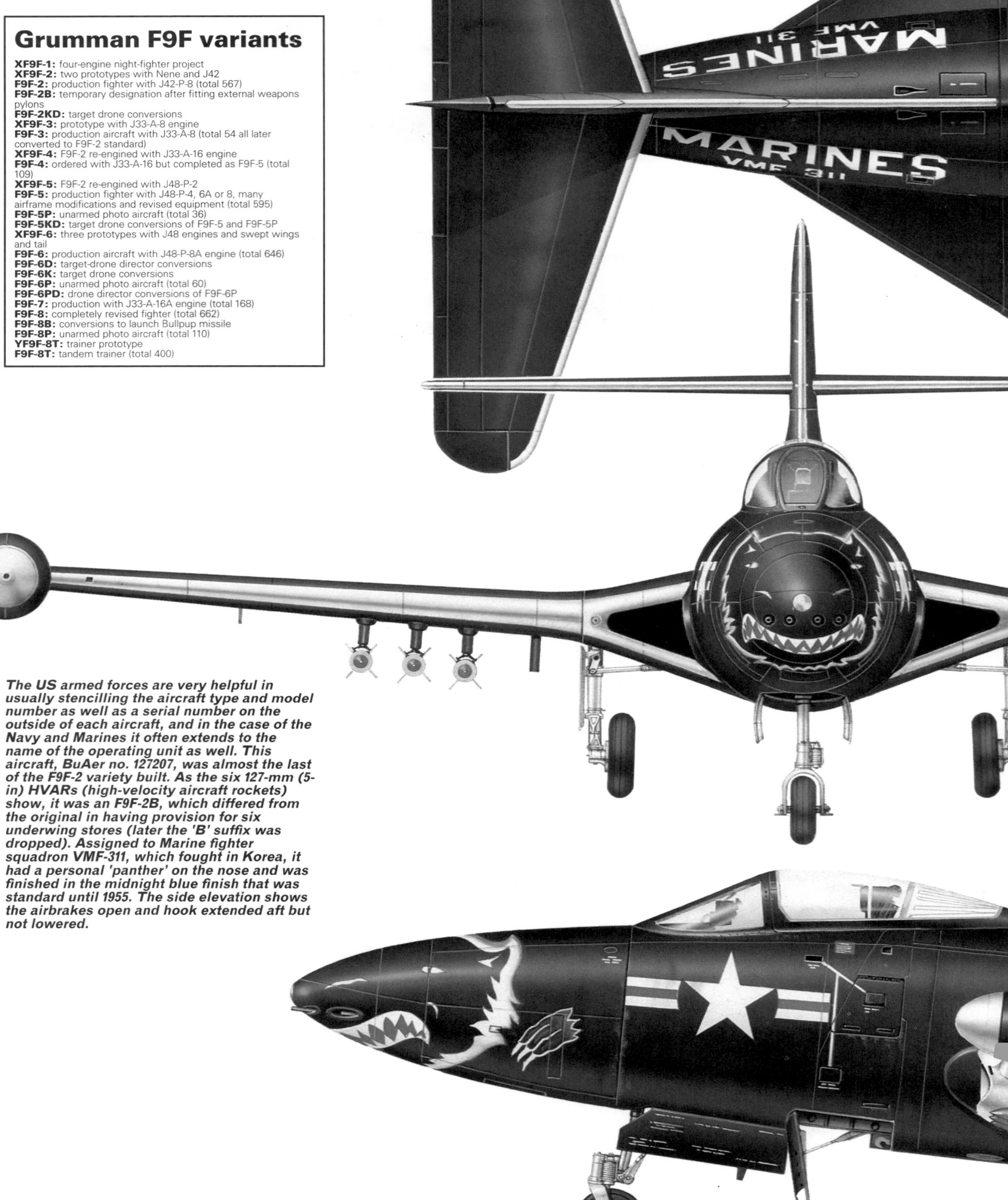

The US armed forces are very helpful in usually stencilling the aircraft type and model number as well as a serial number on the outside of each aircraft, and in the case of the Navy and Marines it often extends to the name of the operating unit as well. This aircraft, BuAer no. 127207, was almost the last of the F9F-2 variety built. As the six 127-mm (5-in) HVARs (high-velocity aircraft rockets) show, it was an F9F-2B, which differed from the original in having provision for six underwing stores (later the 'B' suffix was dropped). Assigned to Marine fighter squadron VMF-311, which fought in Korea, it had a personal 'panther' on the nose and was finished in the midnight blue finish that was standard until 1955. The side elevation shows the airbrakes open and hook extended aft but not lowered.

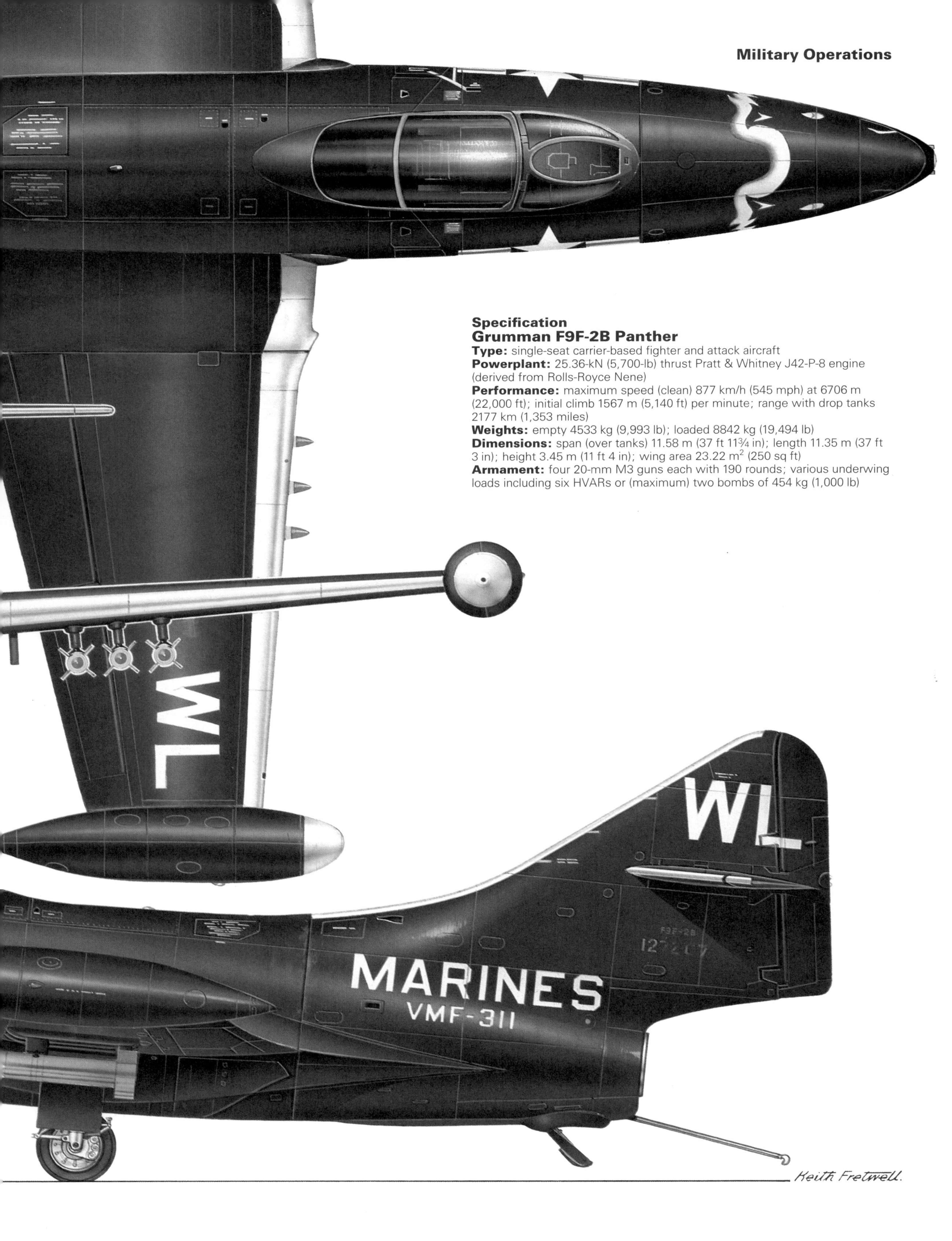

Specification
Grumman F9F-2B Panther

Type: single-seat carrier-based fighter and attack aircraft
Powerplant: 25.36-kN (5,700-lb) thrust Pratt & Whitney J42-P-8 engine (derived from Rolls-Royce Nene)
Performance: maximum speed (clean) 877 km/h (545 mph) at 6706 m (22,000 ft); initial climb 1567 m (5,140 ft) per minute; range with drop tanks 2177 km (1,353 miles)
Weights: empty 4533 kg (9,993 lb); loaded 8842 kg (19,494 lb)
Dimensions: span (over tanks) 11.58 m (37 ft 11¾ in); length 11.35 m (37 ft 3 in); height 3.45 m (11 ft 4 in); wing area 23.22 m^2 (250 sq ft)
Armament: four 20-mm M3 guns each with 190 rounds; various underwing loads including six HVARs or (maximum) two bombs of 454 kg (1,000 lb)

Supermarine Seafire

Always overshadowed by its glorious land-based cousin, the Seafire nevertheless played an important part in World War II, and pushed advancement of the basic Spitfire family to its ultimate expression. Here we tell the story from the first hasty Spitfire conversions to the fearsome Mk 47.

Everyone knows about the Spitfire, but what about the Seafire? From the end of World War II until after the Korean War, successively more potent marks of Seafire played a central role in the fighter squadrons of the Royal Navy. How strange, then, to recall that until 1942 the Seafire did not even exist!

In the crucial final years of peace, 1937-39, when Britain worked frantically to strengthen its air power, the Admiralty had what seem in retrospect to be odd views about carrier-based fighters. In the US Navy the superiority of the monoplane over the biplane was recognised in spring 1936; Brewster continued with the F2A and rival Grumman dropped the F4F biplane and began a new F4F as a monoplane (later to serve with distinction in many theatres as the Wildcat). But in London Their Lordships dismissed the whole idea of a monoplane, and seemed content with the 245 mph Sea Gladiator. When they did at last order a monoplane fighter it was the Blackburn Roc, with a top speed of 194 mph! The notion that the ballerina-like Spitfire could go to war from a carrier deck seems never to have been thought worth investigating!

Why the possibility was ignored is probably impossible to determine, but the naval air staff may have been shaken slightly out of their inactivity by the fact that on Christmas Day 1940 two pilots from Fleet Air Arm No 804 Sqn shot down a Ju 88 over Scapa Flow whilst flying fast monoplanes. These useful fighters were known to the FAA as Grumman Martlet Is, but they had never been ordered by Britain. They were in fact F4F-3s ordered by France, and diverted to Britain on the collapse of that country. This made it difficult to continue to ignore the idea of a modern naval fighter, especially seeing that in May 1940 regular RAF squadron Hurricanes (without any naval equipment) had operated from a carrier off Norway! So in early 1941 the idea of a Sea Hurricane was born, and this was so free from trouble that at the end of 1941 the FAA dared to arrange trials with a carrier-equipped Spitfire.

Carrier trials

At Christmas 1941 Lt-Cdr Peter Bramwell carried out arrested landings, free take-offs and catapult launches aboard *Illustrious*, with a modified Spitfire VB, BL676. Though he expressed reservations about operations from small escort carriers, the trials encountered no difficulty. Accordingly, while RAF Maintenance Units quickly began converting 48 Spitfire VBs into Seafire IBs, with an A-frame arrester hook and naval radio, Cunliffe-Owen and Air Service Training began converting a further 166 Seafire IBs with two further modifications, slinging points (and catapult spools) and a homing receiver. Engines remained the 1,415 hp Merlin 46. Supermarine was contracted to build 262 Seafire IICs, these being new Spitfire VCs with the universal C-type wing, incorporating all the Seafire IB modifications plus further strengthening. The Woolston (Southampton) works did so well that the first IIC reached the FAA on the same day as the first IB (15 June 1942).

Virtually all available FAA Seafire squadrons (801, 807, 880, 884 and 885) took part in the invasion of North Africa in November 1942, one of the air engagements confirming that the Sea-

Deck hands rush towards a Seafire Mk IIC to clear it from the arrester gear before another aircraft lands. The early Seafires had a simple A-frame arrester hook.

No 778 Squadron was a Service Trials unit, evaluating most Fleet Air Arm aircraft and equipment types. Consequently it had a long associaton with the Seafire, having examples of each successive mark. This is a Mk 17, as seen when the unit was at Lee-on-Solent.

fire IIC was much slower than the Ju 88! To rectify this, the Seafire L.IIC was produced, with the low-rated Merlin 32 with cropped supercharger and four-blade propeller. Though of course it was inferior at high altitudes, at low levels the L.IIC was vastly superior, and some had speed and roll rate further improved by having the wings clipped. Westland built 110 L.IICs, and almost all the earlier IICs were converted to L.IIC standard in early 1943. Westland was appointed design authority for the Seafire, and by spring 1943 no fewer than 14 FAA squadrons had been equipped.

Folding wings

So far the Seafire had proved a success story, restricted only by the fact that the wings did not fold so aircraft at sea had to remain on deck. Supermarine had begun work on this problem in early 1942, and in November of that year, as the early marks were going into action off North Africa, the first IIC, MA970, made a second "maiden flight" as the first Seafire with folding wings. Despite the thin profile there was little loss in strength or torsional rigidity and the penalty of the two folds – one at the outer end of the wheel well and the other at the tip – was only 125lb. Folding was manual, the tip fold being needed to fit inside carrier hangars. The production aircraft, the first fully developed Seafire, was the Mk III, and it had the 1,585hp Merlin 55 driving a four-blade Rotol propeller. Ratog (rocket-assisted take-off gear), in the form of a single jettisonable solid motor on each side above the wing root, could be fitted (and was retrofitted to some IICs), but this method of boosting a free non-catapult take-off was never to be used on operations.

Westland began deliveries of 870 Mk IIIs in late September 1943, followed a few weeks later by the first of 350 from Cunliffe-Owen (whose first 20 Mk IIIs had three-blade propellers). Flying a Mk III was little different from a IIC, but the new mark was about 17kt faster at all altitudes. Like most IICs they normally had two 20-mm guns each, with 120 rounds, and four 0.303-in Brownings each with 350 rounds. A flush-fitting 30-, 45- or 90-gal drop tank could be carried, and there was provision for two 250-lb or one 500-lb bomb to be carried. Late production IIIs could launch four 60-lb rockets. Quite early in production the engine was changed to the cropped-blower Mk 55M, giving 1,585hp at low altitudes and enhancing low-level performance. Another change, retrofitted on as many earlier Seafires as possible, was to replace the big ejector exhausts by small individual ejectors from each cylinder. Among other things this improved

With the carrier making good speed the Seafire did not require a catapult to launch, its efficient wing and powerful Merlin engine lifting it off in sufficient time.

pilot view of the deck and batsman without having to make quite such a curved or crabbing approach.

No less an authority than Jeffrey Quill recommended the smaller exhaust stacks as one means of reducing the unacceptably high level of Seafire deck-landing accidents. During the Salerno (Italy) landings on 9 September 1943 the number of serviceable Seafires was reduced from 106 to 39 in the first 48 hours, almost entirely because of accidents. To a small degree the problem was simply that the original Spitfire airframe and landing gear had not been designed for the harsh stresses of carrier operation. To this were added the need for great care in deck landing – more than was needed with, say, the tough F6F Hellcat – and the fact that the Seafire had bad ditching qualities, which added up to pilot apprehension at this crucial stage of the war, when Seafires were becoming available in large numbers. Despite this, Seafires played a major role in all Allied amphibious landings, and after D-day (6 June 1944) Seafire IIIs of 808, 885, 886 and 897 Sqns were assigned to 2TAF and were among the very first Allied air units to go ashore and fly from hastily rolled strips only a few kilometres from the German troops.

The Mk IIC was the first true Seafire, the earlier Mk IBs being conversions of Spitfire Mk Vs. These first naval Spitfires did not feature wing-folding, so they had to remain on deck when not flying.

A Seafire Mk 17 launches from **Triumph**. *The 'teardrop' canopy gave the pilot much better all-round vision.*

The Mk 47 was the last Seafire, and although the rival Hawker Sea Fury was faster, it was the advent of the jet-powered Sea Vampire and Sea Hawk which ended the Seafire's career.

Above: An early Seafire floats over the ramp of a carrier. The type's low landing speed made it suitable for carrier operations, although landing accidents were regular.

Below: This Seafire Mk IIC belonged to No 885 Sqn, flying from HMS **Formidable**. *During November 1942 No 885 provided air cover for the 'Torch' landings in North Africa.*

In late 1942 Their Lordships began considering the prospects for a Seafire with the bigger Rolls-Royce Griffon. On 21 February Jeffrey Quill visited RNAS Arbroath in a clipped-wing Spitfire XII. Famed test pilot 'Winkle' Brown flew it, and found it "sheer magic". On 9 March he put the same aircraft through 15 troublefree landings aboard a carrier. The result was the Seafire XV, and just over a year later, on 26 March 1944, Brown made the first deck landing with one of the new Griffon-Seafires. Though they hardly affected the war, these aircraft opened a new and even more successful chapter in the Seafire story and kept this by now well-liked aircraft in FAA service until long after the Korean war (No 764 Sqn finally disbanded on 23 November 1954).

Tilted engine

Basically the Mk XV retained the airframe of the Mk III, though it naturally looked totally different with the huge Griffon VI engine with cylinder blocks causing large bulges above the nose. View ahead for carrier landing was maintained by tilting the engine slightly downwards. Though not having a two-stage engine, the Mk XV was given symmetric radiators, and other changes included further strengthening of the structure and A-frame hook, the tail of the Spitfire VIII with bigger pointed rudder and retractable tailwheel, and the wing-root tanks of the Spitfire IX. Many other changes were incorporated into the 250 Westland and 134 Cunliffe-Owen production aircraft, notably the switch to a much stronger hook of the tail-mounted 'sting' type, which replaced the lower portion of the rudder. Other changes included a better throttle arrangement, ultra-fine propeller pitch for greater braking on landing, Ratog, and, in the last 30 aircraft, a cut-down rear fuselage and beautiful teardrop canopy.

This new canopy, together with the associated sharply raked windscreen with different framing, was standard on the next version, the Mk XVII. This was also able to house a 33-gal tank in the rear fuselage (except in the FR.XVII when it was replaced by an F.24 camera), because of the weight saved by the cut-down top decking. The biggest advance in the XVII was a redesigned main landing gear, much stronger than before and with longer oleo stroke, which at last made the Seafire the sort of fighter ordinary squadron pilots could land on

Like the Spitfire Mk 20 series, the Seafire Mk 40 series crammed a two-stage Griffon into the basic airframe. The Mk 45 seen here was basically a 'hooked' Spitfire Mk 21.

a carrier. The greater leg stroke both avoided hitting the propeller on the deck and also killed bounce which previously ensured that the aircraft missed all the wires and went into the barrier.

Though it just missed the war the Seafire XVII was widely regarded as the first Seafire that satisfied everyone. Westland delivered 212 and Cunliffe-Owen 20. A very small number had four 20-mm Hispanos and all were equipped to carry eight rockets or underwing bombs or 22.5-gal underwing slipper tanks. The very popular Mk XVII remained long after nearly all the even more powerful Mk 45, 46 and 47 Seafires had gone, notably with second-line squadrons and the RNVR.

During the mid-war years Supermarine had been working on an "ultimate Spitfire", envisaged as the Mk XX with a totally redesigned wing and two-stage Griffon engine. One of the underlying reasons for the new wing was the endemic problem of aileron control reversal at high speeds, and the new Supermarine Type 356 of 1942 had a wing so torsionally stiff it was reckoned aileron control would remain positive to 825 mph! The new metal ailerons had geared tabs, and another change was a new armament scheme with four 20-mm cannon, the inners ahead of the outers, with 150 rounds per gun. The engine was the two-stage Griffon 61, lengthening the nose, driving a five-blade propeller and needing deep symmetric radiators. Eventually the first member of the new family went into production as the Spitfire 21, first delivered from 1944, with traditional canopy and rear fuselage and a tail like a Spitfire XIV.

Massive brute

Naturally the Admiralty showed interest in this very powerful new family, and in November the first Seafire 45 arrived at Farnborough for testing. It was virtually a Spitfire 21 with a sting-type hook and naval radio. The massive brute had plenty of performance and strength but lost a little in handling qualities. Obviously an interim type, 50 were built by Vickers-Armstrongs at Castle Bromwich in 1945. Supermarine's South Marston (Swindon) factory also built 24 Seafire 46s, with the windscreen, canopy and rear fuselage of the XVII. Most had the bigger tail of the Spitfire 24 and a six-blade contraprop, which once and for all eliminated the frightening tendency (uncontrollable by the pilot) of these two-stage Griffon Seafires to slide to the right on take-off, quickly scrubbing the tread off the right tyre and threatening to hit a carrier island!

At last, in early 1947, FAA units began receiving the ultimate Seafire, the F.47, of which South Marston delivered 90, ending in March 1949. Powered by a 2,375 hp Griffon 85, driving a contraprop and with the engine air inlet moved forward immediately behind the propeller, the superb Mk 47 had hydraulically folding wings, with different features from earlier marks and no folding tips. In every way the 47, most of which were FR.47s with an F.24 camera in the rear fuselage, was a bit "more" than its predecessors. It had more fuel, could carry three 500-lb bombs or eight rockets and had fantastic performance despite weighing considerably more than double the loaded weight of early Spitfires. No. 800 Sqn fought with them in Malaya in 1949 and then sailed on to action in Korea. Chief designer Joe Smith once pointed out that the Seafire 47 was over 100 mph faster than early Spitfires despite carrying extra weight equal to "25 passengers and their baggage".

Serving only briefly in the war, the Griffon-engined Seafire served for some years after. These No 800 Sqn Mk 17s are seen on HMS Triumph sailing in the Mediterranean in 1948.

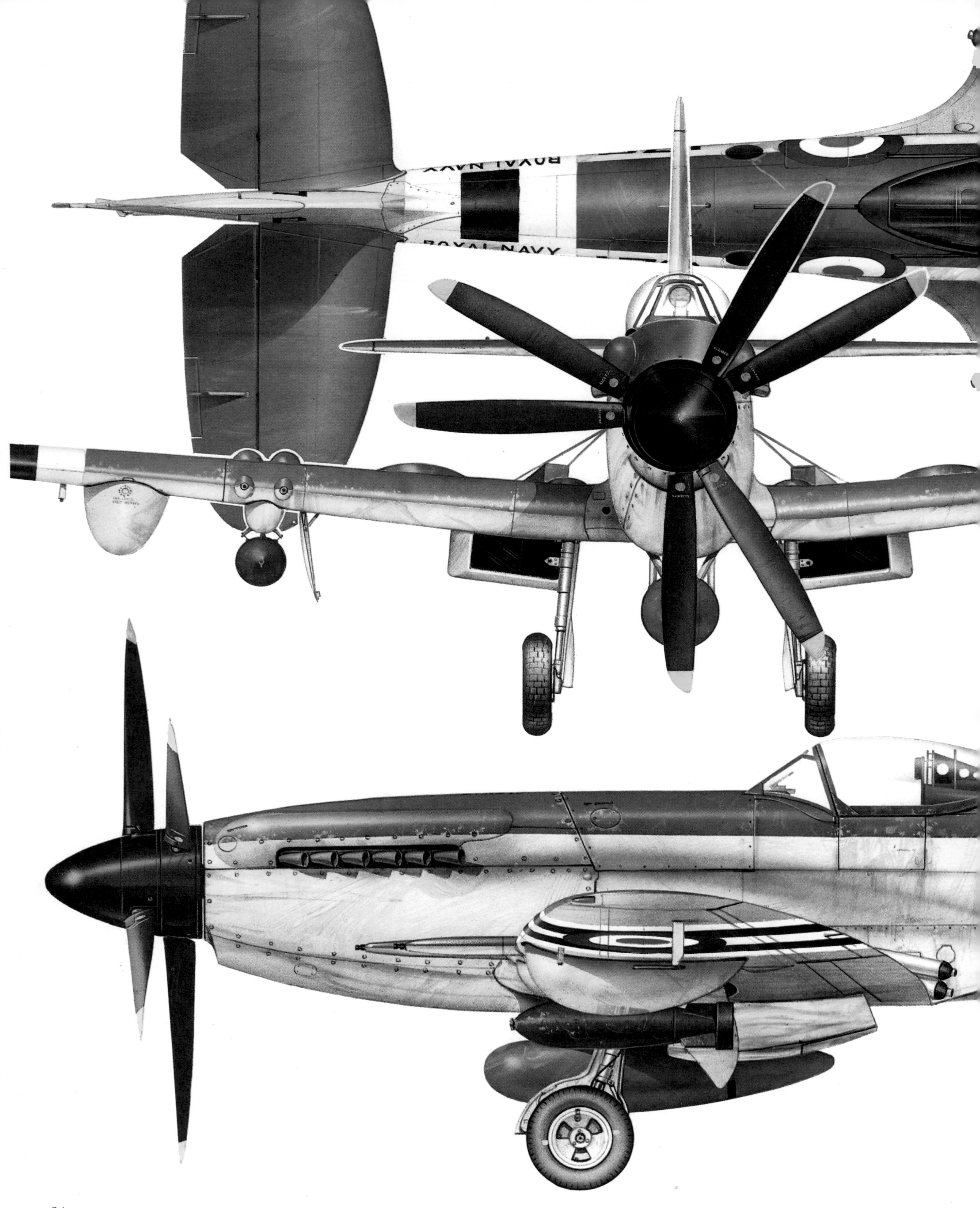
ROYAL NAVY
ROYAL NAVY

The ultimate variant of the Spitfire family was the Seafire Mk 47, incorporating a fearsome Griffon 85 engine driving contra-rotating propellers. These saw service during the Korean War, wearing black-and-white recognition stripes for service with the United Nations forces. Serving with No 800 Squadron, the Seafires flew from Triumph's decks, making its first attack on 4 July 1950 against Haeju airfield. By 25 September the squadron had been withdrawn to Hong Kong, and by the end of the year was back in the United Kingdom. Here it disbanded, and the Seafire passed from front-line service.

Westland Wyvern

During the mid- to late-1940s, the piston-engined warplane reached the peak of its long career, and aircraft such as the Sea Fury and Bearcat attained the height of piston performance. Rapidly overtaking them were the new temperamental breed of jets. Wedged in between was the turboprop-powered warplane, of which very few were produced. The most famous was the Wyvern.

During World War II the British Royal Navy invented a strange species of aircraft called a torpedo fighter. One 'TF', the Beaufighter, was a great success. Another, the Firebrand, spent the entire war under development and finally proved totally unsuitable when it reached the squadrons after the war had ended. The last of the breed, the Westland Wyvern, began life with the world's most powerful piston engine, gave years of problems and seven years later reached the Fleet Air Arm with the piston engine replaced by a turboprop and with a maximum speed reduced by 118 km/h.

Like most of the TF designs the Wyvern was a rather unhappy compromise. It could not fly the missions generally required of a torpedo-and-attack aircraft because it was a single-seater with modest fuel capacity, and no navigator, radar or bad-weather equipment. As a fighter, it could operate in day visual conditions, especially if homed back to its carrier, but was crippled by its size and weight, which made it almost bound to lose in close air combat.

Most seriously, it served as the test-bed for three of the most powerful propeller-driving engines of its era. This was a time when the technology of advanced gearboxes and propellers was moving ahead rapidly, and it was only the bravery of the test pilots of four companies – Westland Aircraft, Rolls-Royce Ltd, Armstrong Siddeley Motors and Rotol Ltd – that the Wyvern ever entered service at all. As it was, seven pilots made forced landings and three others were killed. (Yet, given a choice between the first Westland helicopter and the sole two-seat Wyvern for a flight in 1950, the author picked the Wyvern, and enjoyed it!)

The story began in November 1944 and the issue of Air Ministry (Naval Air Staff) Specification N.11/44. This called for a single-seat long-range day fighter to be powered by the new Rolls-Royce Eagle piston engine, but to be capable – if possible without change to the wings and tail – of being redesigned to take one of the new turboprops then being developed. Obviously, the aircraft had to be fully

***The S.Mk 4 was the principal production version of the Wyvern, and featured a cut-back front fuselage which revealed more propeller spinner and small fins on the tailplane to improve directional stability. This aircraft is landing on* Eagle.**

The prototype Wyvern flew for the first time on 12 December 1946 with Harald Penrose at the controls. Note the Eagle piston engine which initially powered the type, giving the nose an ungainly look.

Upon the adoption of turboprop power, the Wyvern was considerably redesigned. This was the only Clyde-powered example – this engine driving a six-bladed contra-rotating propeller. The Clyde was a good engine, yet it was misguidedly cancelled.

equipped for carrier operation, and armament was to comprise four 20-mm cannon and eight rockets, three 454-kg bombs, an 826-kg mine or a 457-mm torpedo.

In 1945 the RAF issued a requirement for a long-range escort fighter which could be based on the same design, but this was fairly soon abandoned. The RAF wisely decided that future fighters should be jets. But, as the history of the A-1 Skyraider shows, this was cer-

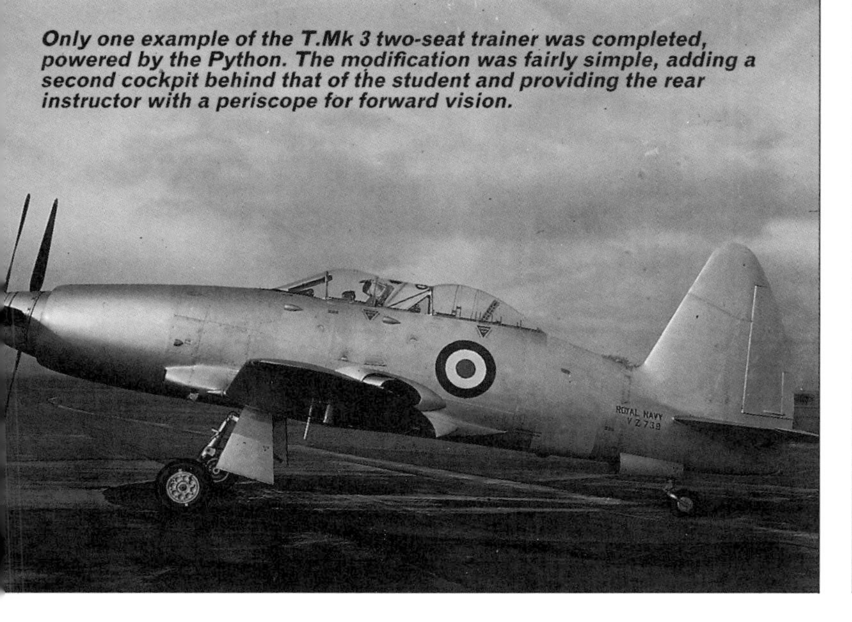

Only one example of the T.Mk 3 two-seat trainer was completed, powered by the Python. The modification was fairly simple, adding a second cockpit behind that of the student and providing the rear instructor with a periscope for forward vision.

This early Wyvern was originally ordered as a TF.Mk 2, but was completed on the production line as an S.Mk 4. However, during its early test flying it had yet to receive the auxiliary finlets on the tailplane. Note the wing-mounted four 20-mm cannon.

The Wyvern was ungainly from any angle, but it appeared even more so on the ground. The short undercarriage never looked strong enough to carry the bulky aircraft, but was in fact a beefy affair designed to withstand the rough punishment of carrier landings.

tainly not the case with naval attack aircraft.

Westland convention

N.11/44 was responded to by General Aircraft and by Westland Aircraft. The latter company's design, the W.34, was chosen as showing greater promise and being more conventional. Chief designer John Digby adopted a totally straightforward approach, resulting in something resembling a big Spitfire or Tempest. The low wing had a slightly tapered centre section and outer panels with curved trailing edges which folded upwards hydraulically to reduce span to 6.1m. Wing profile was 65-212 modified. The centre section had slight anhedral and carried large hydraulically driven Youngman high-lift flaps. The outer panels had 6° dihedral and were fitted with large manual ailerons with spring tabs and, inboard, plain flaps. The mighty 24-cylinder sleeve-valve Eagle 22 piston engine, rated initially at 2,690hp and later at 3,500hp, drove a Rotol contra-rotating propeller with eight blades and a diameter of 4m. Cooling of the liquid coolant for the cylinder blocks and intercooler was handled by a radiator which curved around the front of the engine, except on top (rather like the Shackleton, which is still flying), and the oil was cooled by two quite small radiators under the centre section just ahead of the flaps (very like a Bf 109 or Spitfire). The landing gears were designed for vertical rate of descent of 3.66m/s, the wing structure being stressed to 4.27m/s, and Dowty Liquid Spring shock struts were used to link the upper and lower legs which together formed a levered type of suspension. The deck arrester hook was of the sting type, mounted under the tail, aft of the fully retractable tailwheel. There was provision for the required armament, two of the guns being inboard of the wing fold and the others just outboard.

With eight thrashing blades, howling turboprop and loaded to the teeth, the Wyvern at full bore was an impressive and fearsome sight. Underwing armament consisted of unguided rockets or bombs, but under the centreline a torpedo could be carried.

First flight

Westland built six W.34 prototypes to N.11/44, the type being named Wyvern in 1946. The first, TS371, made its first flight in the hands of Harald Penrose on 12 December 1946. It was completely unpainted, like the second prototype, TS375, which was fitted with the Malcolm pilot-ejection type seat. Other prototypes were TS378,

380, 384 and 387. They were followed by 10 pre-production aircraft designated Wyvern TF.Mk 1, serial numbers VR131-140. Built to Specification 17/46P, they had Martin-Baker Mk 1W ejection seats, full armament and many minor improvements. At the same time, both the engine and propeller were extremely immature. Westland, Rolls-Royce and Rotol test pilots suffered numerous forced landings, two of these being with the aircraft on fire – the Wyverns were grounded on two occasions. In any case, effort on the TF.1 tapered off from 1948 in view of the transfer of interest to turboprops. It had been hoped from the outset that such engines would become available, and by the end of 1945 two candidate engines were running on the testbed.

These engines, the first two high-power turboprops in the world, were the Rolls-Royce Clyde and the Armstrong Siddeley Python. The former was the first two-shaft gas turbine aero engine, one turbine driving a centrifugal compressor and the second driving an axial compressor and the reduction gear to the propeller. This was an odd arrangement, but the Clyde worked well from its first run on 5 August 1945. Soon it was giving well over 4,000 hp; the ninth Clyde gave 4,543 hp and others were cleared for flight at full throttle at 805 km/h at sea level; a severe test.

Westland carried out considerable redesign of the Wyvern to take the new turboprops; the forward fuselage was completely new, the underwing radiators were removed, the vertical tail was made taller, and the cockpit was slightly raised above the jetpipes on each side, which discharged just above the wing trailing edge. The Westland type number was W.35 and the relevant specification N.12/45.

The first W.35 was VP120, powered by the Clyde, rated at 4,030 hp but actually cleared to much higher powers, even though it drove a Rotol contraprop with only six blades. This aircraft flew on 18 January 1949, and was immediately popular with the test pilots. The whole aircraft performed so well that the Ministry of Supply placed an order for 100 Clydes to power the production Wyverns. In what was surely one of his very rare strategic mistakes Lord Hives, head of Rolls-Royce, refused the contract. In his view the Avon jet would be 'the Merlin of the jet age' and the Clyde could never be important. Had the Clyde gone into production there is no doubt it would, with changes, soon have delivered 5,500 hp, and among other things it would have transformed the Princess and Britannia.

As it was Westland was forced to fall back on the rival Python. This was based on a long history of designs and studies going back to work done at Farnborough in the 1920s! It had a reverse-flow layout, with the 14-stage axial compressor arranged back-to-front. Though heavy, bulky and in many ways archaic, the Python had such a long background that it seemed reasonable to expect it to mature rapidly. It was already flying in large testbed aircraft, and on 22 March 1949 it flew in Wyvern TF.2 VP109. This looked almost identical to the Clyde aircraft except for having an eight-blade Rotol contraprop.

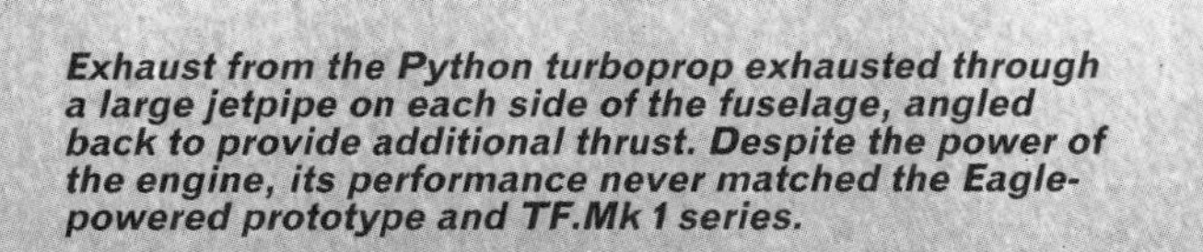

Exhaust from the Python turboprop exhausted through a large jetpipe on each side of the fuselage, angled back to provide additional thrust. Despite the power of the engine, its performance never matched the Eagle-powered prototype and TF.Mk 1 series.

Westland Wyvern

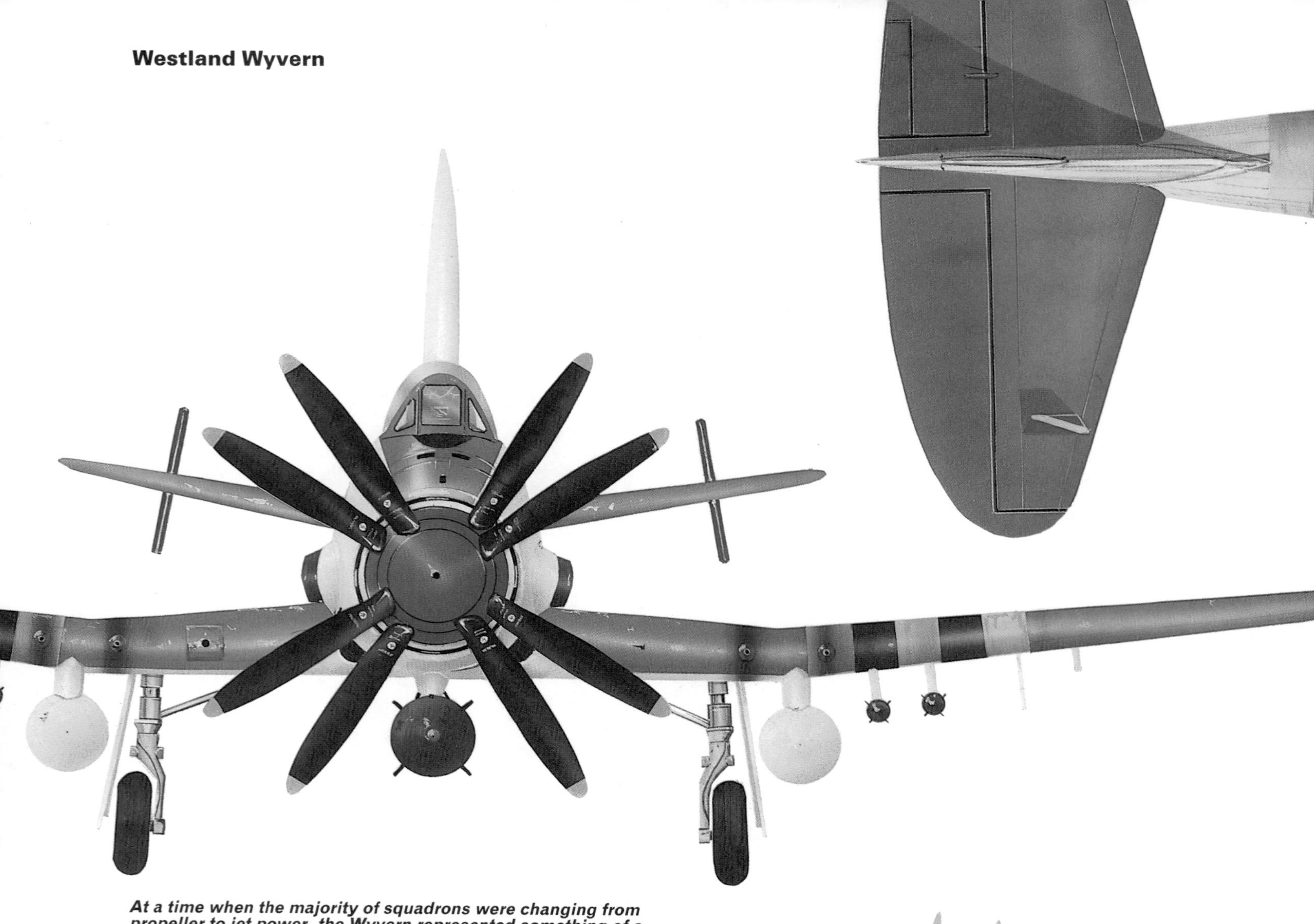

At a time when the majority of squadrons were changing from propeller to jet power, the Wyvern represented something of a compromise, being one of the few front-line combat aircraft to be powered by a turboprop. However, the engine did not perform as well as some of the later 24-cylinder piston engines it had been designed for, and comparative jet aircraft easily outperformed it. Elsewhere turboprop-powered attack aircraft (such as the Douglas A2D Skyshark) were shelved in favour of either jets or powerful piston types (like the Douglas AD Skyraider).

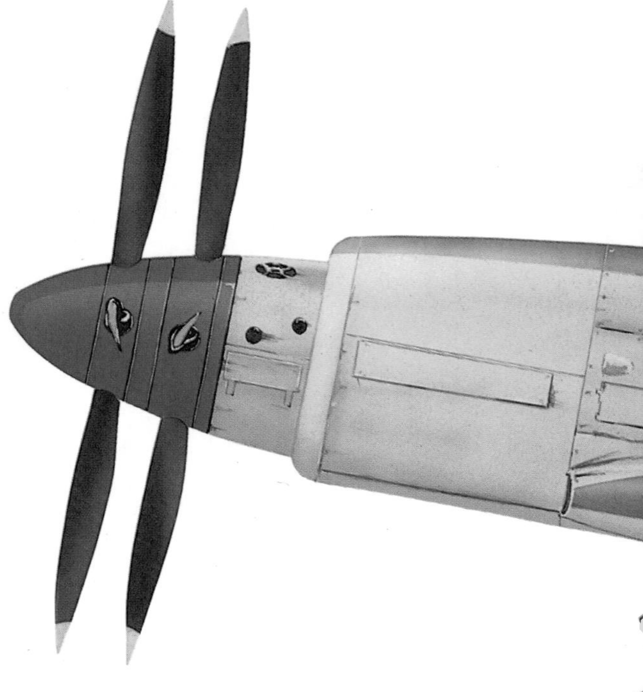

GRANT RACE

Specification

Westland Wyvern S.Mk 4

Type: single-seat carrierborne strike fighter

Powerplant: one Armstrong Siddeley Python 3 axial-flow turboprop, rated at 2736 kW (3,760 shp) plus 536 kg (1,180 lb) jet thrust for take-off, driving eight-blade contra-rotating Rotol airscrew

Dimensions: span 13.42 m (44 ft); length 12.88 m (42 ft); height (wings spread) 4.57 m (15 ft); height (wings folded) 5.11 m (16 ft 9 in); max width (wings folded) 6.1 m (20 ft)

Armament: four 20-mm cannon in wings, one inboard and one outboard of each wing-fold; underwing racks for unguided rockets and bombs; centreline rack for aerial torpedo

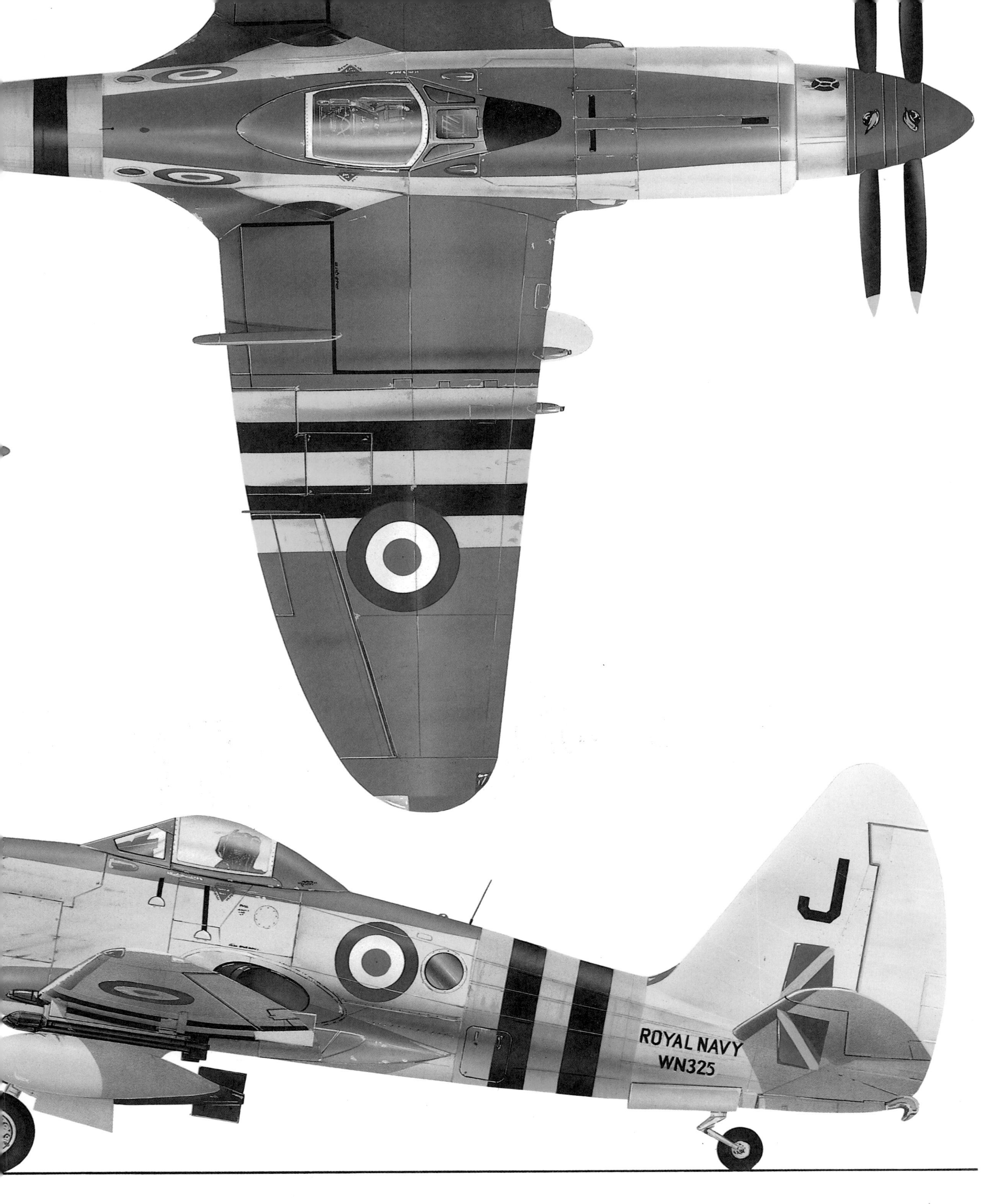
J
ROYAL NAVY
WN325

***No. 813 Squadron was the first front-line unit to get the Wyvern, having previously operated another little-known strike aircraft, the Blackburn Firebrand. Throughout its five-year association with the Wyvern it flew from Ford, but also took its aircraft aboard* Eagle *and* Albion.**

Westland built a second Python-engined prototype, as well as a single example of the T.3 tandem-seat trainer to Specification T.12/48. The trainer, VZ739, first flew on 11 February 1950. The rear (instructor) cockpit had a tall and prominent periscope to provide acceptable forward view on the approach. The author flew this aircraft at Merryfield, the grass satellite of Yeovil, in summer 1950. It was a very impressive machine. However, the flight test programme was punctuated by problems with the engine, gearbox and propeller. Two experienced test pilots crashed fatally, and several times aircraft made dead-stick landings. One of the main problems was the need for high drag on the approach yet the availability of instant high power for a carrier overshoot. The answer was finally found in what Rotol called an inertia controller, but this was not fully developed until 1953. Until then the Wyvern had a reputation for dangerous propulsion difficulties.

Rather against Westland's better judgement the Python had to be accepted as the production engine, and an initial 20 Wyvern TF.2s were ordered as VW867-886. These differed from the prototypes in small details, and in having horizontal tails with dihedral and provision for 410-litre drop tanks under the inboard ends of the outer wings. Oil coolers were mounted in ram air ducts projecting ahead of the wing roots. The ailerons and rudder had electrically operated trim tabs, and there were various improvements to the equipment. But the continued procession of changes resulted in VW868, 870, 871 and 873 being converted into a new mark, at first called TF.4 and from 1952 called S.4, for 'strike'. Aircraft VW880-886 were completed as S.4s from the outset.

No. 830 Squadron took part in the Suez campaign in November 1956, its Wyverns being used to carry out attacks against Egyptian positions. In order to distinguish the diverse aircraft of the Anglo-French-Israeli allies, yellow and black stripes were applied.

The S.4 was the main production version of the Wyvern, 87 in all being delivered. There were many minor differences, but the only externally obvious ones concerned the nose and the tailplane. The air inlet surrounding the nose was immediately behind the propeller in the TF.2, but in the S.4 it was cut back by 460 mm to make it much easier to load fresh cartridges into the remotely situated breeches of the BTH turbo starter for the main engine. The tailplane was fitted with auxiliary fins to improve yaw (directional) stability, especially at low airspeeds at high angles of attack. Other small differences were that the seat was a Martin-Baker Mk 2B, the canopy was stiffened and fitted with a heavier metal frame, the aileron tabs were modified and small fences were added between the ailerons and the flaps.

Wyvern matures

Production S.4s, apart from those ordered as TF.2s, were VZ745-766, VZ772-799, WL876-888, WN324-336 and WP336-346. By this time the Wyvern S.4 was quite a mature and refined aircraft, but there were still a few shortcomings to be rectified. After delivery all aircraft in service were retrofitted with flush perforated airbrakes extended hydraulically from under the wing centre section on each side, ahead of the main flaps. Previously it had been thought that the patented Youngman flaps would be sufficiently effective as airbrakes in dive attacks. Another modification was to replace the curved windscreen with a flat bulletproof type. The last major modification was to make provision for Venom-type wingtip auxiliary fuel tanks, though these were seldom seen.

Seven years after its first flight the Wyvern entered service with No. 813 Squadron, previously equipped with Firebrands, in May 1953. At this time Fleet Air Arm first-line aircraft were painted dark sea grey above and duck-egg green elsewhere. The CO, Lt-Cdr C.E.Price, worked the squadron up at *HMS Peregrine* (RNAS Ford, Sussex) and in 1954 embarked in *HMS Eagle,* and later transferred to *HMS Albion.* The second squadron was No. 827, which embarked in *Eagle* in May 1955. In November 1955 Nos 830 and 831 Squadrons were re-formed with the Wyvern at Ford, going to sea with *Eagle* in April 1956.

Nos 830 and 831 Squadrons took part in the Suez campaign in November 1956, with their aircraft painted in black/yellow 'invasion stripes'. From 1957 the Fleet Air Arm was progressively run down, and the last Wyvern unit, No. 813, was disbanded in March 1958. No service Wyverns have been preserved, the only remaining example being a TF.Mk 1 at the Fleet Air Arm Museum at Yeovilton.

It was probably inevitable that the Wyvern should have suffered such a halting and protracted history. The piston-engined TF.1 of 1946 had a speed of 734 km/h, service ceiling of 10,000 m and range of 1900 km. The production S.4 of 1953 had a speed of 616 km/h, service ceiling of 8535 m and range of 1445 km. Moreover, it cost 2.5 times as much.

Curtiss SB2C Helldiver

For a carrier-based aircraft of its day the Helldiver was a very big machine. Packed with new technology and advanced features it was intended by Curtiss to be a major wartime project. However to those who flew it, the SB2C became known as the 'Son of a Bitch 2nd Class'. Plagued with structural faults and immature design it never succeeded the earlier SBD and while its military career continued through sheer numbers alone, frequent modifications really never overcame its inherent failings.

The Curtiss SB2C, one of the few members of the long and proud series of Curtiss dive-bombers to bear the name Helldiver (officially or unofficially), was intended to be a great war-winner to replace the ancient SBD. Unlike the Douglas product, created by Ed Heinemann working under John K. Northrop, the marvellous new Curtiss had a mighty new two-row engine, an internal weapon bay and a mass of fuel and new equipment all packaged into a tight space. After Pearl Harbor it became the focus of a gigantic nationwide production programme intended to blast the Japanese from the Pacific. The only thing wrong was the aircraft itself. To a man, the US Navy preferred the old SBD, which simply kept on in the forefront of the battle.

The other mass-produced navy Curtiss of World War II was the SO3C Seamew, and it is doubtful if two less-successful aircraft have ever been built in numbers. This experience played a major part in the decline of the once pre-eminent names of Curtiss and Wright in the immediate post-war era, and this was allowed to happen by the US Army and US Navy customers.

In fact the Seamew was designed by a team under the famed chief engineer, Don R. Berlin, while the SB2C was the creation of a newly formed group under Raymond C. Blaylock. As its designation reveals, the SB2C was planned as a scout bomber, for operation from US Navy carriers. The 1938 specification was extremely comprehensive and allowed little room for manoeuvre. The type had to be a stressed-skin cantilever monoplane, and the wing had to be raised from the low position in order to allow the accommodation of an internal weapon bay beneath it. This bay did not have to accommodate a torpedo, but it did have to take a 454-kg (1,000-lb) bomb and a wide range of other stores, and be closed by hydraulically-operated bomb doors. There had to be tandem accommodation for a crew of two, a large amount of fuel (various ranges and mission radii were specificed) and comprehensive radio and other gear including a hefty camera in the rear cockpit. The structure had to be stressed for dive-bombing, and the aircraft had to be carrier-compatible, with folding wings, catapult hooks and an arrester hook. The specified engine was the Wright R-2600 14-cylinder Cyclone.

Not unnaturally the prototype XSB2C-1 came out looking rather like its rival, the Brewster XSB2A-1 Buccaneer; and, if such a thing were possible, the latter was an even poorer aircraft than the Curtiss. In fact the US Navy had such faith in the Buffalo-based company that it placed a firm order for 200 SB2C-1s before the prototype made its first flight on 18 December 1940. The single prototype, BuNo. 1758, had been ordered on 15 May 1939, and the big production order came on 29 November 1940. Thus, as 1941 dawned Curtiss had a single shiny prototype which occasionally flew, on the strength of which 14,000 workers were being hired for a vast new plant rapidly taking shape at Columbus, Ohio (later NAA and today Rockwell). Plans were already afoot for two further giant production programmes, at Canadian Car & Foundry at Fort William and Fairchild Aircraft at Longueil, Montreal. Curtiss announced that 'The Helldiver is the world's most efficient dive-bomber; it carries twice the bomb load, has double the fire-power, is at least 100 mph faster,

A Curtiss SB2C-3 Helldiver banks hard over a carrier in the Pacific. The aircraft has entered the landing pattern and has its hook down ready for the trap. The aircraft on the deck are Grumman TBF Avengers and F6F Hellcats which fought alongside the Helldiver during the fiercest fighting of the Pacific war.

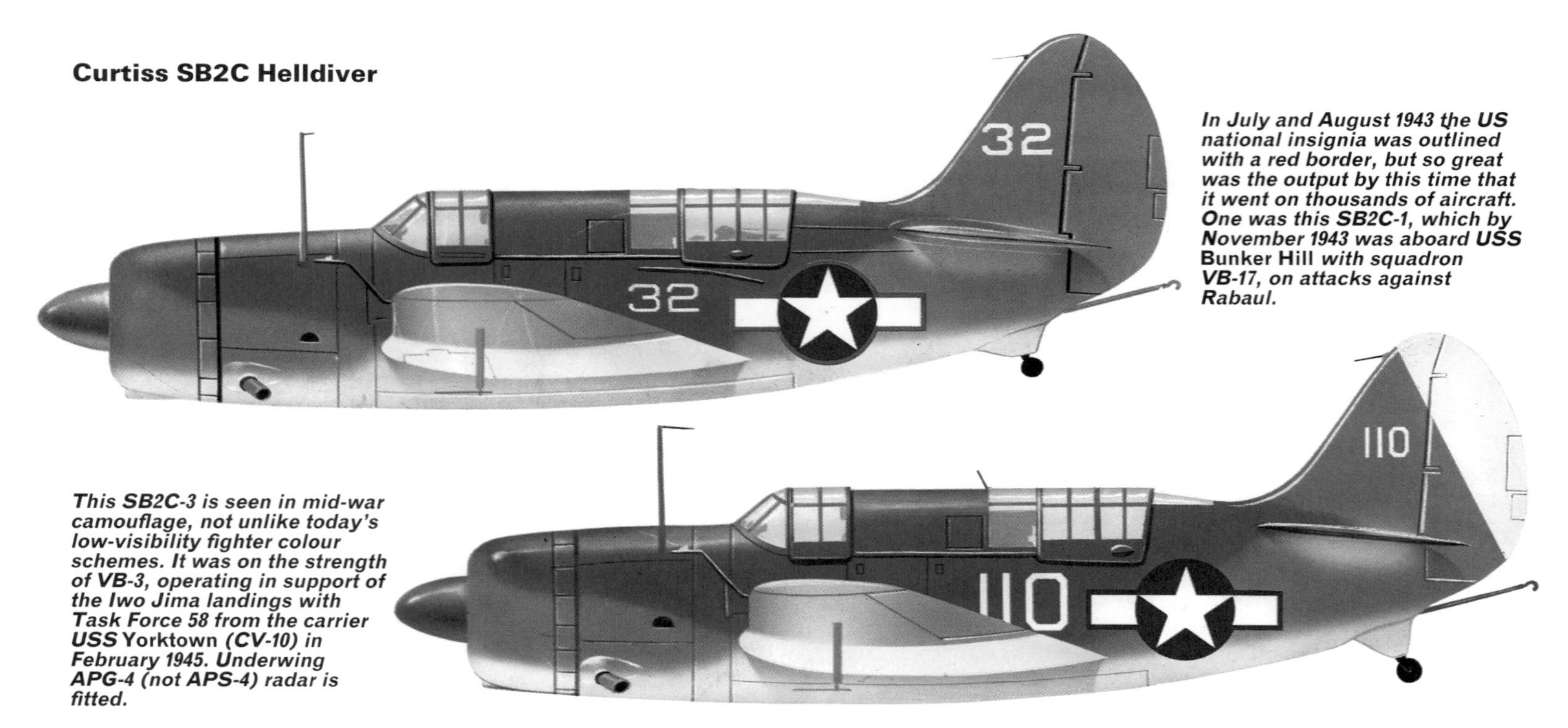

In July and August 1943 the US national insignia was outlined with a red border, but so great was the output by this time that it went on thousands of aircraft. One was this SB2C-1, which by November 1943 was aboard USS Bunker Hill *with squadron VB-17, on attacks against Rabaul.*

This SB2C-3 is seen in mid-war camouflage, not unlike today's low-visibility fighter colour schemes. It was on the strength of VB-3, operating in support of the Iwo Jima landings with Task Force 58 from the carrier USS Yorktown *(CV-10) in February 1945. Underwing APG-4 (not APS-4) radar is fitted.*

remains in flight 4½ hours longer and can operate 600 miles further away from its base than any type now in use. We will build 1,000 or more, at the rate of 80 a month.'

Such confidence overlooked the fact that the SB2C was riddled with problems. Some were the normal ones of immaturity, affecting almost all the functioning items and particularly the R-2600-8 engine and 3.66-m (12-ft) Curtiss Electric three-blade propeller. More serious were the deeper faults of the aircraft itself, which resulted in structural weaknesses, generally poor handling, shockingly inadequate stability (especially in yaw and pitch) and unacceptable stall characteristics. Yet the strange thing is that the first prototype looked almost the same as all the production machines. Even the fact that the tail had to be enlarged was not immediately obvious.

Features of the XSB2C-1 included a large wing with all its taper on the trailing edge. On the trailing edge were large flaps split into lower and upper portions, again divided into inboard and outboard sections on the manually folded outer wings. In normal flight the upper flap sections were hydraulically locked to form the upper surface of the wing, the lower part functioning as a normal split flap. For dive-bombing the upper flaps were unlocked by moving the selector lever to a different position, the hydraulic jacks then opening both flaps fully above and below. This held the dive to 354 km/h (220 mph) but buffeted the tail so violently that the pilot feared structural failure (which often did occur, though not necessarily from the buffet). The ailerons, which in most versions had greater chord than the flaps, were unusual in having aluminium skin above and fabric below. In line with the ailerons on the leading edge were large slats which were pulled open by a cable connection to the landing gears, so that at low speeds in the traffic pattern the handling, especially lateral control, was almost acceptable. The US Navy did pass the sluggish ailerons, but in 1944 the British rejected it out of hand, and that was after four years of improvement.

Prototype crash

Unfortunately, BuNo. 1758 crashed quite early, on 8 February 1941, the cause being engine failure on the approach. Like many aircraft of its day the SB2C suffered violent changes in trim with application of flap, dive brakes, gear down or changes in engine power. In the case of this aircraft the forces needed on the stick were at the limit of what most pilots could apply, and very high friction in the control circuits did not help, so it was small wonder that control was lost when the engine cut. But with a gigantic production programme fast taking shape Curtiss simply had to carry on with flight test, so 1758 had to be urgently rebuilt. Almost every part was changed, the fuselage being about 0.305 m (1 ft) longer, the tail areas almost 30 per cent larger and numerous shapes subtly altered. The poor stability led to the expensive addition of an autopilot. Thanks to combat reports from Europe the fuel tanks in the fuselage and inner wings were made of the self-sealing type, local armour was added and the forward-firing armament changed from two 12.7-mm (0.5-in) guns above the cowling to four of these guns in the wings. The rear cockpit was redesigned with improved collapsible decking to improve the field of fire of the observer's single 12.7-mm (0.5-in) gun. Later this gun was replaced by observer armament of twin 7.62-mm (0.3-in) guns, each with no less than 2,000 rounds, with traverse round the mounting ring effected by an hydraulic motor. Wing racks were added for bombs of up to 147-kg (325-lb) depth-bomb size. These and other changes did not all come in at once but most had at least been agreed on paper by the time the prototype resumed flight testing on 20 October 1941.

So enormous was the production scheme that, coming on top of dozens of others throughout North America, it fell seriously behind. Curtiss had agreed to begin deliveries in December 1941, but by this time no production machine was even being assembled. Worse, on 21 December 1941 the sole prototype broke up in the air while on dive-bombing tests, pilot B. T. Hulse managing to escape by parachute. By this time further changes had been demanded, and another 900 Helldivers had been ordered for the US Army Air Force as A-25 Shrikes, with carrier gear deleted, pneumatic tailwheels and

The XSB2C-1 prototype (no. 1758) is seen during flight tests, wearing one of the many pre-war US Navy colour schemes and pre-war national insignia. Design problems were to delay service entry until late 1943.

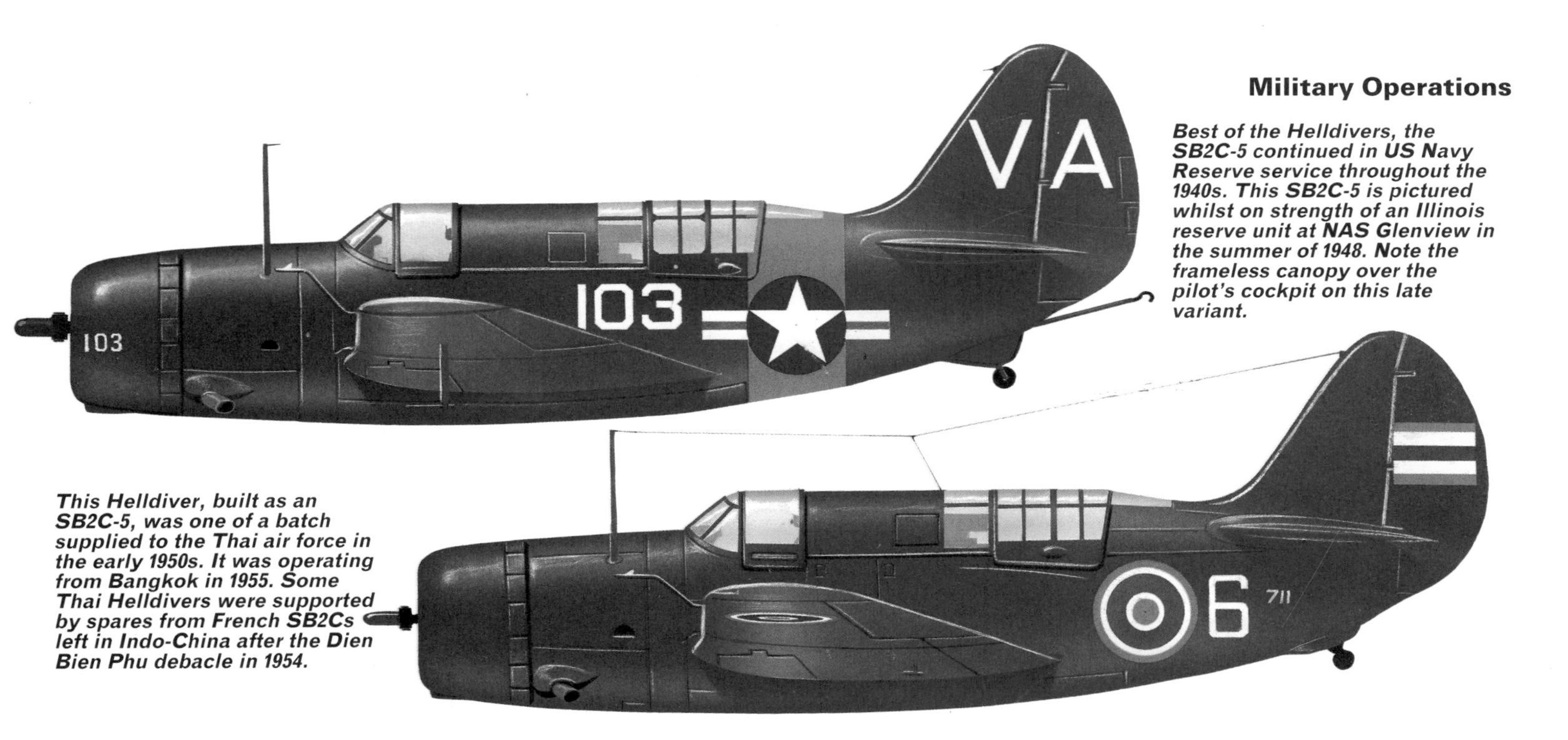

Best of the Helldivers, the SB2C-5 continued in US Navy Reserve service throughout the 1940s. This SB2C-5 is pictured whilst on strength of an Illinois reserve unit at NAS Glenview in the summer of 1948. Note the frameless canopy over the pilot's cockpit on this late variant.

This Helldiver, built as an SB2C-5, was one of a batch supplied to the Thai air force in the early 1950s. It was operating from Bangkok in 1955. Some Thai Helldivers were supported by spares from French SB2Cs left in Indo-China after the Dien Bien Phu debacle in 1954.

many other changes. Everyone worked round the clock to try to speed the programme, and eventually the first SB2C-1 was completed at Port Columbus in June 1942. The US Navy did not fail to notice that 10 days earlier the far better Grumman TBF Avenger had gone into action, though its design was begun almost two years later than the bug-ridden SB2C.

Disappointing results

Urgent testing of the first six production machines revealed that in many respects they were worse than the prototype, the great increase in weight (empty weight rose from 3230 kg/7,122 lb to some 4636 kg/10,220 lb) without change in the engine resulting in an aircraft described at NAS Anacostia as 'extremely sluggish'. But by this time the trickle of production machines was fast building up, and to avoid political scandals some had to be delivered, so US Navy attack squadron VS-9 began to equip with SB2C-1s in December 1942. In fact political scandals had to be accepted; this was wartime, and there seemed to be so many poor or late programmes that the Truman Committee on the National Defense Program was set up to examine what was going on. This committee finally compiled a damning report on the SB2C, and among other things managed to divert the A-25s to other customers, though many did briefly wear US Army colours.

Subsequently production of the SB2C progressed through the many variants listed separately. Only the original order for 200 applied to the SB2C-1 model, and all of these were retained in the USA for training purposes. The SB2C-1A, which appeared in 1943, was the non-navalised A-25A after transfer to the US Marine Corps, where many saw action still painted olive-drab. The SB2C-1C introduced several armament improvements, including the option of removing the bomb doors and carrying a torpedo on an external truss, but little use appears to have been made of this. The major SB2C-1C change was to replace the four wing guns by two 20-mm cannon, each with 400 rounds loaded from above the wing. Immediately ahead of the magazines were extra 170-litre (37.4-Imp gal) auxiliary tanks, and at full load the SB2C-1C, the first model to go into action, was inferior in many performance respects to the old SBD, which was far nicer to fly, and safer.

Rabaul strike

The first action was flown by a bomber squadron, VB-17, operating from USS *Bunker Hill*. The SB2Cs flew the second strike mounted on 11 November 1943 against the big Japanese base at Rabaul, New Guinea. They were painted in the sea blue and white scheme then common, though by this time aircraft on the line were being finished in gloss Midnight Blue, usually with a bold white three-figure Modex number on the nose.

A welcome small improvement in performance resulted in the SB2C-3 from fitting the more powerful R-2600-20 engine, its extra power being absorbed by an improved Curtiss Electric propeller with four blades and fitted with root cuffs. Towards the end of the war it became common to omit the spinner, though this was often done at unit level. Certainly by 1944, when the SB2C-3 appeared, the Helldiver was well established in service, and at least was becoming operationally effective, though crashes, inflight break-ups and carrier landing accidents continued at the very top of the 'league

The lone XSB2C-2, no. 00005, was the only Helldiver seaplane. A conversion of the fifth production SB2C-1 with twin Edo floats and a ventral fin, it flew in September 1942 but never led to a combat-ready machine, the 287 planned production SB2C-2s (nos 03862/04148) being cancelled before any had flown.

A line-up of US Army RA-25A Helldivers, either serving as utility hacks and for target towing or abandoned to the elements. Note the crudely overpainted insignia, the camouflaged rudder (possibly a replacement part) and the 'BOX' chalked on the cowlings of several aircraft in the line. Prefix 'R' meant 'Restricted'.

Curtiss SB2C Helldriver

With 'S2C-5' stencilled on its fin, this SB2C-5 was one of the first combat aircraft to be supplied to the post-war Italian Marinavia, serving with 86° Gruppo Antisom (antisommergibli, which means anti-submarine). The 86° unit badge appears on the fin. The tailwheel mount is unusual, and no hook is fitted.

table'. To everyone in the US Navy this aircraft was The Beast, though gradually pilots who became experienced on it came to think this appellation unfair.

Like most wartime programmes, production became a flood after most of the tougher fighting had been done, and the SB2C-4, which did not appear until summer 1944, was the most numerous version of all. From the pilot's viewpoint the chief new feature of this model was that both upper and lower wing flaps were perforated, looking like a sieve. This had virtually no effect on their drag in dive-bombing but did slightly reduce the tremendous tail buffet, which many pilots claimed affected their ability to see the target and aim the dive! Operational effectiveness was considerably increased in this version by strengthening the wing and providing for the carriage of either two drop tanks, two 227-kg (500-lb) bombs or eight 127-mm (5-in) rockets.

End of the line

The final production Helldiver was the SB2C-5, with slightly increasd internal fuel capacity (an extra 132 litres/29 Imp gal). As listed under Variants, most of the Columbus versions had more or less exact counterparts built by the two Canadian companies.

Curtiss was only too keenly aware of the indifferent qualities of the SB2C, and many years after the war the company president, Guy Vaughan, said it was 'one of the biggest of the wartime crosses we had to bear'. Don Berlin left the company in 1942 to join Fisher Body, and Blaylock, possibly working with director of engineering G. A. Page Jr, designed the much better-looking SB3C and corresponding US Army A-40. A single-seater, the SB3C was expected to reach 571 km/h (355 mph) even carrying two torpedoes or a heavy internal bomb load, powered by an R-3350; but the two SB3C prototypes were cancelled.

After the war Helldivers did not vanish overnight. A few continued flying with the US Navy Reserves and with various test units until at least 1947, often being used to tow targets. Others were operated in the attack role by the French Aéronavale, the navies of Italy and Portugal and the air forces of Greece and Thailand. French Helldivers played a significant role in the war in Indo-China, which did not collapse until 1954. One cannot blame the SB2C for that.

JW117 was the Helldiver Mk I used for the ground and air photography sessions at the Aeroplane & Armament Experimental Establishment at Boscombe Down, England, in October 1944. Much of its air evaluation was handled by famed test pilot Lieutenant-Commander E. M. 'Winkle' Brown, RN. His opinion was adverse.

Curtiss SB2C-4 Helldiver cutaway drawing key

1 Curtiss Electric four-bladed constant-speed propeller
2 Spinner
3 Propeller hub mechanism
4 Spinner backplate
5 Propeller reduction gearbox
6 Carburettor intake
7 Intake ducting
8 Warm air filters
9 Engine cowling ring
10 Oil cooler intake
11 Engine cowlings
12 Wright R-2600-20 Cyclone 14 radial engine
13 Cooling air exit louvres
14 Exhaust collector
15 Exhaust pipe fairing
16 Oil cooler
17 Engine accessories
18 Hydraulic pressure accumulator
19 Boarding step
20 Cabin combustion heater
21 Engine oil tank (25 US gal/ 94.6 litre capacity)
22 Engine bearer struts
23 Hydraulic fluid tank
24 Fireproof engine compartment bulkhead
25 Aerial mast
26 Starboard wing fold hinges
27 Wing fold hydraulic jack
28 Gun camera
29 Rocket projectiles (4.5-in/ 11.43-cm)
30 Starboard leading edge slat (open)
31 Slat roller tracks
32 Slat operating cables
33 Starboard navigation light
34 Formation light
35 Starboard aileron
36 Aileron aluminium top skins
37 Aileron control mechanism
38 Starboard dive brake (open position)
39 Windshield
40 Bullet proof internal windscreen
41 Reflector gunsight
42 Instrument panel shroud
43 Cockpit coaming
44 De-icing fluid tank
45 Instrument panel
46 Pilot's pull-out chart board
47 Rudder pedals
48 Control column
49 Cockpit floor level
50 Engine throttle controls
51 Pilot's seat
52 Oxygen bottle
53 Safety harness
54 Armoured seat back
55 Headrest
56 Pilot's sliding cockpit canopy cover
57 Jury strut
58 Wing folded position
59 Fixed bridge section between cockpits
60 Fuel tank filler cap
61 Fuselage fuel tank (110 US gal/416 litre capacity)
62 Fuselage main longeron
63 Handhold
64 Fuselage frame and stringer construction
65 Autopilot controls

66 Sliding canopy rail
67 Aerial lead-in
68 Radio equipment bay
69 Life raft stowage
70 APG-4 low-level bombing radar
71 Gunner's forward sliding canopy cover
72 Gun mounting ring
73 Gunner's seat
74 Footrests
75 Ammunition boxes
76 Armour plate
77 Wind deflector
78 Twin 0.3-in (7.62-mm) machine-guns
79 Retractable turtle decking
80 Gun rest mounting
81 Folding side panels
82 Upper formation light
83 Fin root fillet
84 Starboard tailplane
85 Deck handling handhold
86 Fabric-covered elevator
87 Remote compass transmitter
88 Tailfin construction
89 Aerial cable
90 Sternpost
91 Rudder construction
92 Fabric skin covering
93 Trim tab
94 Balance tab
95 Elevator trim tab
96 Elevator construction
97 Tailplane construction
98 Tailplane spar root fixing
99 Deck arrester hook
100 Arrester hook damper
101 Tail navigation light
102 Tailwheel leg strut
103 Solid tyre tailwheel
104 Leg fairing
105 Rear fuselage frames
106 Tailplane control cables
107 Lifting bar
108 Gunner's floor level
109 Wing root trailing edge fillet
110 Aft end of bomb bay
111 Rear spar centre section fixing
112 Wing walkway
113 Port upper surface flap dive brake
114 Rear spar hinge joint
115 Split trailing edge flaps
116 Balance tab
117 Aileron hinge control
118 Aileron trim tab
119 Lower surface fabric skinning
120 Wing rib construction
121 Wing tip construction
122 Port navigation light
123 Pitot tube
124 Automatic leading edge slat (opens with undercarriage operation)
125 Slat riblets
126 Slat operating cables
127 Main spar
128 Leading edge nose ribs
129 500-lb (226.8-kg) bomb
130 Rocket projectiles (4.5-in/ 11.43-cm)
131 Drop tank (58 US gal/219.5 litre capacity)
132 Wing fold joint line
133 Main undercarriage leg fairing doors
134 Drag strut
135 Port mainwheel
136 Shock absorber leg strut
137 20-mm wing cannon
138 Cannon barrel fairing
139 Undercarriage leg pivot mounting
140 Wing fold spar hinge joint
141 Cannon ammunition box
142 Auxiliary fuel tank (45 US gal/170 litre capacity)
143 Fuel filler cap
144 Centre section fuel tank (105 US gal/397.5 litre capacity)
145 Front spar/fuselage attachment joint
146 Main undercarriage wheel well
147 Retractable catapult strop
148 Approach light
149 Bomb doors (open)
150 Bomb door hydraulic jack
151 Displacement gear jack
152 H-type bomb displacement arm
153 1,000-lb (453.6-kg) bomb

Curtiss SB2C Helldiver variants

XSB2C-1: single prototype (BuNo. 1758) with R-2600-8, several times rebuilt or modified
SB2C-1: first production version; total 200; first block to receive the new 1940 scheme of Assigned Serial Numbers (00001/00200)
SB2C-1A: designation applied to **A-25A**; subsequently used again for 410 ex-USAAF A-25A for US Marine Corps
A-25A Shrike: US Army version of SB2C-1 with various changes; total 900, of which 410 to US Marine Corps, 270 to US Navy and 10 to RAAF
SBF-1: Fairchild-built SB2C-1; total 50
SBW-1: CCF-built SB2C-1; total 38
SBW-1B: CCF-built Lend-Lease aircraft of SB2C-1C standard for the UK; total 28 of which 26 delivered (see next entry)
Helldiver Mk I: Fleet Air Arm SBW-1B, 26 delivered as JW100/125, most to No. 1820 Sqn but rejected for operational use
SB2C-1C: first version with 20-mm wing guns; total 778
XSB2C-2: single aircraft (00005) tested September 1942 with twin Edo floats; intended as reconnaissance bomber
SB2C-3: improved model with 1,900-hp (1417-kW) R-2600-20, four-blade propeller and fitted from start with APG-4 low-level auto bomb system (also retrofitted to many other versions); total 1,112
SBF-3: Fairchild-built SB2C-3; total 150
SBW-3: CCF-built SB2C-3; total 413
SB2C-3E: SB2C-3 aircraft fitted with APS-4 3-cm radar; over 180
SB2C-4: wing hardpoints for two 500-lb (227-kg) bombs or eight 5-in (127-mm) rockets, perforated wing flap/dive brakes and equipment changes; total 2,045
SB2C-4E: SB2C-4 aircraft fitted with APS-4 radar
SBF-4E: Fairchild-built SB2C-4E; total 100
SBW-4E: CCF-built SB2C-4E; total 270
SB2C-5: improved aircraft with increased internal fuel and other minor changes; total 970 from February 1945 (BuNo. 83128 onwards) and 2,500 cancelled
SBW-5: CCF-built SB2C-5, total 85; 165 cancelled
XSB2C-6: two SB2C-3s (BuNos 18620/18621) completely rebuilt as longer aircraft with increased fuel capacity and 2,100-hp (1566-kW) Pratt & Whitney R-2800-28 Double Wasp engines

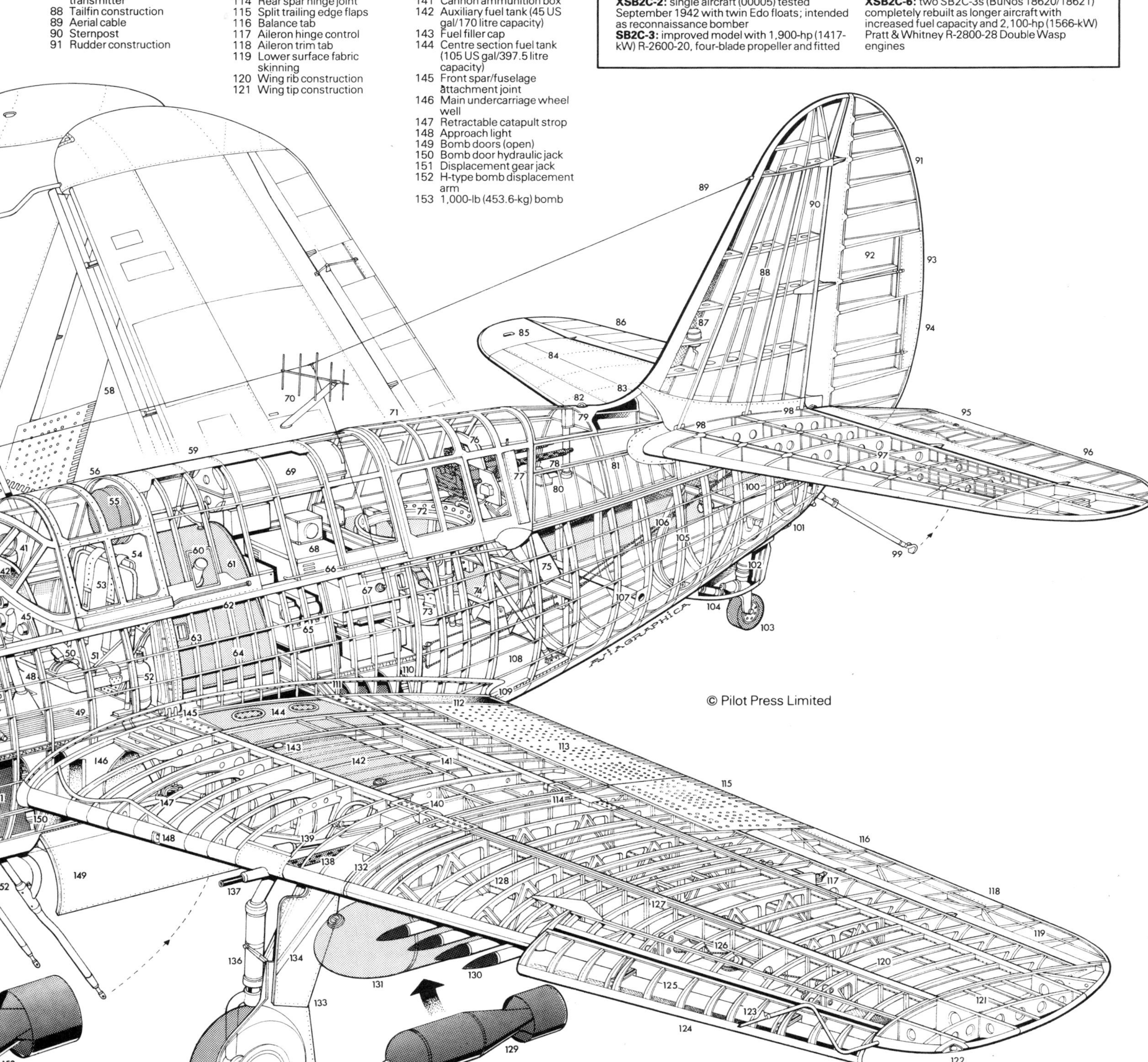

Hawker Sea Hawk

Sturdy and straight-winged, the Sea Hawk was a good example of early British jet design, which had proceeded ignorant of the advances made by German aerodynamicists. It went to war at Suez, but by the 1950s it was falling into obsolescence. Despite this, Sea Hawks would be found on Indian carrier decks for another two decades.

Towards the end of World War II the Hawker design staff, having produced over a period of two decades a series of successful piston-engine aircraft, began to turn its attention to the problems (and advantages) of jet propulsion. Various proposals for fighter designs were put forward, including a version of the Fury (P.1035) fitted with a Rolls-Royce B.41 Nene engine, but no official support was forthcoming. Convinced of the merits of its ideas, the company decided to construct a machine as a private venture, and in October 1945 work started on the P.1040, a single-engine jet fighter fitted with a bifurcated jet pipe, for either RAF or RN use. Three months later a tender based on this design was submitted to the Ministry of Aircraft Production, and in May 1946 an order was received for three prototypes and a static test airframe, thus justifying the company's enterprise. RAF interest in Hawker's proposals had by then waned, however, contracts having been placed instead for the Gloster Meteor F.Mk 4.

The first P.1040 to fly was VP401, which took to the air at Boscombe Down on 2 September 1947 with W. Humble at the controls, this being used only for aerodynamic purposes, no armament or other military equipment being fitted. Powered by a single Rolls-Royce Nene 1 engine of 20-kN (4,500-lb) thrust, the P.1040 had unswept wings merged into the circular fuselage. The wing roots incorporated air inlets and jet pipe exhausts as well as the main landing gear units. This configuration enabled it to carry four internal fuel tanks within the fuselage, with a total capacity of 1796 litres (395 Imp gal). Trials were transferred to Farnborough on 5 September, and improvements incorporated in the prototype included new pointed 'pen-nib' type heat-shield fairings in place of the original rectangular design, to cure handling problems, and the fitting of the uprated Nene 2, which produced 22.2 kN (5,000 lb) of thrust. Another modification, incorporated in production aircraft, was the addition of a bullet or acorn fairing to the fin at its intersection with the tailplane. This aircraft participated in the National Air Races at Elmdon in 1949, winning the SBAC Challenge Cup on 1 August at an average speed of 821 km/h (510 mph). Soon afterwards it returned to the manufacturers to be fitted with an Armstrong Siddeley Snarler liquid-fuel rocket motor in the rear fuselage, in which form it became the P.1072, flying for the first time with this engine in use on 20 November 1950, following a conventional flight four days earlier.

The second and third aircraft were completed to naval Specification N.7/46 of 17 October 1946, and as such were fully equipped with folding wings, catapult spools and an armament of four 20-mm Hispano cannon mounted in the belly. The first of these (VP413) took to the air at Boscombe Down on 3 September 1948, and following dummy deck assessment trials there it made a number of landings on HMS *Illustrious* during 1949. These revealed a tendency for the arrester hook to miss the wires, and a lengthened hook was fitted for the later tests. This modification proved successful, and was accordingly fitted also to the third prototype (VP422), which first flew on 17 October 1949. This latter machine incorporated other modifications, including pick-up points for the fitment of underwing drop tanks and provision for RATOG (rocket-assisted take-off gear).

It had become apparent from the earlier trials that the design would meet current RN needs, and on 21 January 1949 production Specification 25/48/P was issued for 151 machines (serialled WF143

This is a quartet of Sea Hawk FB.Mk 3s of No. 806 Sqn, allocated to HMS* Centaur *in 1954. This squadron adopted as its insignia the Ace of Diamonds, which it carried on successive marks of Sea Hawk. For pioneering the use of the Sea Hawk in carriers, in HMS* Eagle *with F.Mk 1s, the squadron was awarded the 1955 Boyd Trophy.

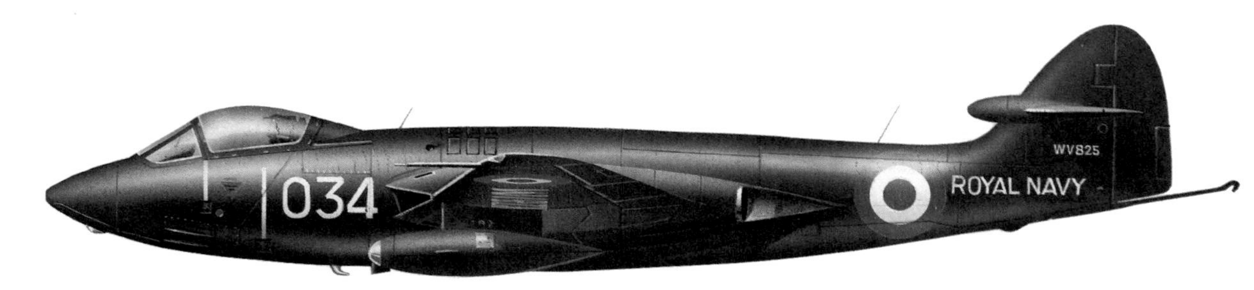

Hawker Sea Hawk FGA.Mk 6 of the Airwork Fleet Requirements Unit at Hurn around 1966-67. Converted in 1958 from an FGA.Mk 4, it was painted gloss black overall and was fitted with a powerful Harley light in the port drop tank to enable RN ships' gunners to pick up the approaching aircraft easily.

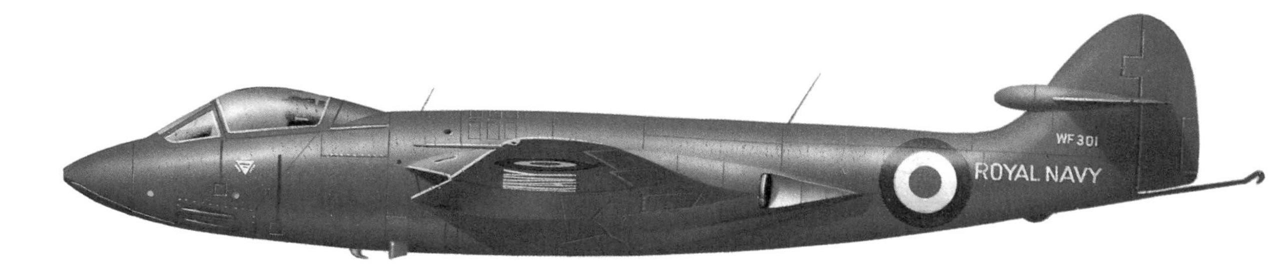

Hawker Sea Hawk FB.Mk 3 of No. 738 Sqn, FAA, painted red overall as part of the 'Red Devils' Aerobatic Team. The five aircraft of this team participated in the SBAC Display at Farnborough in September 1957, landing and taking off in formation, and performing aerobatics using coloured smoke.

onwards) to be known as the Sea Hawk F.Mk 1, and constructed by Hawker Aircraft Ltd at its Kingston works. Fitted with the 22.2-kN (5,000-lb) thrust Nene Mk 101, these aircraft were to have increased wing span to improve performance during take-off and landing, a pressurised cockpit and Martin-Baker ejection seats. The first nine machines were reserved for development purposes, being flown at Dunsfold, Boscombe Down, Farnborough and elsewhere on spinning, control, RATOG, catapult, arrester, cooling equipment, target towing, engine-proving and armament trials, as well as carrier trials aboard HMS *Eagle* and cold-weather trials with the Climatic Department of the RCAF's Central Experimental Proving Establishment at Namao, Alberta.

By the time production got under way, Hawker had also gained a contract for the large-scale production of the Hunter for the RAF. Capacity was insufficient at Kingston for both production lines, and consequently only 30 Sea Hawk F.Mk 1s were built there before development and production of the type was transferred to Coventry, where Armstrong Whitworth was short of work for its Baginton factory. A new Specification 25/48/P2 was issued on 1 February 1951 for Coventry-built aircraft, and the first machine (WF162) flew on 18 December 1952. In the meantime WF147 had been modified to Sea Hawk F.Mk 2 standard, with fully powered ailerons to correct lateral control problems with the earlier version. This modification proved successful, and was introduced on the Coventry production line, WF240-279 being produced as Sea Hawk F.Mk 2s; the first to fly was WF241 on 5 January 1954.

Ground-attack version

The final variant in this initial order was the Sea Hawk FB.Mk 3 fighter-bomber (WF280 onwards), of which 116 were built, with strengthened wings able to take two 227-kg (500-lb) bombs or mines in place of the drop tanks of the earlier versions, the underwing pylons being modified for this purpose. The final Nene Mk 101-powered version was the Sea Hawk FGA.Mk 4 ground-attack aircraft equipped with modified outer wings fitted with hardpoints. These enabled the variant to carry a variety of loads for close support work, including four 227-kg (500-lb) bombs or up to 16 76-mm (3-in) rocket projectiles with 27-kg (60-lb) warheads, or any combination of the two. The additional drag from this load adversely affected performance, but nevertheless production was ordered commencing at WV792, which first flew on 26 August 1954, and eventually 97 machines were built to this standard.

Trials were carried out with an inflight-refuelling probe fitted in a drop tank, to improve range, and one aircraft had a forward-facing F.94 camera in a similar position, but neither of these ideas was further developed. Meanwhile, Rolls-Royce had been improving the powerplant, and in 1954 the Nene Mk 103 became available, giving 24 kN (5,400 lb) of thrust. Over the next few years, the RN Aircraft Yard at Fleetlands re-engined many of the surviving Sea Hawk FB.Mk 3s and Sea Hawk FGA.Mk 4s, and these emerged as Sea Hawk FB.Mk 5s and Sea Hawk FGA.Mk 6s respectively. In addition, the remaining orders for Sea Hawk FGA.Mk 4s were delivered direct from Armstrong Whitworth as Sea Hawk FGA.Mk 6s, the first of 86 machines so to emerge being XE339 which first flew on 18 February 1955. This latter version also incorporated the 'Green Salad' navigational aid.

Initial service trials of the Sea Hawk were carried out from September 1952 by No. 703 Squadron, the Service Trials Unit at Ford, these continuing after the unit merged into No. 700 Squadron in August 1955. The first operational unit to receive the type was No. 806 'Ace of Diamonds' Squadron at RNAS Brawdy, which had eight Sea Hawk F.Mk 1s initially, the first being delivered on 10 March 1953. Three months later the squadron participated in the Coronation Review flypast at Spithead, and soon afterwards the commanding officer, Lieutenant Commander P. C. S. Chilton, made the first landing of a British aircraft on the deck of a fully angled carrier

The Hawker P.1040 prototype VP401 first flew on 2 September 1947, and was used for aerodynamic purposes. The second and third prototypes, VP413 and VP422, were navalised versions completed to Specification N.7/46, and were essentially the prototype Sea Hawks. VP401 was later fitted with an Armstrong Siddeley rocket motor.

A line-up of No. 806 Sqn Sea Hawk FB.Mk 3 fighter-bombers simultaneously start their engines at Hal Far, Malta, during 1954. A Short Sturgeon target-tug can be seen climbing out behind the Sea Hawks, which then represented the Fleet Air Arm's most advanced equipment. The aircraft saw operational service at Suez and in India.

when on 23 June he landed on USS *Antietam*. His squadron eventually embarked in HMS *Eagle* in February 1954, two other squadrons (Nos 804 and 898) having by then been equipped with the type. Experience in the *Eagle* led to the introduction of a redesigned crash barrier, less likely to damage the fuselage and particularly the cockpit.

The Sea Hawk F.Mk 2 reached No. 802 Squadron at RNAS Lossiemouth in April 1954, and the following month it joined No. 807 Squadron at RNAS Brawdy. It was quickly followed by the Sea Hawk FB.Mk 3, which first entered service in July 1954. Most of these early aircraft were relegated to second-line use when the later versions became available, and by mid-1956 the Sea Hawk FGA.Mk 6 was the main first-line equipment, supplemented by a few uncoverted Sea Hawk FB.Mk 3s and Sea Hawk FGA.Mk 4s. Operational units using the type at that time were Nos 800, 801, 802, 804, 810, 811, 895, 897, 898 and 899 Squadrons.

Suez campaign

That year the Sea Hawk had an opportunity to prove its effectiveness, when the Royal Navy participated in Operation Musketeer, the joint Anglo-French Suez operations in November. Three British carriers were available in the eastern Mediterranean in anticipation of events, all with Sea Hawk squadrons aboard. In HMS *Albion* were Nos 800 and 802 Squadrons, while HMS *Eagle* carried Nos 810 and 897 Squadrons, and HMS *Bulwark* had Nos 804, 895 and 899 Squadrons. There had been some rearrangement immediately before the operation, Nos 895 and 897 Squadrons having exchanged their respective Sea Hawk FGA.Mk 6s and Sea Hawk FB.Mk 3s. These aircraft were involved in attacks on airfields and various military installations in the Canal Zone, as well as providing the Allied forces with close support. Two aircraft were shot down during the operation and others suffered damage by fire from enemy ground forces, but by the time the ceasefire came the Sea Hawk had proved its value in the ground-attack role.

The Sea Hawk eventually ended its first-line career on 15 December 1960, when No. 806 Squadron disembarked its Sea Hawk FGA.Mk 6s to Brawdy after spending much of the year in the Far East in the *Albion*. A few Sea Hawks had entered service with the RNVR squadrons during 1956, but these units were all disbanded on 10 March 1957 as part of the sweeping defence cuts at that time. However, the type soldiered on for some time with second-line units, the last to fly it being the civilian-operated Fleet Requirements Unit at Hurn. Run by Airwork Ltd, the unit's Sea Hawk FGA.Mk 6s were employed on radar calibration duties with ships of the Royal Navy, being painted gloss black overall and fitted with a Harley light in the port drop tank. The last machine to fly with this unit (XE390) finally departed for the RN Aircraft Yard on 18 February 1969. One restored Sea Hawk FGA.Mk 6 (WV908) survives with the RN Historic Flight at Yeovilton.

Efforts to sell the Sea Hawk abroad were only partially successful. Neither Australia nor Canada was convinced that the type met their needs, Australia preferring the de Havilland Sea Venom and Canada the American-built McDonnell F2H Banshee. A demonstration on 12 April 1954, by J. O. Lancaster of Armstrong Whitworth, at the French navy base at Lann-Bihoué near Lorient, was equally unproductive. However, the Marine Luchtvaartdienst (MLD, or Dutch naval air service) was more impressed and, with US Offshore Procurement providing the necessary financial backing, the production line was restarted for the supply of 22 Sea Hawk Mk 50s, the

This Sea Hawk FGA.Mk 4 of No. 898 Sqn is seen on the flight deck of HMS* Ark Royal *early in 1957. In the background are two Sea Hawk FGA.Mk 6s of No. 804 Sqn, still carrying 'Suez bands' in yellow and black, as applied to all aircraft participating in the campaign against Egypt in November 1956.

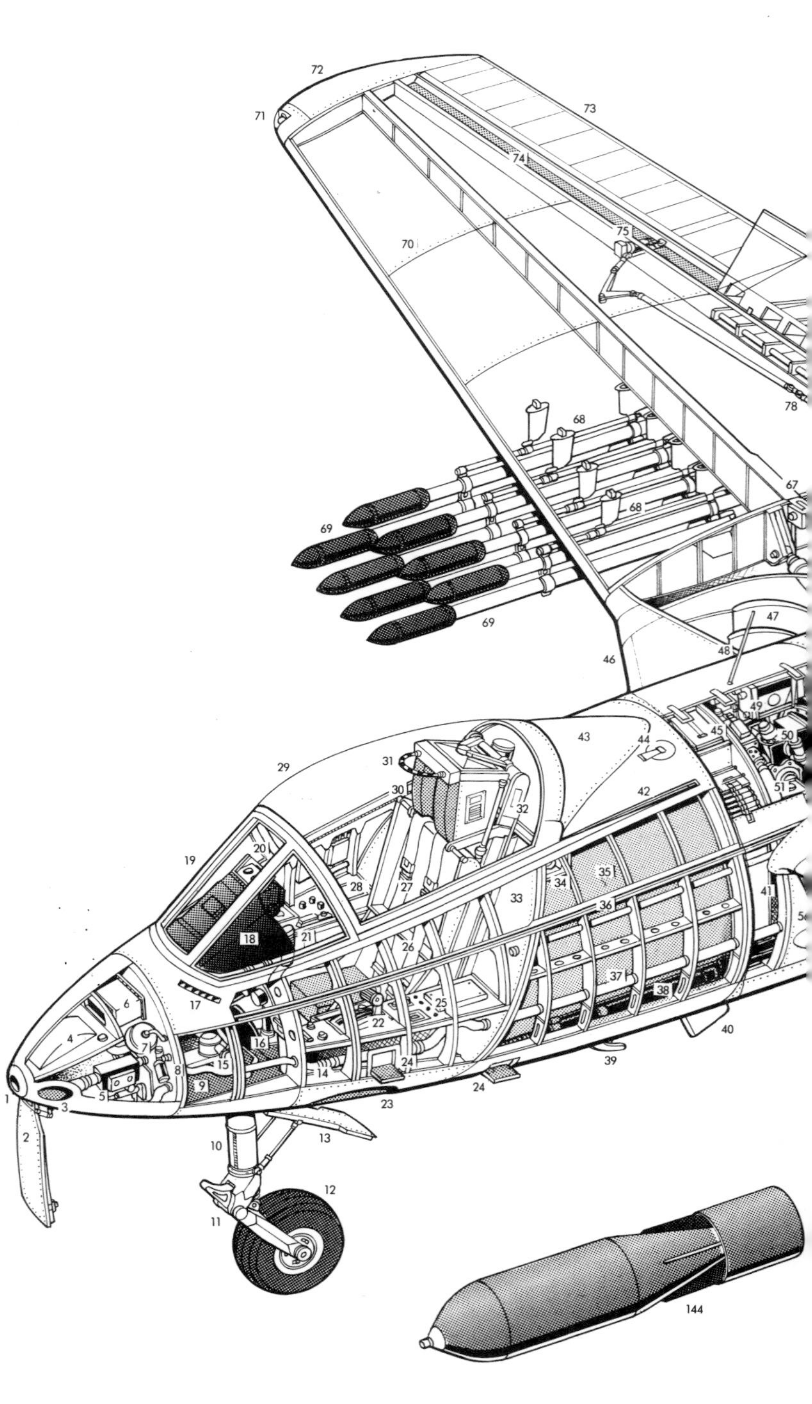

Hawker Sea Hawk Mk 100 of MFG 1 of the West German navy. Orders for 34 of this type were fulfilled from 1958, to be shore based at Schleswig for Baltic air defence. A further 34 aircraft were supplied as Mk 101s, fitted out for long-range radar reconnaissance. The surviving aircraft were sold to India.

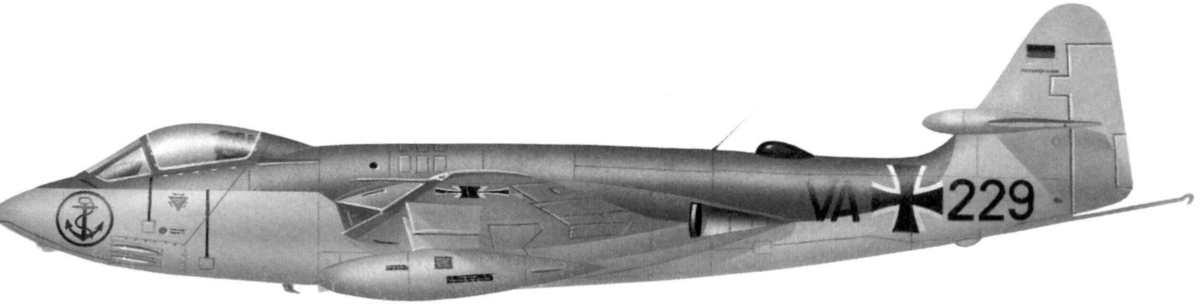

Hawker Sea Hawk FGA.Mk 4 cutaway drawing key

1 Ram air intake
2 Nosewheel door
3 Camera aperture
4 Nosewheel housing
5 Gun camera
6 Air conditioning system heat exchanger
7 Pressurization valve
8 Front pressure bulkhead
9 Cockpit floor level
10 Nose undercarriage leg strut
11 Nosewheel forks
12 Forward retracting nosewheel
13 Nosewheel leg door
14 Heating air duct
15 Rudder pedals
16 Oxygen bottle
17 Heating air spill louvres
18 Instrument panel shroud
19 Bullet proof windscreen
20 Reflector gunsight
21 Control column
22 Engine throttle
23 Cannon muzzle blast trough
24 Boarding steps
25 Port side console panel
26 Pilot's Martin-Baker ejection seat
27 Safety harness
28 Starboard side console panel
29 Cockpit canopy cover
30 Ejection seat headrest
31 Face blind firing handle
32 Ejection seat launch rails
33 Sloping rear pressure bulkhead
34 Canopy winding gear
35 Forward fuselage fuel tank (total internal capacity 395 Imp gal/1796 litres)
36 Upper main longeron
37 Air system ducting
38 British Hispano 20-mm cannon (four)
39 Retractable catapult strop hook
40 Used cartridge case ejection chute
41 Ammunition feed chute
42 Sliding canopy rail
43 Canopy aft fairing
44 Fuel filler cap
45 Ammunition tanks (200 rounds per gun)
46 Starboard air intake
47 Intake duct flow vanes
48 HF aerial
49 Forward radio and electrical equipment racks
50 Engine accessory compartment
51 Fire extinguisher
52 Cartridge starter magazine (six rounds)
53 Starter exhaust duct
54 Boundary layer bleed air spill duct
55 Bleed air system spill louvres
56 Boundary layer splitter plate
57 Port air intake
58 Intake duct framing
59 Engine bay access door
60 Fireproof bulkhead
61 Compressor intake filter screens
62 Rolls-Royce Nene Mk 101
63 Engine flame cans
64 Engine bearer struts
65 Intake plenum suction relief doors
66 Starboard wing folding hydraulic jack
67 Main spar hinge joint
68 Rocket launch rails
69 25-lb (11.3-kg) air-to-ground rockets

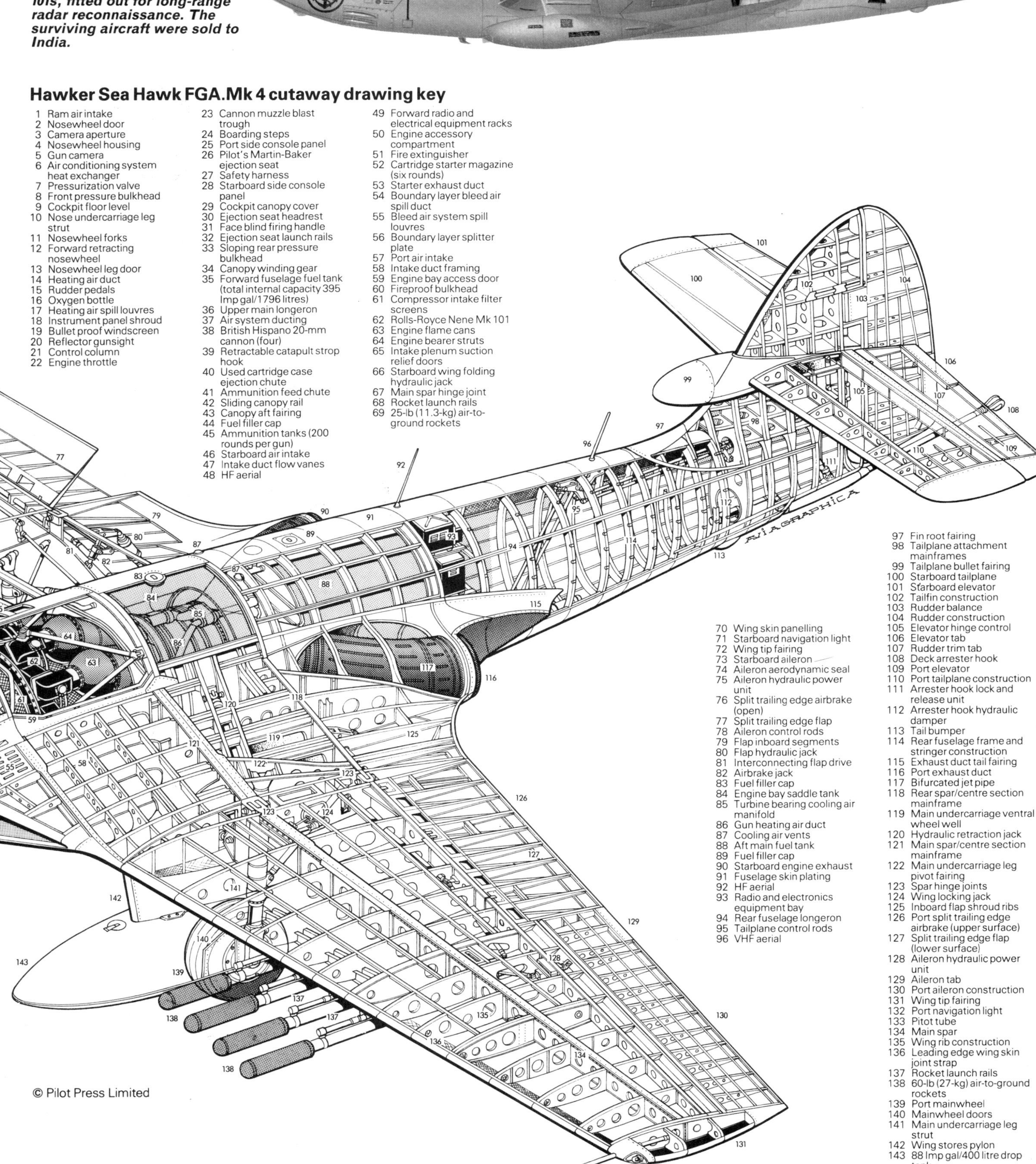

70 Wing skin panelling
71 Starboard navigation light
72 Wing tip fairing
73 Starboard aileron
74 Aileron aerodynamic seal
75 Aileron hydraulic power unit
76 Split trailing edge airbrake (open)
77 Split trailing edge flap
78 Aileron control rods
79 Flap inboard segments
80 Flap hydraulic jack
81 Interconnecting flap drive
82 Airbrake jack
83 Fuel filler cap
84 Engine bay saddle tank
85 Turbine bearing cooling air manifold
86 Gun heating air duct
87 Cooling air vents
88 Aft main fuel tank
89 Fuel filler cap
90 Starboard engine exhaust
91 Fuselage skin plating
92 HF aerial
93 Radio and electronics equipment bay
94 Rear fuselage longeron
95 Tailplane control rods
96 VHF aerial
97 Fin root fairing
98 Tailplane attachment mainframes
99 Tailplane bullet fairing
100 Starboard tailplane
101 Starboard elevator
102 Tailfin construction
103 Rudder balance
104 Rudder construction
105 Elevator hinge control
106 Elevator tab
107 Rudder trim tab
108 Deck arrester hook
109 Port elevator
110 Port tailplane construction
111 Arrester hook lock and release unit
112 Arrester hook hydraulic damper
113 Tail bumper
114 Rear fuselage frame and stringer construction
115 Exhaust duct tail fairing
116 Port exhaust duct
117 Bifurcated jet pipe
118 Rear spar/centre section mainframe
119 Main undercarriage ventral wheel well
120 Hydraulic retraction jack
121 Main spar/centre section mainframe
122 Main undercarriage leg pivot fairing
123 Spar hinge joints
124 Wing locking jack
125 Inboard flap shroud ribs
126 Port split trailing edge airbrake (upper surface)
127 Split trailing edge flap (lower surface)
128 Aileron hydraulic power unit
129 Aileron tab
130 Port aileron construction
131 Wing tip fairing
132 Port navigation light
133 Pitot tube
134 Main spar
135 Wing rib construction
136 Leading edge wing skin joint strap
137 Rocket launch rails
138 60-lb (27-kg) air-to-ground rockets
139 Port mainwheel
140 Mainwheel doors
141 Main undercarriage leg strut
142 Wing stores pylon
143 88 Imp gal/400 litre drop tank
144 500-lb (226.8-kg) HE bomb

Hawker Sea Hawk

Specification
Hawker Sea Hawk FGA.Mk 6

Type: single-seat carrierborne ground-attack fighter
Powerplant: one 24-kN (5,400-lb) thrust Rolls-Royce Nene Mk 103 turbojet
Performance: maximum speed 964 km/h (599 mph) at sea level; initial climb rate 1737 m (5,700 ft) per minute; service ceiling 13565 m (44,500 ft); range 2253 km (1,400 miles) with drop tanks
Weights: empty 4336 kg (9,560 lb); maximum take-off 7348 kg (16,200 lb) with two drop tanks and two 227-kg (500-lb) bombs
Dimensions: span 11.89 m (39 ft 0 in); length 12.09 m (39 ft 8 in); height 2.64 m (8 ft 8 in); wing area 25.83 m^2 (278 sq ft)
Armament: four 20-mm Hispano cannon each with 200 rounds, plus various external loads including 16 rocket projectiles or two 227-kg (500-lb) bombs beneath the wings as well as two 455-litre (100-Imp gal) drop tanks

Hawker P.1040 Sea Hawk variants

P.1040: first prototype (VP401); non-navalised
P.1040: second and third prototypes (VP413 and VP422) with Nene 2 engine and increased wing span; navalised to conform with Specification N.7/46
Sea Hawk F.Mk 1: first production version to Specification 25/48P with increased wing span and tail area, new canopy, fitted with Nene Mk 101
Sea Hawk F.Mk 2: improved version with power-boosted ailerons
Sea Hawk F.Mk 3: fighter-bomber variant with strengthened wing and racks for two bombs
Sea Hawk FGA.Mk 4: ground-attack fighter variant equipped for close-support work, with four underwing pylons
Sea Hawk FB.Mk 5: conversion of FB.Mk 3 fitted with Nene Mk 103
Sea Hawk FGA.Mk 6: conversion of FGA.Mk 4 fitted with Nene Mk 103; late production machines produced to this standard
Sea Hawk FGA.Mk 6: new production for Indian Navy, also some converted and refurbished RN aircraft
Sea Hawk Mk 50: ground-attack fighter version for Marine Luchtvaartdienst, essentially as FGA.Mk 6, but fitted with US radio
Sea Hawk Mk 100: close-support version for West German navy, based on Mk 6, but with larger vertical surfaces, extra tankage and US radio equipment; some later to Indian Navy
Sea Hawk 101: long-range radar reconnaissance fighter for West German navy, similar to Mk 100 but with EkcoType 34 search radar in pod under starboard wing; some later to Indian Navy

This Sea Hawk FGA.Mk 6 of No. 804 Sqn, FAA, is shown carrying the special black and yellow stripes which were applied for the Suez operation in November 1956. Operating from HMS* Bulwark*, the squadron made attacks on Egyptian airfields and provided support for ground troops. On returning home early in 1957 the squadron transferred to HMS* Ark Royal*, and its fin code changed accordingly from 'B' to 'O', but evidently the Suez markings were not immediately painted out.

61
O
XE409
ROYAL NAVY

Chris Davey

Hawker Sea Hawk

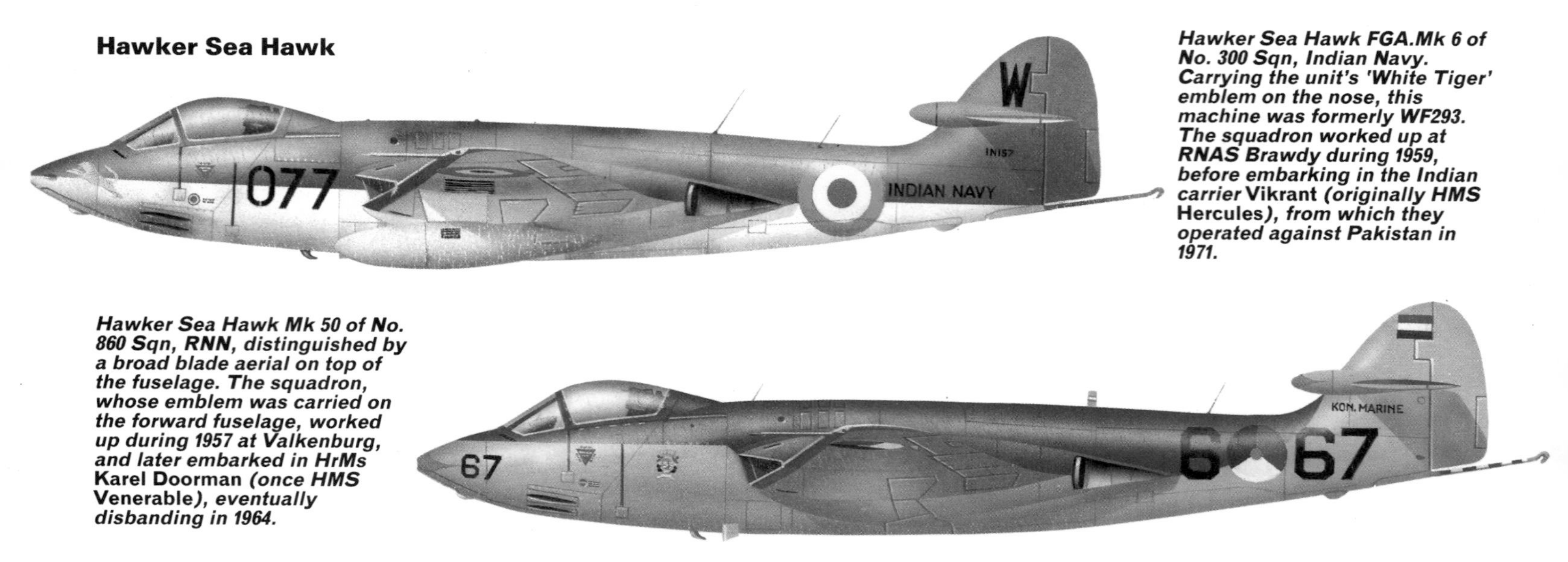

Hawker Sea Hawk FGA.Mk 6 of No. 300 Sqn, Indian Navy. Carrying the unit's 'White Tiger' emblem on the nose, this machine was formerly WF293. The squadron worked up at RNAS Brawdy during 1959, before embarking in the Indian carrier* Vikrant *(originally HMS* Hercules*), from which they operated against Pakistan in 1971.

Hawker Sea Hawk Mk 50 of No. 860 Sqn, RNN, distinguished by a broad blade aerial on top of the fuselage. The squadron, whose emblem was carried on the forward fuselage, worked up during 1957 at Valkenburg, and later embarked in HrMs* Karel Doorman *(once HMS* Venerable*), eventually disbanding in 1964.

first of which (6-50) was delivered in July 1957. This version was essentially the same as the Sea Hawk FGA.Mk 6, differing only by the provision of American UHF radio equipment. They were later fitted with Sidewinder 1A air-to-air guided missiles on the outer wing pylons, and in this form served with No. 860 Squadron at Valkenburg, embarking at intervals in HrMs *Karel Doorman* (the former HMS *Venerable*). No. 3 Headquarters Squadron at Valkenburg also used the type, as well as some Gloster Meteor T.Mk 7s, for training purposes. The aircraft were withdrawn in October 1964.

West German order

West Germany also took an interest in the type during the mid-1950s, resulting in an order for 34 Sea Hawk Mk 100s and the same number of Sea Hawk Mk 101s. Based on the Sea Hawk FGA.Mk 6, the Sea Hawk Mk 100 was a versatile close-support day aircraft capable of fulfilling the fighter/bomber/ground-attack roles, being fitted with a taller fin and equipped with UHF radio. The Sea Hawk Mk 101 was basically similar, but being intended as a long-range radar reconnaissance fighter it carried Ekco Type 34 search radar on the starboard wing pylon. The first 12 Sea Hawk Mk 100 aircraft (starting with VA-220) were despatched from 13 February 1958 to RNAS Lossiemouth, where Marinefliegergeschwader 1 (MFG 1) formed and worked up, before departing on 22 July for Schleswig to undertake Baltic air defence. The remainder were delivered direct to Germany, the last to fly being Sea Hawk Mk 101 RB-376 which arrived on 21 April 1959, all being shore-based as Germany had no aircraft-carriers. Only MFG 1 and MFG 2 received Sea Hawks, and these aircraft were withdrawn when Lockheed F-104G Starfighters arrived during 1964-65; 28 surviving aircraft were sold to an Italian company during 1966.

On completion of the Dutch and West German orders, the production line was again closed and the jigs dismantled in 1959. However, the Indian Navy then chose the Sea Hawk for its new angled-deck carrier INS *Vikrant*, under conversion by Harland & Wolff from the laid-up HMS *Majestic*. The first nine Sea Hawk FGA.Mk 6 aircraft (IN151-IN159) were produced by Armstrong Whitworth from refurbished and re-engined RN Sea Hawk FB.Mk 3 aircraft, but these were followed by 14 new Sea Hawk FGA.Mk 6s (IN160-IN173) from a resurrected production line. Seven further machines refurbished by Armstrong Whitworth became IN174-IN180, and 16 more by Short Brothers at Belfast became IN181-IN196. In addition, the 28 former West German aircraft were purchased later to become IN230-239 (Sea Hawk Mk 100) and IN-240-257 (Sea Hawk Mk 101). The Indian Sea Hawks went into service with No. 300 'White Tiger' Squadron, which formed up at RNAS Brawdy on 7 July 1960, embarking in its parent carrier a year later. A shore-based support unit, No. 551 Squadron at Dabolim, was also equipped with the type. Indian Sea Hawks saw operational service in December 1971, during the war with Pakistan, attacks being made on shipping and coastal installations in the Chittagong area. The *Vikrant* has now been converted for V/STOL aircraft operation, using BAe Sea Harrier FRS.Mk 51s as replacement for the long-serving Sea Hawks.

A trio of Sea Hawk Mk 100s of MFG 1 of the West German navy. Thirty-four of this variant were supplied, being distinguished from their FAA counterparts by a revised fin and rudder. Some of these aircraft later went to the Indian Navy, as did a few of the 34 supplied Mk 101s.

SEA HARRIER: Ocean Raptor

Blooded in the Falklands war, Britain's Sea Harrier has proved itself to be a flexible and versatile means of providing air defence for the fleet without the need for large, vulnerable and expensive conventional aircraft carriers.

Few, indeed, are the types of aeroplane which have singly decided the outcome of a military campaign, and by that criterion the BAe Sea Harrier is a very special aircraft. Had it not existed in 1982, the successful mission by the Royal Navy Task Force to eject Argentine invaders from the Falkland Islands would not have taken place.

Of course, the prospects for victory at the start of this unexpected war would have been greater if the UK had possessed full-size aircraft-carriers operating several squadrons of Phantoms, Buccaneers, Gannets and Westland Sea Kings. However, defence cuts during the 1960s included abandonment of aircraft-carriers as an instrument of British naval power, and for a time it appeared that the Fleet Air Arm would soon be only a helicopter force. Into this potential vacuum stepped the Harrier, an aircraft which had been demonstrating vertical landings on vessels of varying sizes since February 1963. Having formerly opposed vectored-thrust aircraft because they would remove the *raison d'être* of large carriers, the Admiralty now backed the navalised Harrier for fear of having no jet combat aircraft under its direct control.

The ship type which made the Sea Harrier aircraft possible was the 'Invincible'-class anti-submarine cruiser. Displacing 19,500 tons and variously also known as the CAH and 'through-deck' cruisers, the three vessels of this type are the HMS *Invincible, Illustrious* and *Ark Royal*, commissioned in 1980, 1982 and 1985, respectively. Instead of catapults their short decks incorporate at the forward end a ramp (angled at 7° on the first two vessels, and 12° on the *Ark*) to permit rolling take-offs at maximum weight. As first deployed, the ships carried one squadron of anti-submarine Westland Sea King helicopters and another of five Sea Harriers.

Navalising the Harrier

When commissioned to produce the Sea Harrier, what is now the Kingston plant of British Aerospace was instructed to make minimal changes to the Harrier GR.Mk 3, which had been in RAF service since 1969. This was a tall order, for the RAF Harrier is optimised for ground attack and reconnaissance, whereas the FAA wanted to add interception capability and an associated radar. The chosen radar is the Ferranti Blue Fox which has been developed from the Seaspray used in the Westland Lynx HAS.Mks 2/3, but with air-to-air modes added. Operating in the I-band and employing frequency agility to increase immunity to jamming, the Blue Fox is optimised for single-crew aircraft in that flight parameters (speed, heading, attitude, etc.) are superimposed on its display screen. The pilot is therefore able to study the radar picture without having to make constant references to the instrument panel.

Naturally the Blue Fox is located in the Sea Harrier's nose, the need to place a comparatively large amount of avionics equipment in this area leading to a raised pilot's seat compared with that of the RAF Harrier, and a useful consequence is an improved field of view for

An innovation introduced in connection with the Sea Harrier is the ski-jump, allowing the aircraft to launch with greater combat loads from the carrier deck. Carrier landings are made vertically.

14

This Sea Harrier FRS.Mk 1 (XZ457) is seen how it appeared immediately after the Falklands conflict, the drab scheme broken only by the roundels, a few warning marks and three kill markings on the nose, depicting two Daggers and a Skyhawk. It is armed with a pair of AIM-9L 'Nine-Lima' Sidewinders, and has two 30-mm Aden cannon pods under the fuselage. The overall dark sea-grey colour led to the 'Shar' being nicknamed 'Muerta Negro' ('Black Death') by the Argentines.

No. 800 Sqn put up this neat quintet. The middle aircraft demonstrates the post-Falklands twin-Sidewinder launcher, while three of the others carry Sidewinder acquisition rounds for air combat practice.

air fighting. The radome and its attached pitot probe fold to port in order to fit deck-lifts aboard the 'Invincible'-class ships. Further equipment additional to RAF standards includes Doppler, a transponder and a new Ferranti HARS, which is a twin-gyro platform operating in conjunction with Doppler as a replacement for the same firm's INAS. The HARS is required to provide additional accuracy because of the lack of en-route surface-reference points over the sea, and has the further advantage that it can be aligned on a moving deck.

Behind the cockpit, Harrier and Sea Harrier have more in common. Dangers of salt water corrosion have resulted in the naval aircraft having additional protection, whilst the Rolls-Royce Pegasus Mk 104 is a parallel to the RAF's Mk 103 except for similar proofing. Both aircraft have three weapon-attachment points under the fuselage and two beneath each wing (strengthened on the Sea Harrier), and a measure of self-protection is provided by the Marconi ARI 18223 radar-warning receiver antenna mounted on the fin and in the extreme tail. As built, Sea Harriers were equipped with a 'pop-out' ram-air turbine in the upper fuselage to provide emergency power in the event of a flame-out. These have since been removed on the principle that ejection is the healthiest option for a pilot confronted by engine failure.

Triple-role aircraft

The designation Sea Harrier FRS.Mk 1 indicates the Fighter, Reconnaissance and Strike/attack roles assigned to the aircraft by the FAA. For interception the prime weapon is currently the AIM-9L Sidewinder infra-red AAM (from European licensed production by BGT), assisted at close ranges by two cannon. At first, one all-aspect AIM-9L was applied to each outer wing pylon, but capacity has been doubled by rapid production of a twin adaptor which was just too late to see action in the Falklands war. The cannon are of the well-tried Aden 30-mm type, fitted in RAF-type pods carrying 100 rounds each and attached to the fuselage shoulder hardpoints. The gun pods also perform an aerodynamic function in preventing air recirculation and consequent loss of lift when hovering close to the ground, and so are replaced by strakes if removed.

Leading the Sea Harrier's surface attack armoury is the BAe Sea Eagle, an all-weather 'fire-and-forget' anti-ship missile. Powered by a small Microturbo TRI 60 turbojet, the Sea Eagle extends its carrier's reach by up to 100 km (62 miles).

Performance:

Maximum speed at high altitude	Mach	1.25
Maximum speed at low altitude	640 kts	(1185 km/h; 736 mph)
Intercept radius, with three minutes combat and vertical landing on return	740 km	(460 miles)
Strike radius	463 km	(288 miles)

Carrier approach speed

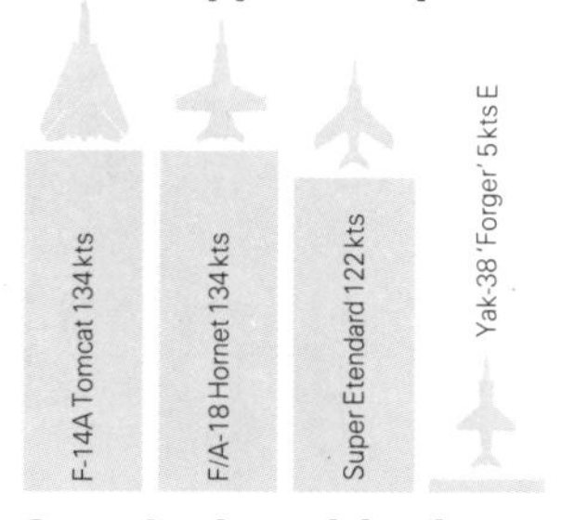

Service ceiling

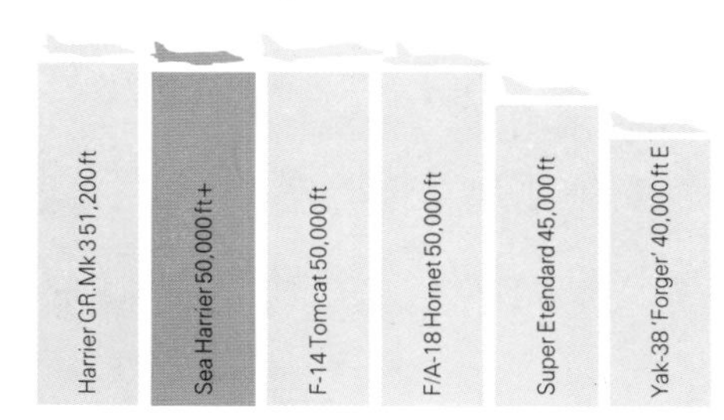

Speed at high altitude

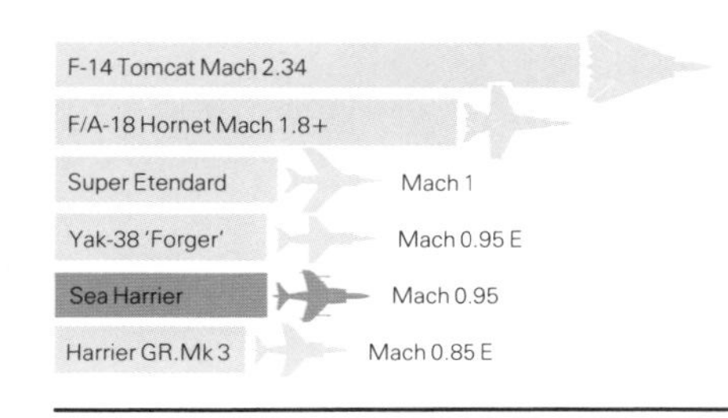

Speed at low altitude

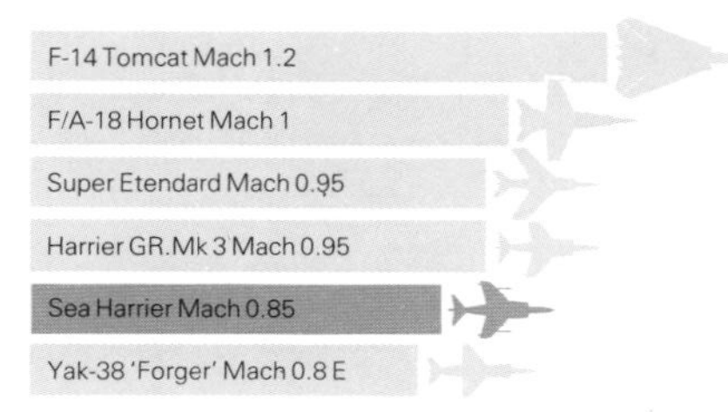

Operational range (internal fuel)

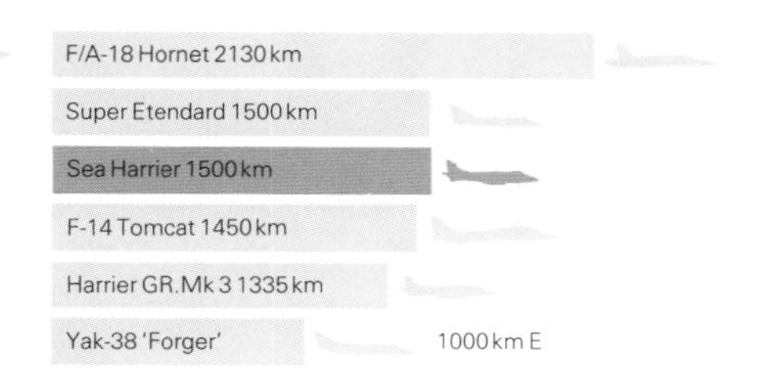

Specification: British Aerospace Sea Harrier FRS.Mk 1

Wings

Span	7.70 m	(25 ft 3 in)
Area	18.68 m^2	(201.1 sq ft)
Wing sweep	34° at quarter chord	

Fuselage and tail unit

Accommodation	1 pilot	
Length overall	14.50 m	(47 ft 7 in)
Height overall	3.71 m	(12 ft 2 in)
Tailplane span	4.24 m	(13 ft 11 in)

Landing gear

Retractable bicycle landing gear, single nosewheel, twin mainwheels, outriggers on wingtips

Wheelbase, nosewheel to mainwheels	3.45 m	(11 ft 4 in)
Outrigger wheel track	6.76 m	(22 ft 2 in)

Weights

Empty	5897 kg	(13,000 lb)
Maximum take-off	11884 kg	(26,200 lb)
Maximum external load	3629 kg	(8,000 lb)

Powerplant

One Rolls Royce Pegasus vectored thrust turbofan

Thrust	9752 kg	(21,500 lb)

British Aerospace Sea Harrier recognition features

Sea Harrier is similar in appearance to its land-based progenitor and to the American development, the McDonnell Douglas AV-8B. It can also be confused with the Soviet Yakovlev Yak-38 'Forger'.

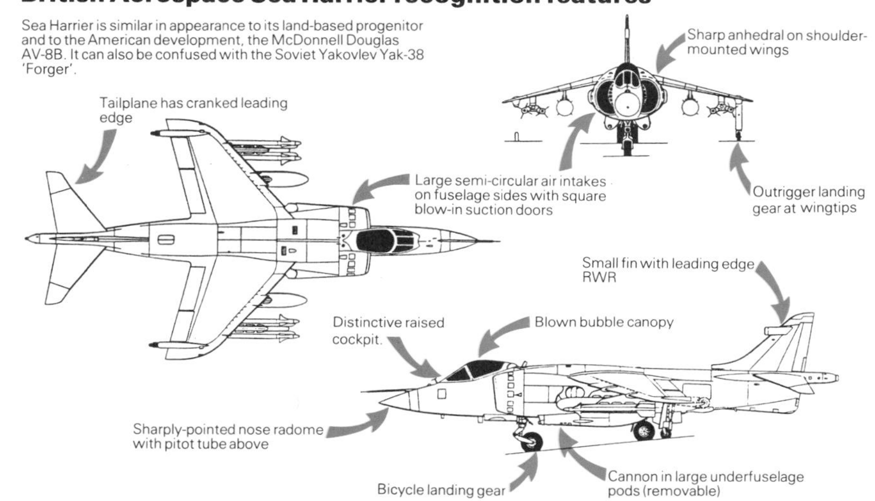

Sea Harrier variants

Sea Harrier FRS.Mk 1: multi-role variant of the Harrier for the Royal Navy; redesigned forward fuselage and different avionics systems; Pegasus 104 with improved corrosion resistance and increased capacity gearbox

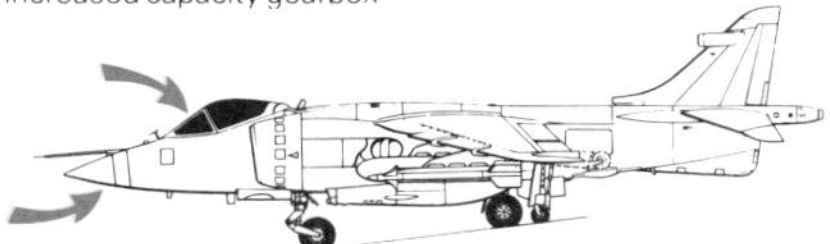

Sea Harrier T.4N: two-seat conversion trainer for the Royal Navy

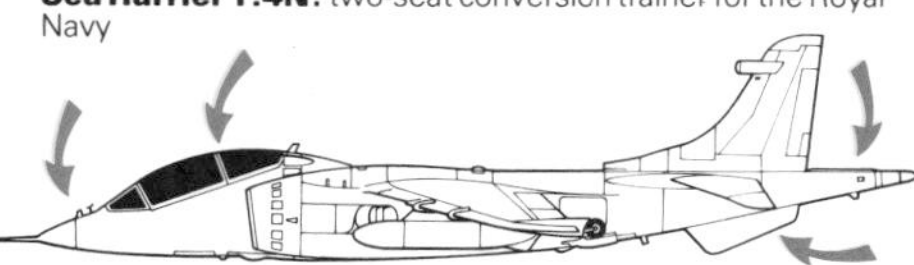

Sea Harrier FRS.Mk 51: designation of Sea Harriers delivered to Indian Navy. Planned procurement is for 48 aircraft
Harrier T.Mk 60: two-seat trainer for Indian Navy; full Sea Harrier equipment except Blue Fox radar
Sea Harrier FRS.Mk 2: redesignation of Royal Navy FRS.Mk 1s after Mid-Life Update; they will receive Blue Vixen radar in a reconfigured radome and will be adapted to carry AIM-120 AMRAAM missiles; avionics improvements also planned

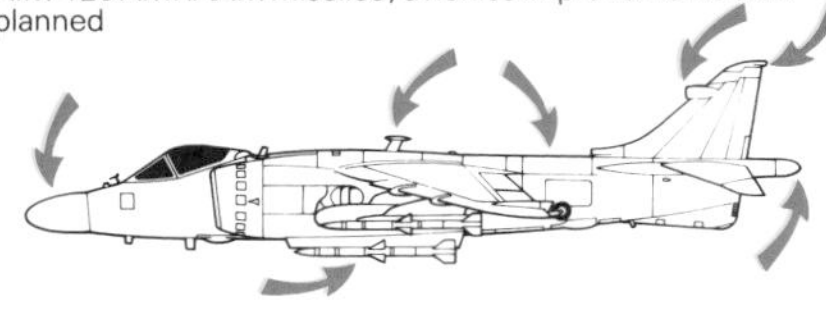

Sea Harrier: Ocean Raptor

units and example aircraft

Royal Navy

No. 800 Squadron

Base: RNAS Yeovilton and HMS *Illustrious*
Formed: 31 March 1980
Task: maritime fighter/ attack/reconnaissance
Aircraft: XZ455 '127/L', XZ492 '125/L', ZA175 '124/L', ZA190 '126/L', ZA191 '123/L'

No. 801 Squadron

Base: RNAS Yeovilton and HMS *Invincible*
Formed: 28 January 1981
Task: maritime fighter/ attack/reconnaissance
Aircraft: XZ451 '000/N', XZ459 '001/N', XZ495 '003/ N', XZ499 '002/N', ZA193 '004/N'

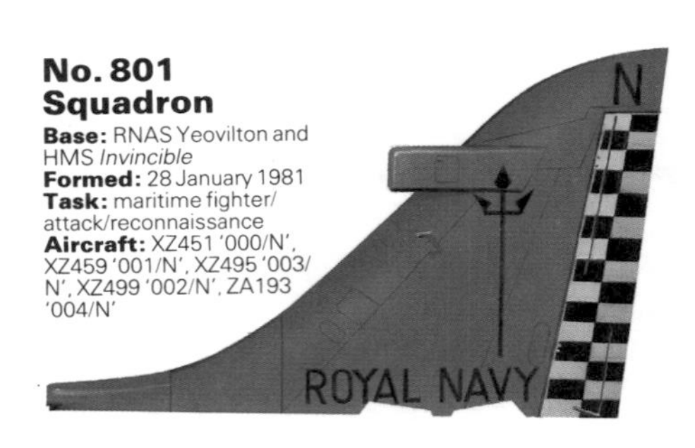

No. 899 Squadron

Base: RNAS Yeovilton
Formed: 31 March 1980 (ex 700A squadron)
Task: maritime fighter/ attack/reconnaissance and training
Aircraft: XZ457 '715', XZ460 '714', XZ493 '713', XZ494 '716', ZA176 '712', ZA195 '710', ZD578 '711'

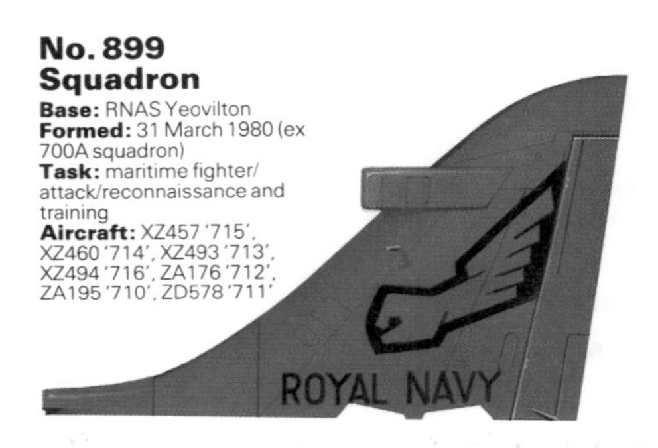

Indian Navy

No. 300 Squadron

Base: Goa/Dabolim
Formed: 22 December 1982 (as Indian Navy Training Unit, Yeovilton)
Task: maritime fighter/ attack/reconnaissance
Aircraft: IN601, IN602, IN603, IN604, IN605, IN606

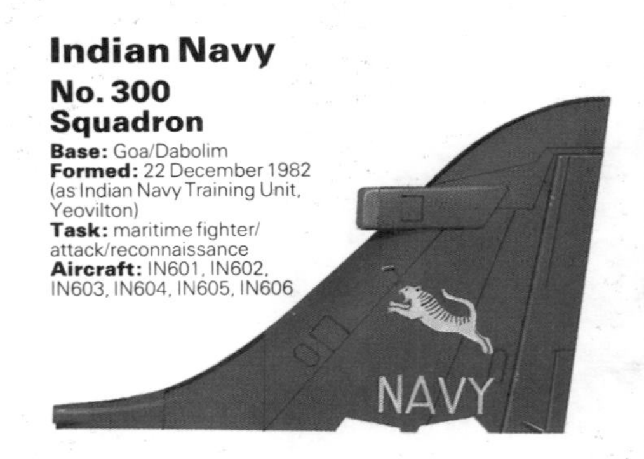

The cockpit of the Sea Harrier FRS.Mk 1 is dominated by the display for the Ferranti Blue Fox radar, on the right of the main instrument panel. The rest of the cockpit bears a strong family resemblance to that of the land-based Harrier, with armament selection switches at the bottom of the left hand side of the panel and Sidewinder operation controlled from a panel in front of the control column. The head-up display is newer and larger than that fitted to the Harrier GR.Mk 3.

Sea Harrier warload

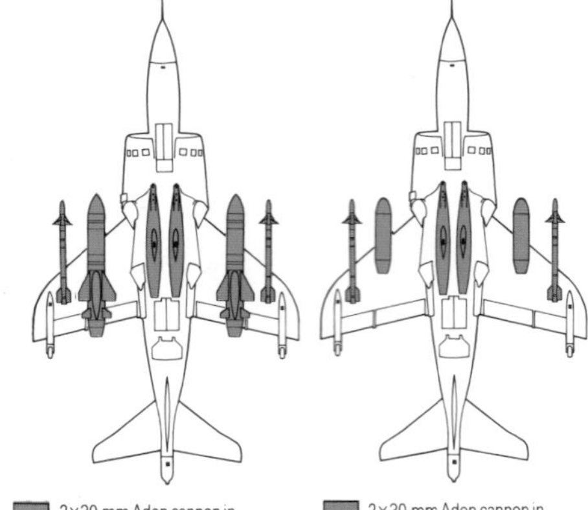

2×30-mm Aden cannon in underfuselage pods
2×BAe Sea Eagle anti-shipping missiles on inboard underwing pylons
2×AIM-9L Sidewinder air-to-air missiles on outer pylons

Royal Navy anti-shipping (provisional)

Highly resistant to ECM, the Sea Eagle is an advanced sea-skimming anti-ship missile. Sea Harriers have played an important part in development trials, sinking an obsolete destroyer in July 1984. Sea Harrier units will receive the Sea Eagle after the RAF's Buccaneer squadrons.

2×30-mm Aden cannon in underfuselage pods
2×Royal Navy 36-round 2-in (50.8-mm) rocket pods on inboard pylons
2×AIM-9L Sidewinder air-to-air missiles on outer pylons

Royal Navy ground attack

The Sea Harrier is an extremely useful close-support tool, and can be armed with SNEB or RN rocket pods, retarded and cluster bombs, etc.

2×30-mm Aden cannon in underfuselage pods
4×AIM-9L Sidewinder air-to-air missiles on twin launchers on outer pylons
2×864-litre (190-Imp gal) fuel tanks on inboard pylons

Royal Navy fighter

Royal Navy Sea Harriers are currently being refitted with multiple Sidewinder pylons, to allow the carriage of more than two AAMs on combat air patrol.

2×30-mm Aden cannon in underfuselage pods
2×Matra Magic air-to-air missiles on outer pylons
2×864-litre (190-Imp gal) fuel tanks on inboard pylons

Indian Navy fighter

Indian Navy Sea Harriers are equipped to fire Matra Magics in place of the Sidewinder, a strange choice in view of the success of the Sidewinder in the Falklands war, against aircraft which often mounted Magics. Indigenous bombs and rockets will also be used.

British Aerospace Sea Harrier FRS.Mk 1 cutaway drawing key

1 Pitot tube
2 Radome
3 Flat plate radar scanner
4 Scanner tracking mechanism
5 Ferranti Blue Fox radar equipment module
6 Radome hinge
7 Nose pitch reaction control valve
8 Pitch feel and trim mechanism
9 Starboard side oblique camera
10 Inertial platform
11 Pressurization spill valve
12 IFF aerial
13 Cockpit ram air intake
14 Yaw vane
15 Cockpit front pressure bulkhead
16 Rudder pedals
17 Cockpit floor level
18 Tacan aerial
19 Ventral Doppler navigation aerial
20 Canopy external latch
21 Control column
22 Windscreen de-misting air duct
23 Instrument panel
24 Instrument panel shroud
25 Birdproof windscreen panels
26 Windscreen wiper
27 Head-up display
28 Starboard side console panel
29 Nozzle angle control lever
30 Engine throttle lever
31 Underfloor control linkages
32 Lower UHF aerial
33 Radome, open position
34 Detachable in-flight refuelling probe
35 Pre-closing nosewheel doors
36 Ejection seat rocket pack
37 Radar hand controller
38 Fuel cock
39 Cockpit rear pressure bulkhead
40 Cabin air discharge valve
41 Canopy handle
42 Pilot's Martin-Baker Type 10H zero-zero ejection seat
43 Sliding canopy rail
44 Miniature detonating cord (MDC) canopy breaker
45 Starboard engine-air intake
46 Cockpit canopy cover
47 Ejection seat headrest
48 Drogue parachute container
49 Parachute release mechanism
50 Boundary layer spill duct
51 Cockpit air conditioning plant
52 Intake centre-body fairing
53 Ram air discharge to engine intake
54 Hydraulic accumulator
55 Nose undercarriage hydraulic jack
56 Boundary layer bleed air duct
57 Nose undercarriage wheel bay
58 Port engine air intake
59 Landing/taxiing lamp
60 Nosewheel forks
61 Pivoted axle beam
62 Nosewheel, forward retracting
63 Supplementary air intake doors (fully floating)
64 Intake duct framing
65 Air refuelling probe mounting and fuel connector
66 Engine intake compressor face
67 Air conditioning system ram air intakes
68 Boundary layer air spill duct canopy cut-out
69 UHF homing aerials
70 Engine bay access doors
71 Rolls-Royce Pegasus Mk 104 vectored thrust turbofan engine
72 Hydraulic filters
73 Engine oil tank
74 Forward fuselage integral fuel tank, port and starboard
75 Engine bay venting air scoop
76 Hydraulic system ground connections
77 Cushion augmentation strake, port and starboard, fitted in place of gun pack

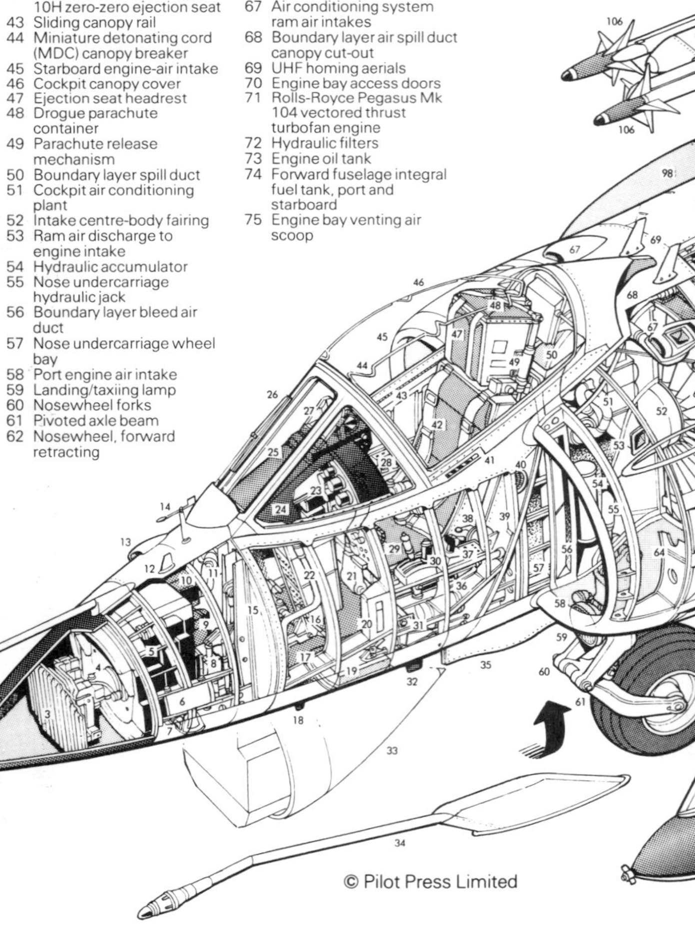

78 Engine monitoring and recording equipment
79 Forward nozzle fairing
80 Fan air (cold stream) swivelling nozzle
81 Nozzle bearing
82 In-flight refuelling floodlight
83 Venting air intake
84 Alternator cooling air duct
85 Hydraulic pumps
86 Engine accessory equipment gearbox
87 Single alternator on starboard side
88 GTS/APU exhaust
89 Gas turbine starter/ Auxiliary Power Unit (GTS/ APU)
90 Aileron control rod
91 Wing front spar carry-through
92 Nozzle bearing cooling air duct
93 Engine turbine section
94 Wing panel centreline joint rib
95 Wing centre section fairing panels
96 GTS/APU air intake
97 Alternator cooling air exhaust
98 864-litre (190-Imp gal) jettisonable external fuel tank
99 Starboard inner stores pylon
100 Leading-edge dog-tooth
101 Reaction control air ducting
102 Aileron control rod
103 Starboard wing integral fuel tank; total internal fuel capacity 2864 litre (630 Imp gal)
104 Fuel system piping
105 Inboard pylon attachment hardpoint
106 Starboard twin Sidewinder installation
107 Starboard outer stores pylon
108 Wing fences
109 Vortex generators
110 Outer pylon hardpoint
111 Aileron hydraulic power control unit
112 Roll control reaction air valve
113 Starboard navigation light
114 Wing-tip fairing
115 Starboard outrigger fairing
116 Outrigger wheel, retracted position
117 Sea Harrier FRS.Mk 2 ventral view
118 Blue Vixen radar
119 AIM-120 advanced medium range air-to-air missiles (AMRAAM), four
120 Fuel tank-mounted missile pylon
121 Rear fuselage stretched avionics equipment bay
122 Ventral gun packs
123 Starboard aileron
124 Fuel jettison pipe
125 Starboard plain flap
126 Trailing-edge root fairing
127 Water-methanol filler cap
128 Wing slinging point
129 Anti-collision light
130 Water-methanol injection system tank
131 Engine fire extinguisher bottle
132 Flap operating rod
133 Flap hydraulic jack
134 Fuel contents transmitters
135 Rear fuselage integral fuel tank
136 Ram air turbine housing
137 Turbine doors
138 Emergency ram air turbine (being removed)
139 Rear fuselage frames
140 Ram air turbine jack
141 Cooling system ram air intake
142 Air system heat exchanger
143 HF tuner
144 HF notch aerial
145 Rudder control linkage
146 Starboard all-moving tailplane
147 Temperature sensor
148 Tailfin construction
149 Forward radar warning receiver
150 VHF aerial
151 Fin tip aerial fairing
152 Rudder
153 Rudder top hinge
154 Honeycomb core construction
155 Rudder trim jack
156 Rudder tab
157 Tail reaction control air ducting
158 Yaw control port
159 Aft radar warning receiver
160 Rear position light
161 Pitch reaction control air valve
162 Tailplane honeycomb trailing-edge
163 Extended tailplane tip
164 Tailplane construction
165 Tail bumper
166 IFF notch aerial
167 Tailplane sealing plate
168 Fin spar attachment
169 Tailplane centre-section carry-through
170 All-moving tailplane control jack
171 Radar altimeter aerials
172 UHF stand-by aerial
173 Ram air exhaust
174 Equipment air conditioning plant
175 Ground power supply socket
176 Twin batteries
177 Chaff and flare dispensers
178 Dispenser electronic control units
179 Avionics equipment racks
180 Avionics bay access door
181 Ventral airbrake
182 Airbrake hydraulic jack
183 Liquid oxygen converter
184 Nitrogen pressurizing bottle for hydraulic system
185 Flap drive torque shaft
186 Rear spar/fuselage attachment point
187 Nozzle blast shield
188 Rear (hot stream) swivelling exhaust nozzle
189 Wing rear spar
190 Port flap honeycomb core construction
191 Fuel jettison valve
192 Fuel jettison pipe
193 Aileron honeycomb core construction
194 Outrigger wheel fairing
195 Wing tip fairing
196 Hydraulic retraction jack
197 Shock absorber leg strut
198 Port outrigger wheel
199 Torque scissor links
200 Outrigger wheel leg fairings
201 Port navigation light
202 Roll control reaction air valve
203 Wing rib construction
204 Outer pylon hardpoint 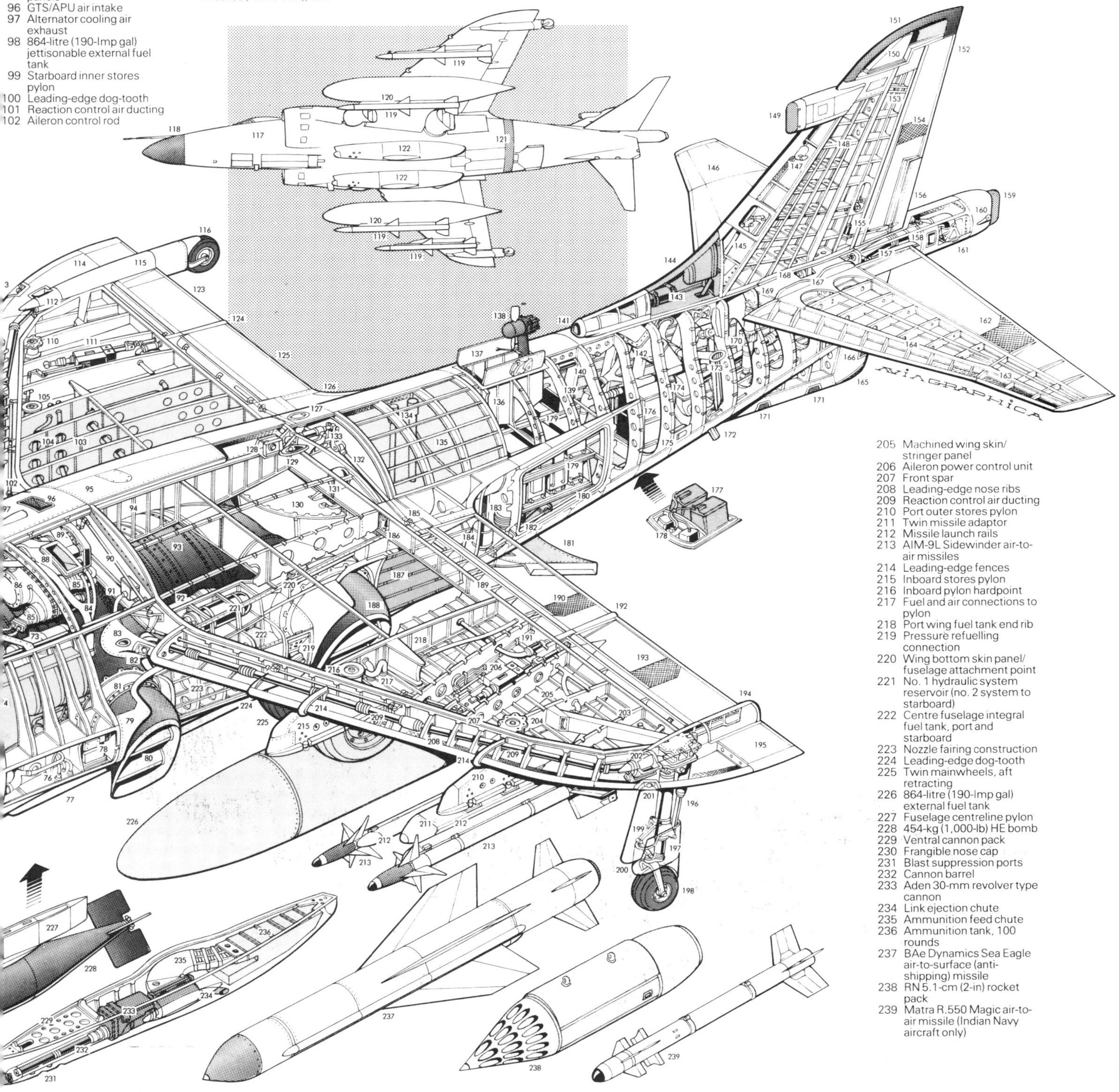
205 Machined wing skin/ stringer panel
206 Aileron power control unit
207 Front spar
208 Leading-edge nose ribs
209 Reaction control air ducting
210 Port outer stores pylon
211 Twin missile adaptor
212 Missile launch rails
213 AIM-9L Sidewinder air-to-air missiles
214 Leading-edge fences
215 Inboard stores pylon
216 Inboard pylon hardpoint
217 Fuel and air connections to pylon
218 Port wing fuel tank end rib
219 Pressure refuelling connection
220 Wing bottom skin panel/ fuselage attachment point
221 No. 1 hydraulic system reservoir (no. 2 system to starboard)
222 Centre fuselage integral fuel tank, port and starboard
223 Nozzle fairing construction
224 Leading-edge dog-tooth
225 Twin mainwheels, aft retracting
226 864-litre (190-Imp gal) external fuel tank
227 Fuselage centreline pylon
228 454-kg (1,000-lb) HE bomb
229 Ventral cannon pack
230 Frangible nose cap
231 Blast suppression ports
232 Cannon barrel
233 Aden 30-mm revolver type cannon
234 Link ejection chute
235 Ammunition feed chute
236 Ammunition tank, 100 rounds
237 BAe Dynamics Sea Eagle air-to-surface (anti-shipping) missile
238 RN 5.1-cm (2-in) rocket pack
239 Matra R.550 Magic air-to-air missile (Indian Navy aircraft only)

Against landing craft, other 'soft' ships and land targets, the Sea Harrier can employ guns, bombs and rockets. The standard 454-kg (1,000-lb) bomb, free-fall or retarded, may be carried on inner wing pylons and the centreline attachment, whilst Royal Navy 50.8-mm (2-in) rocket pods form an alternative underwing load. Where range is the dominant factor in a mission, inboard pylons are equipped with 455-litre (100-Imp gal) or 864-litre (190-Imp gal) drop-tanks. Ferrying is accomplished with 1364-litre (300-Imp gal) tanks, which must live up to the 'drop' in their name if the flaps are to be lowered for landing. The inboard wing stations can each carry up to 907 kg (2,000 lb) of weaponry, and those outboard are stressed for 454 kg (1,000 lb), but aircraft weight restrictions for carrier operation are such that full capacity cannot be exploited under normal circumstances.

Naval service

The initial Sea Harrier FRS.Mk 1 contract covered 24 aircraft, of which the first three were assigned to development work. Strangely, because of a combination of delays, the maiden flight of a Sea Harrier was undertaken from Dunsfold by the first production (overall fourth) aircraft on 20 August 1978. This aeroplane lost little time in becoming the first to land on a ship, duly arriving aboard HMS *Hermes* on 13 November of that year. The last of the Royal Navy's 'real' aircraft-carriers, the *Hermes* had been converted to a commando ship and so was without catapults. She was, however, re-fitted with a 12° ramp and served as a 'Harrier-carrier' until 1983. It was aboard the *Hermes* that No. 700A Squadron, the Sea Harrier IFTU, conducted a first seaborne deployment in October-November 1979, following the hand-over of the FAA's first aircraft on 18 June. No. 700A Squadron was later redesignated No. 899 Squadron at the aircraft's home base of RNAS Yeovilton and currently acts as a headquarters unit.

Three further squadrons have formed to fly Sea Harriers: Nos 800, 801 and 809, of which the last was a temporary unit established for the Falklands war. Assigned five aircraft each for carrier deployment, the two current seagoing squadrons will increase their complement to eight, this being the number of aircraft found necessary to enable a round-the-clock two-aircraft CAP to be maintained. Constant vigilance over the fleet was the prime requirement in the South Atlantic campaign, when 28 Sea Harriers made 1,100 CAPs and 90 offensive support sorties in the course of 2,376 flights, 2,088 deck landings and 2,675 hours 25 minutes of airborne time. They destroyed 23 Argentine aircraft (nine IAI Daggers, eight McDonnell Douglas Skyhawks, two Dassault-Breguet Mirage IIIs, an English Electric Canberra and a Lockheed Hercules) without a single air-to-air combat loss, although two were shot down by ground fire and four destroyed in accidents. Incredibly, aircraft availability was over 80 per cent despite cramped conditions on the hangar deck, foul weather and minor battle damage, and only one per cent of planned missions had to be abandoned because of aircraft unserviceability.

Exports and improvements

This impressive record of combatworthiness unfortunately failed to produce the export orders which might confidently have been expected. The sole firm customer, India, decided on a Sea Harrier purchase as long ago as November 1979, when it ordered six single-seat Mk 51s and two Mk 60 trainers, followed in November 1985 by a further 10 Mk 51s and a single Mk 60. Although a Letter of Intent was signed for seven further Mk 51s and a fourth Mk 60 in October 1986, this has never been turned into a firm order.

For its part, the FAA subsequently increased its Sea Harrier contracts to 57 and the last aircraft was delivered in August 1988. With 17 lost to all causes by the end of 1990, all 40 surviving aircraft are to undergo a mid-life update to FRS.Mk 2 standard. These will be followed down the Dunsfold line in 1994 by 10 new-build Sea Harrier FRS.Mk 2s following a March 1990 order from the Royal Navy. Major features of the FRS.Mk 2 will be the substitution of a Ferranti Blue Vixen radar and addition of Hughes AIM-120 AMRAAMs. The pulse-Doppler Blue Vixen in conjunction with the fire-and-forget AIM-120 will give the Sea Harrier all-important look-down/shoot-down capability against intruding aircraft. Replacing the 30-mm Aden guns, 25-mm Adens or two AIM-120s will be carried under the fuselage. The outer wing pylons will take either an AIM-120 or a Sidewinder.

Avionics improvements will require additional space to be provided through extension of the equipment bay in the rear fuselage. Changes in the cockpit include two multi-function video screens; HOTAS controls for maximum pilot efficiency; provision for the JTIDS secure voice and data transmission system; and a dedicated RWR display. The last is associated with updating of ARI 18223 to Guardian configuration for improved protection. Aircraft will standardise on the Tracor ALE-40 chaff/flare dispenser installed in the lower rear fuselages of some Sea Harriers for the Falklands war. Having achieved world renown during this conflict so early in its operational career, the aircraft may see the remainder of its service life as an anticlimax. However, the far-reaching improvements to be made in the immediate future will ensure that the Sea Harrier remains equal to the tasks which may be demanded of it in both the North and South Atlantic.

Glossary

AAM Air-to-Air Missile
AMRAAM Advanced Medium-Range Air-to-Air Missile
CAH Carrier, Assault, Helicopter
CAP Combat Air Patrol
ECM Electronic CounterMeasures
FAA Fleet Air Arm
HARS Heading and Attitude Reference System
HOTAS Hands-On Throttle And Stick
IFTU Intensive Flight Trials Unit
INAS Inertial Navigation Attack System
JTIDS Joint Tactical Information Distribution System
MLU Mid-Life Update
RNAS Royal Naval Air Station
RWR Radar-Warning Receiver
STOVL Short Take-Off and Vertical Landing
VTOL Vertical Take-Off and Landing

With air brake deployed and nozzles rotated, a No. 801 Sqn 'Shar' manoeuvres prior to landing. The pointed nose of the FRS.Mk 1 is to disappear as aircraft are reworked to FRS.Mk 2 standard with Blue Vixen radar.

GRIFFON SPITFIRES

Sentiment associates the Spitfire with the Merlin engine, but by the end of World War II development had long been concentrated entirely on variants powered by the bigger Griffon engine. These were in many ways quite different aircraft, but they put new life into the great story of one of the world's most famous warplanes.

The Supermarine Type 300, the Spitfire prototype, first flew on 5 March 1936. From the very beginning its flight development was conducted under pressure, and the pressure increased as the years went by. Ten years later well over 20,000 Spitfires (and over 2,000 Seafires) had been delivered to many customers. Only then was it possible to take a breather and discover that the aircraft at the end of the line were twice as heavy, more than twice as powerful and far more capable than the little Model 300, which seemed like a sprightly elf by comparison. Jeffrey Quill, chief test pilot over almost the entire period of Spitfire development, pointed out that, in terms of gross weight, a Seafire Mk 47 was equal to a Spitfire Mk I plus 32 standard airline passengers each with 18 kg (40 lb) of baggage.

Quill also surprised some by commenting that in his opinion the nicest Spitfire to fly was DP845. This was unexpected because, of all the much-rebuilt hack development Spitfires, DP845 beat the lot. Among many other claims to fame it was the very first Spitfire to be powered by a Griffon engine; an odder claim is that the same serial number was carried by a Miles Whitney Straight (G-AEVG in its original civil guise).

Supermarine and Rolls-Royce had discussed the possibility of mating the big Griffon to the little Spitfire as early as August 1939. With a capacity of 36.7 litres (2,239 cu in) compared with the Merlin's 27 litres (1,648 cu in), the Griffon was being developed for the naval Fairey Barracuda and Fairey Firefly. Its potential for fighters was enhanced when Rolls-Royce carefully revised the design to bring down the frontal area to almost the same as that of the Merlin, though it was clear the tops of the cylinder blocks would project slightly above the existing Spitfire cowl line. Pilot view dead ahead, however, could actually be slightly improved. No more could be done at the time, but discussions were not terminated and in 1940 the Air Ministry issued Specification F.4/40 for a single-seat high-altitude fighter. Supermarine managed to get a contract for two special Spitfires to this specification, strengthened to accept 'various engines including the Griffon'.

These two aircraft (DP845 and DP851) had the Supermarine designation Type 337 and much in common with the Spitfire Mk III, though the mark number assigned was IV. By early 1941, however, the same number had been assigned to the Spitfire PR.Mk IV photo-reconnaissance production version, so DP845, the only one to fly at that time, was restyled Spitfire Mk XX. It flew in 1941, with a Griffon IIB and four-bladed propeller. The planned armament was six His-

At the end of World War II, the latest Spitfire in service was the F.Mk 21. This was developed immediately into the F.Mk 22 and later into the F.Mk 24; small numbers of each variant were used after the end of hostilities. Here two F.Mk 22s and an F.Mk 21 are seen flying from the Supermarine test airfield at High Post.

pano cannon, and this armament was mocked-up on DP845. It was hoped to go into production with Griffon Spitfires at once, all with mark numbers of XX or higher, and 750 Spitfire Mk XXs were ordered from the Castle Bromwich factory on 23 August 1941, but somebody in the Ministry of Aircraft Production changed the mark number to the regular Merlin-engined Spitfire Mks VB and VC for these aircraft, whose serials were in the range ER206-ES369.

Thus in 1941-42 there were just two Griffon-engined Spitfires, flying mainly from Rolls-Royce's Hucknall airfield until the new engine could be considered reasonably mature. The engine was variously a Mk IIB or Mk III, with a variety of four-bladed propellers and asymmetric radiators of Morris QCY type, larger than that of the Spitfire Mk V aircraft but looking similar from a distance. The big change from the pilot's viewpoint was that the propeller rotation was reversed. On take-off other Spitfires tended to swing to the left, but with the Griffon there was a much more powerful swing in the opposite direction. The drill was to wind the rudder trim full left before opening the throttle. In a powered landing, varying engine power caused reactions on the rudder pedals. General handling was much like that of other Spitfires, though the extra power was useful at low level in faster and steeper climbs, and to some extent in pulling even tighter turns without any fear of flicking into a high-speed stall. The only real fault of all Spitfires in 1941 was that at high speeds the ailerons froze almost solid, and only a very strong pilot could generate enough stick movement for a fast roll.

By the summer of 1942, while longer-term development of the Griffon-engined Spitfire was in full swing, Focke-Wulf Fw 190As were making hit-and-run raids with single heavy bombs against south coast towns and causing an increasing nuisance. The new Hawker Typhoon was good as a low-level interceptor, but it was obvious that a Griffon-engined Spitfire might be even better. DP845 was modified in a matter of days as the prototype Supermarine Type 366, or Spitfire Mk XII, with two cannon and four machine-guns (standard 'B' armament) plus a broad fin and pointed rudder. Various batches of aircraft already in production were earmarked for completion as Spitfire Mk XIIs. All 100 had been ordered as Spitfire Mk VC aircraft, but they were completed to two slightly differing standards. Basically the Spitfire Mk XII was a Mk VC with a strengthened airframe, and a special attachment at Frame 5 for the completely different semi-cantilever beam on which was placed the 1294-kW (1,735-hp) Griffon III or IV, driving a Rotol propeller with four blades of duralumin or Jablo densified wood. The deep asymmetric radiator and broad pointed rudder were retained, and LF clipped wings were fitted. These wings were of Universal type, but the B-type armament was fitted to all 100 aircraft. The slight difference was that the first 45 (EN221/238 and EN601/627) had fuselages of Mk IX type, with fixed tailwheel, while 55 (MB794/805, 829/863, 875/882) had Mk VIII-type fully retractable tailwheels. Not least of the remarkable features of the Spitfire Mk XII was that empty and normal loaded weight was in each case lighter than that of a Spitfire Mk IX!

Striving for the ultimate Spitfire

Back in 1941, two years before delivery of the Spitfire Mk XIIs, Joe Smith and Alan Clifton had been working on the Type 356 as the ultimate Spitfire. Its mark number was to be 21, but by 1942 the differences were so fundamental that it had become a new fighter altogether, and for a time it was planned to name it the Victor. To assist development of the powerful machine, Rolls-Royce was assigned six Spitfire airframes, JF316/321, originally ordered as Spitfire Mk VIIIs with retracting tailwheels and normal-span Universal wings. They were trucked to Hucknall where the first four were fitted with the Griffon 61, first of the new two-stage Griffons with an intercooler, driving a new Rotol propeller with five broad blades, and with deep symmetrical radiators. The last two aircraft were fitted with the Griffon 85 driving a six-bladed contraprop, usually also of Rotol make. Because of its naval ancestry the Griffon had a cartridge starter with a five-round breech, making the aircraft independent of ground electrical power. The much longer nose of these aircraft necessitated an even larger vertical tail, the first type being an unlovely pointed type with a straight leading edge which gave way to a very broad assembly with a graceful rounded outline.

JF317 was the first of this group to fly, and intensive and often hair-raising development flying took place in the hands of Rolls-Royce and Supermarine test pilots. From the start it was clear that the two-stage Griffon made the Spitfire a real he-man's aeroplane, and what happened next was predictable: there was a crash programme for a

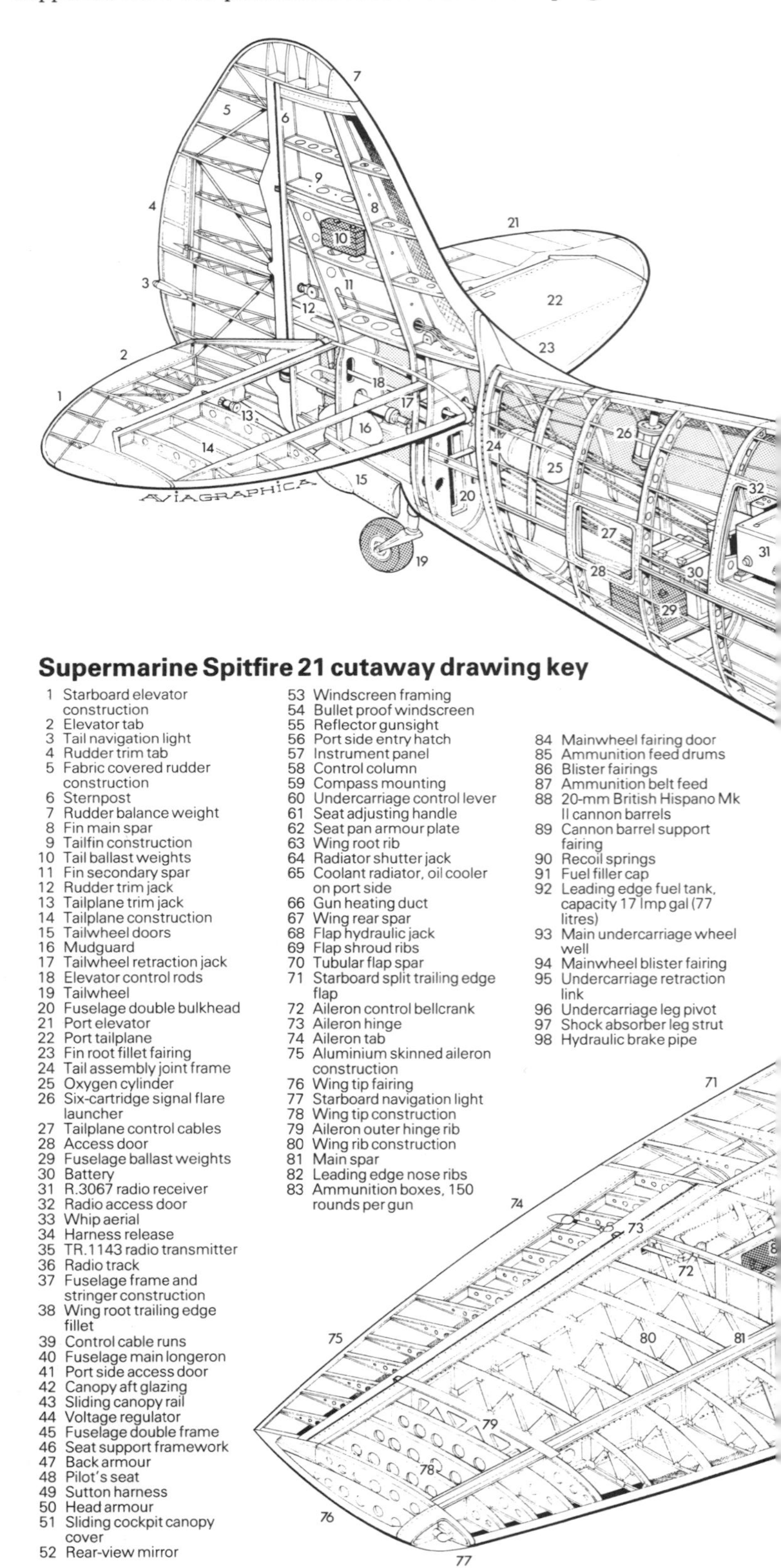

Supermarine Spitfire 21 cutaway drawing key

1 Starboard elevator construction
2 Elevator tab
3 Tail navigation light
4 Rudder trim tab
5 Fabric covered rudder construction
6 Sternpost
7 Rudder balance weight
8 Fin main spar
9 Tailfin construction
10 Tail ballast weights
11 Fin secondary spar
12 Rudder trim jack
13 Tailplane trim jack
14 Tailplane construction
15 Tailwheel doors
16 Mudguard
17 Tailwheel retraction jack
18 Elevator control rods
19 Tailwheel
20 Fuselage double bulkhead
21 Port elevator
22 Port tailplane
23 Fin root fillet fairing
24 Tail assembly joint frame
25 Oxygen cylinder
26 Six-cartridge signal flare launcher
27 Tailplane control cables
28 Access door
29 Fuselage ballast weights
30 Battery
31 R.3067 radio receiver
32 Radio access door
33 Whip aerial
34 Harness release
35 TR.1143 radio transmitter
36 Radio track
37 Fuselage frame and stringer construction
38 Wing root trailing edge fillet
39 Control cable runs
40 Fuselage main longeron
41 Port side access door
42 Canopy aft glazing
43 Sliding canopy rail
44 Voltage regulator
45 Fuselage double frame
46 Seat support framework
47 Back armour
48 Pilot's seat
49 Sutton harness
50 Head armour
51 Sliding cockpit canopy cover
52 Rear-view mirror
53 Windscreen framing
54 Bullet proof windscreen
55 Reflector gunsight
56 Port side entry hatch
57 Instrument panel
58 Control column
59 Compass mounting
60 Undercarriage control lever
61 Seat adjusting handle
62 Seat pan armour plate
63 Wing root rib
64 Radiator shutter jack
65 Coolant radiator, oil cooler on port side
66 Gun heating duct
67 Wing rear spar
68 Flap hydraulic jack
69 Flap shroud ribs
70 Tubular flap spar
71 Starboard split trailing edge flap
72 Aileron control bellcrank
73 Aileron hinge
74 Aileron tab
75 Aluminium skinned aileron construction
76 Wing tip fairing
77 Starboard navigation light
78 Wing tip construction
79 Aileron outer hinge rib
80 Wing rib construction
81 Main spar
82 Leading edge nose ribs
83 Ammunition boxes, 150 rounds per gun
84 Mainwheel fairing door
85 Ammunition feed drums
86 Blister fairings
87 Ammunition belt feed
88 20-mm British Hispano Mk II cannon barrels
89 Cannon barrel support fairing
90 Recoil springs
91 Fuel filler cap
92 Leading edge fuel tank, capacity 17 Imp gal (77 litres)
93 Main undercarriage wheel well
94 Mainwheel blister fairing
95 Undercarriage retraction link
96 Undercarriage leg pivot
97 Shock absorber leg strut
98 Hydraulic brake pipe

The last mark of Spitfire to see active service was the PR.Mk 19, which was not retired until 1954. This mark had flown the last combat mission of the type on 1 April 1954 during the Malayan campaign. The PR.Mk 19 also served in Germany in the late 1940s, where No. 2 Sqn flew this aircraft from Fürstenfeldbrück.

99 Starboard mainwheel
100 Mainwheel leg fairing door
101 Undercarriage torque scissors
102 Fuel pipe runs
103 Main spar stub attachment
104 Lower main fuel tank, capacity 48 Imp gal (218 litres)
105 Upper main fuel tank, capacity 36 Imp gal (164 litres)
106 Fuel filler cap
107 Oil tank vent
108 Oil tank, capacity 9 Imp gal (41 litres)
109 Oil tank access door
110 Engine compartment fireproof bulkhead
111 Port split trailing edge flap
112 Flap hydraulic jack
113 Flap synchronizing jack
114 Port twin 20-mm Hispano cannon
115 Spent cartridge case ejector chute
116 Ammunition feed drums
117 Ammunition belt feeds
118 Ammunition boxes, 150 rounds per gun
119 Aileron control bellcrank
120 Aileron tab

Supermarine Griffon Spitfire and Seafire variants

Spitfire Mk IV: two aircraft (DP845 and 851), latter reserved for Mk 21; first with larger engine, later Mk XX
Spitfire Mk XII: interim low-level fighter based on existing Mk V or Mk VIII; B armament in Universal clipped wing; Griffon III or IV and four-bladed propeller; total 100
Spitfire Mk XIV: interim fighter with two-stage high-altitude Griffon (in production Mk 65 or 67 with five-bladed propeller); strengthened Mk VIII airframe, enlarged tail; Universal wing (often clipped by local action), **Spitfire XIVE** with two 20-mm and two 12.7-mm (0.5-in) guns, later batches with bubble hood, and **Spitfire FR.Mk XIV** versions with cameras and rear-fuselage tank; total 957
Spitfire Mk XVIII (post-war **Spitfire F.Mk 18** and **Spitfire FR.Mk 18**): definitive variant with improved wing with tanks, FR with rear-fuselage fuel and cameras; extruded spar booms used on this mark only (abandoned on Mk 21); total 100 F plus 200 FR
Spitfire Mk XIX (post-war **Spitfire PR.Mk 19**): unarmed photo version with Mk VC wing of 'bowser' type as on Mk XI; first 20 Griffon 65 and unpressurised, followed by 205 Griffon 66 and pressurised
Spitfire Mk XX: further stage in life of Mk IV DP845
Spitfire Mk 21: redesigned aircraft with completely new wing; total 120
Spitfire Mk 22: bubble hood and cut-down rear fuselage; often Mk 85 engine and contraprop; later with Spiteful tail; total 278
Spitfire Mk 23: unbuilt Mk 22 with different wing profile
Spitfire Mk 24: zero-length rocket launchers, two 150-litre (33-Imp gal) rear-fuselage tanks, Mk 5 guns fired electrically; total 54 plus 27 Mk 22 with rear tanks not included under Mk 22
Seafire Mk XV: basic Griffon variant derived from Spitfire Mk XII; total six prototypes plus 250 from Westland and 134 from Cunliffe-Owen
Seafire Mk XVII: (decision to avoid duplicating mark numbers left Mk XVI to Spitfire) as Mk XV with bubble hood, new windscreen, rear-fuselage tank except in **Seafire FR.Mk XVII** *(post-war* **Seafire FR.Mk 17** to complement **Seafire F.Mk 17**) sub-type; total 212 from Westland and 20 from Cunliffe-Owen
Seafire Mk 45: interim model based on Spitfire Mk 21; total 50
Seafire Mk 46: interim model based on Spitfire Mk 22; total 24
Seafire Mk 47: definitive model with many improvements, Mk 87 or 88 engine driving contraprop, folding wings, extra fuel/weapons; total 90

121 Port aileron
122 Wing tip fairing
123 Port navigation light
124 Pitot tube
125 Cannon barrel fairings
126 Cannon barrels
127 Port leading edge fuel tank, capacity 17 Imp gal (77 litres)
128 Upper engine cowling
129 Hydraulic fluid tank
130 Intercooler
131 Compressor intake
132 Generator
133 Heywood compressor
134 Engine bearer attachment
135 Hydraulic pump
136 Coolant pipes
137 Gun camera
138 Camera port
139 Engine air intake duct
140 Port mainwheel
141 Engine bearer
142 Cartridge starter
143 Exhaust stubs
144 2,035 hp (1517-kW) Rolls-Royce Griffon 61 engine
145 Engine magnetoes
146 Coolant header tank
147 Front engine mounting

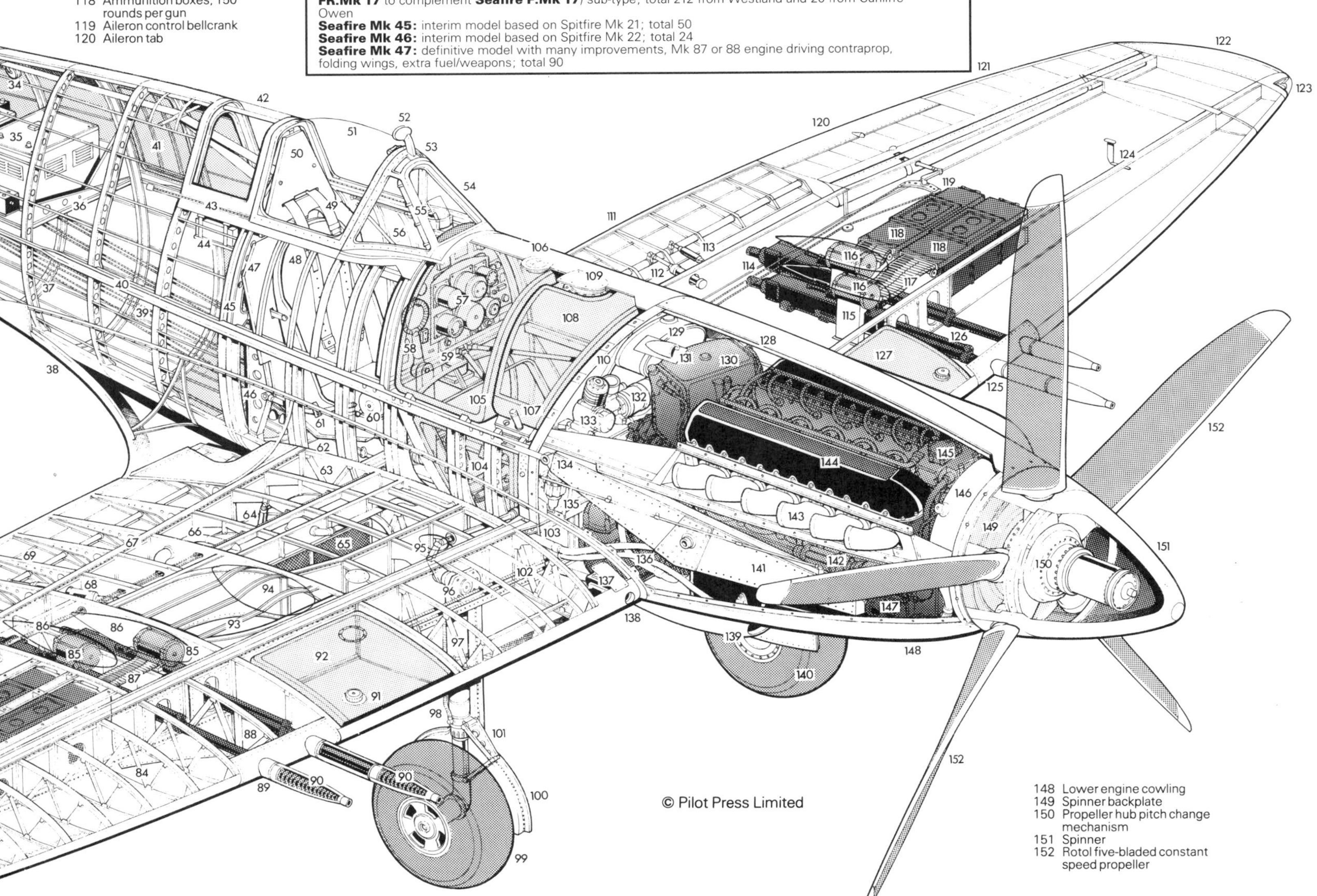

148 Lower engine cowling
149 Spinner backplate
150 Propeller hub pitch change mechanism
151 Spinner
152 Rotol five-bladed constant speed propeller

Griffon Spitfires

The Spitfire Mk XII served with only two squadrons, Nos 41 and 91. No. 41 Sqn was the first to receive the type and used the aircraft's excellent low-altitude capability to counter the hit-and-run raiders encountered along the South Coast. Anti-shipping strikes in the English Channel were also carried out.

Stemming from the original Griffon Seafire, the Seafire Mk XV, the Mk XVII featured several improvements such as tear-drop canopy with steeply raked windscreen, strengthened undercarriage and a rear fuselage tank. These were popular machines and served with the RNVR squadrons until 1954. This example served with No. 778 Sqn at Lee-on-Solent.

lash-up interim fighter to go into the earliest possible production. The load on the designers was immense, for in addition to over a dozen current marks there was the Type 356 and a totally new next-generation fighter with a small laminar wing, for which airframe NN660 had been reserved and which became the Spiteful. To meet the urgent new need the team under Smith hastily contrived the Type 379 as the optimum short-term marriage of the big two-stage engine and the strengthened Spitfire Mk VIII airframe. It was given the mark number XIV.

The first jet kill

Several of the surviving six prototypes were brought up to Spitfire Mk XIV standard, with the Griffon 65 or 67, five-bladed propeller, definitive fin/rudder and new extended horn-balanced elevators (all control surfaces being structurally redesigned). The first 50 were ordered on 14 August 1943 from the Supermarine works, and again there was a compromised serial, the first Spitfire Mk XIV being RB140, which was the serial borne by the last of a batch of Slingsby Cadet gliders for the ATC! The Mk XIV was the dominant Spitfire in the 2nd TAF from mid-1944 over France and Belgium, 957 in all being delivered of which 430 were Spitfire FR.Mk XIVs with a rear-fuselage tank and oblique reconnaissance camera. Those with suffix E had two 20-mm and two 12.7-mm (0.5-in) guns, and other variations, without a separate mark, were a bubble hood and cut-down rear fuselage and clipped wings carried out at unit level for extra speed low down, especially on 'Diver' patrols to shoot down flying bombs. On 5 October 1944 a Spitfire Mk XIV scored the first victory over a Messerschmitt Me 262 twin-jet fighter.

History repeated itself precisely in that, just as the properly designed Merlin-engined Spitfire Mk VIII was continually deferred while lash-up Spitfire Mk IXs poured from the lines, so did the Spitfire Mk XIV join the RAF in hundreds while the planned 'Super Spitfire' version, the Spitfire Mk XVIII, was delayed and never saw action (not until troubles in Israel, that is). It had a stronger airframe, extra wing fuel and the bubble hood, and the Spitfire FR.Mk XVIII (post-war Spitfire FR.Mk 18) added vertical and/or oblique cameras. Last of the regular wartime models was the definitive unarmed photo-reconnaissance version, the Spitfire PR.Mk 19, which was odd in many respects such as having a pressurised cockpit without the familiar hinge-down access door on the left. At 740 km/h (460 mph) it was the fastest Spitfire in service.

High-speed handling difficulties

The type number for the Spitfire Mk 18 was 394, whereas the final sub-family, the Mks 21 to 24, were all based on the Type 356 of 1942 design. Chief test pilot Jeffrey Quill had not appreciated how dreadful was the aileron problem at high speeds until he fought with No. 65 Squadron in the Battle of Britain. No real cure was found until, in the Type 356, the entire wing was redesigned. Instead of having the torsion box comprising the front spar and the skin over the leading edge, the new wing was based on six very strong torque boxes aft of the front spar, and it was calculated that control reversal would not occur until a speed of 1328 km/h (825 mph) was reached! The metal-skinned ailerons were totally new, and had geared tabs. The plan shape was visibly different, and the only armament provided was four 20-mm cannon, in a new installation tested on a Spitfire Mk XIV, JF319. There were many other changes, including new and very strong landing gear, but not all were built into the first interim Spitfire Mk 21, which was none other than DP851, the 'missing' Mk XX. One of its non-standard features was the long-span pointed wing of

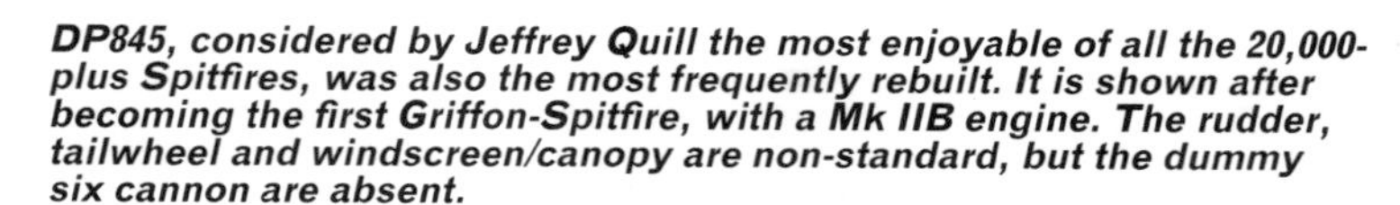

DP845, considered by Jeffrey Quill the most enjoyable of all the 20,000-plus Spitfires, was also the most frequently rebuilt. It is shown after becoming the first Griffon-Spitfire, with a Mk IIB engine. The rudder, tailwheel and windscreen/canopy are non-standard, but the dummy six cannon are absent.

First of the Griffon-engined Spitfires to enter service, the Mk XII was also the only species to have the low-blown single-stage engine (Mk III or IV, with different propeller drive ratios), asymmetric radiators and four-bladed propeller. This Mk XII, seen before delivery, had the Mk VIII airframe.

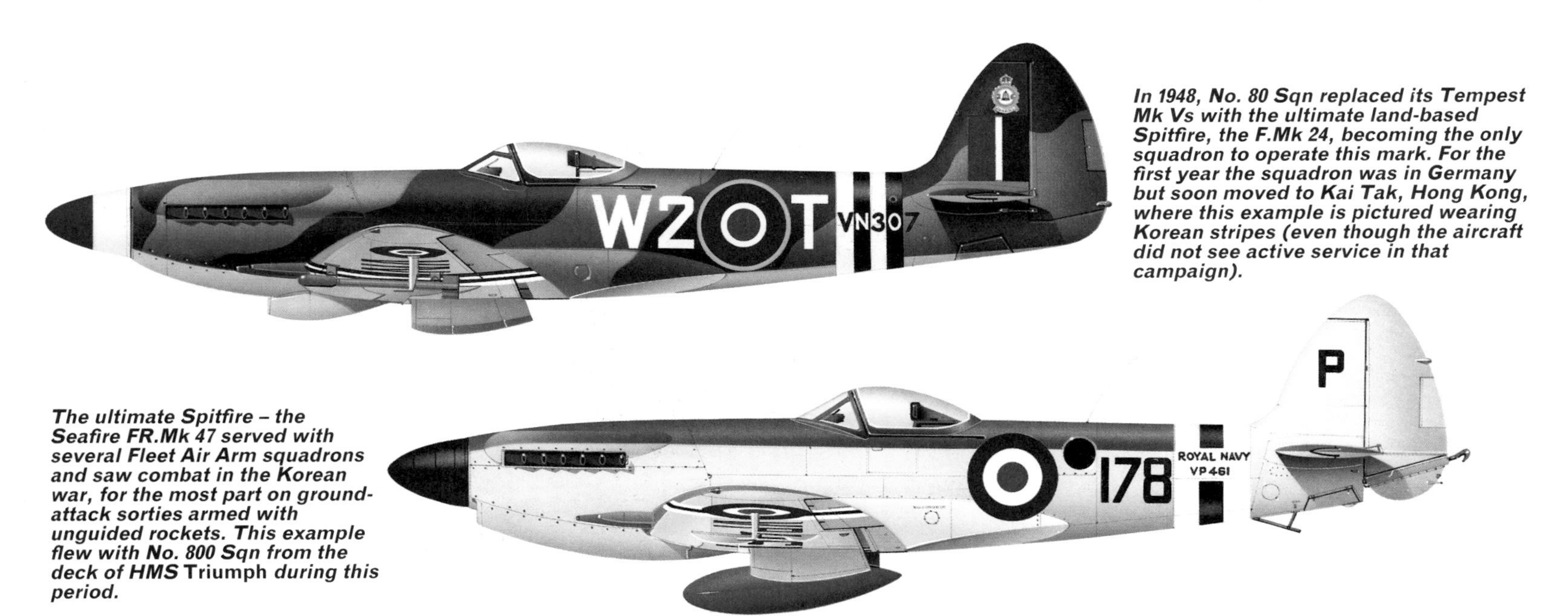

In 1948, No. 80 Sqn replaced its Tempest Mk Vs with the ultimate land-based Spitfire, the F.Mk 24, becoming the only squadron to operate this mark. For the first year the squadron was in Germany but soon moved to Kai Tak, Hong Kong, where this example is pictured wearing Korean stripes (even though the aircraft did not see active service in that campaign).

The ultimate Spitfire – the Seafire FR.Mk 47 served with several Fleet Air Arm squadrons and saw combat in the Korean war, for the most part on ground-attack sorties armed with unguided rockets. This example flew with No. 800 Sqn from the deck of HMS Triumph *during this period.*

the HF.Mk VII, and a similar wing was fitted to the first production Spitfire F.Mk 21 (LA187), which had PRU livery with B-type markings. In between came PP139, yet another compromised serial, the first specially built Spitfire Mk 21. Vast orders were placed with both Supermarine and Castle Bromwich, but the war's ending caused slashing cuts and only 122 were built, variously with 12- or 24-volt electrics and all with the original canopy.

Spitfire F.Mk 21s joined No. 91 Squadron in March 1945, and in the same month the first Spitfire F.Mk 22 (PK312) was delivered from Castle Bromwich, and was distinguishable by its bubble hood. The cut-down rear fuselage caused stability problems of the kind now deliberately designed into 1990s fighters, and the rear-fuselage tank had to be sealed off until, during the run of 278 of this mark, the much bigger Spiteful-type tail was fitted. Last of all, bringing the Spitfire total up to 20,351, was the Spitfire F.Mk 24, with operative rear tank, short Mk 5 guns, rocket launchers and various other detail modifications. VN496, the 81st Spitfire F.Mk 24, emerged from the South Marston works on 20 February 1948.

As the Griffon was intended for the Fleet Air Arm it naturally was considered for the Seafire. Following discussions in 1942, Specification N.4/43 was raised to cover a naval edition of the Spitfire Mk XII. The Type 377 emerged with a manually folding wing with extra wing tankage, Griffon VI driving a four-bladed Rotol and (though not a two-stage engine) with symmetric radiators, and an A-frame hook and catapult spools. Six prototypes were built, starting with NS487, and by late 1944 Westland were beginning a run of 250 and Cunliffe-Owen its batch of 134. From no. 51 the hook was of the sting type, and the final two batches (from SW876) had the bubble hood. The latter was standard with the Seafire Mk XVII, the prototype of which was the modified third Seafire Mk XV (NS493), and other features included a steeply raked windscreen with extra framing, long-stroke strengthened main legs, rocket-assisted take-off attachments as standard and, except in the FR version, a rear-fuselage tank.

From land bases to carrier decks

The Seafire Mk XVII was a popular machine which served post-war in the RNVR as the Seafire F.Mk 17 and Seafire FR.Mk 17 until the end of 1954. This was two years after the withdrawal of the later Seafire Mks 45, 46 and 47, which were based on the Type 356 (Spitfire Mk 21). Castle Bromwich built 50 Seafire Mk 45s, to Specification N.7/44, as an interim navalised Spitfire Mk 21 with a hook and tailwheel cable deflector. Cunliffe-Owen developed the Seafire Mk 46, with bubble hood and later with the Spiteful tail, the small production batch coming from South Marston. The ultimate variant was the Seafire Mk 47, a naval Spitfire Mk 24, the first two off the South Marston line (PS944/945) serving as prototypes. The installation of the Griffon 85 and contraprops used on many Seafire Mk 45s and Mk 46s was made standard, though on production it became the Mk 87 or Mk 88 engine with Stromberg or Rolls-Royce injection carburettor and the carburettor air inlet extended right to the front of the cowling. Early in production a folding wing was introduced, without the extra folding tips of earlier Seafires, and later still the fold was made hydraulic. Almost all were Seafire FR.Mk 47s with oblique cameras and 105-litre (23-Imp gal) blister tanks under the outer wings. The last of 90, VR972, was delivered in March 1949, and these fine machines served with No. 800 Squadron in Malaya and Korea.

Almost all surviving Spitfires are Merlin-engined. An exception is N20E, registered in the USA, seen here when it was flying in Canada. Before that it had come third in the Tinnerman Trophy at Cleveland, Ohio, in 1949. Earlier still it had been FR.Mk XIV TZ138 on winterisation tests in Canada.

Among the last Spitfires to continue serving in the RAF in the fighter role, these FR.Mk 18s (post-war designation) are seen parked on pierced-steel planks at Butterworth in 1950. No. 60 Sqn flew the very last Spitfire strike against bandit camps on 1 January 1951. The PR.Mk 19 went on until 1 April 1954 in the reconnaissance role.

MV349 was a Spitfire F.Mk XIVE built by Supermarine and delivered in late 1944. As the markings show it immediately went out to the Far East Air Force, being shipped to Bombay and flown to Burma, where it operated with RAF No. 28 Sqn on the Malayan front until the end of the war. The actual end of fighting came just as No. 28 Sqn, with the other squadrons, was being readied to go aboard carriers from where they were to fly off to Malayan airfields during the final assault in that theatre. As can be seen, MV349 was fitted with a low-level oblique camera aft of the cockpit, as in the FR.Mk XIVE, but did not have the latter's clipped wings. Standard E armament was fitted: two 20-mm Hispano Mk II cannon and two 12.7-mm (0.5-in) Browning machine-guns. The vertical tail had had to be increased in area to counter the longer nose, and the rear-view hood and cut-down rear fuselage ideally needed even greater fin area in compensation.

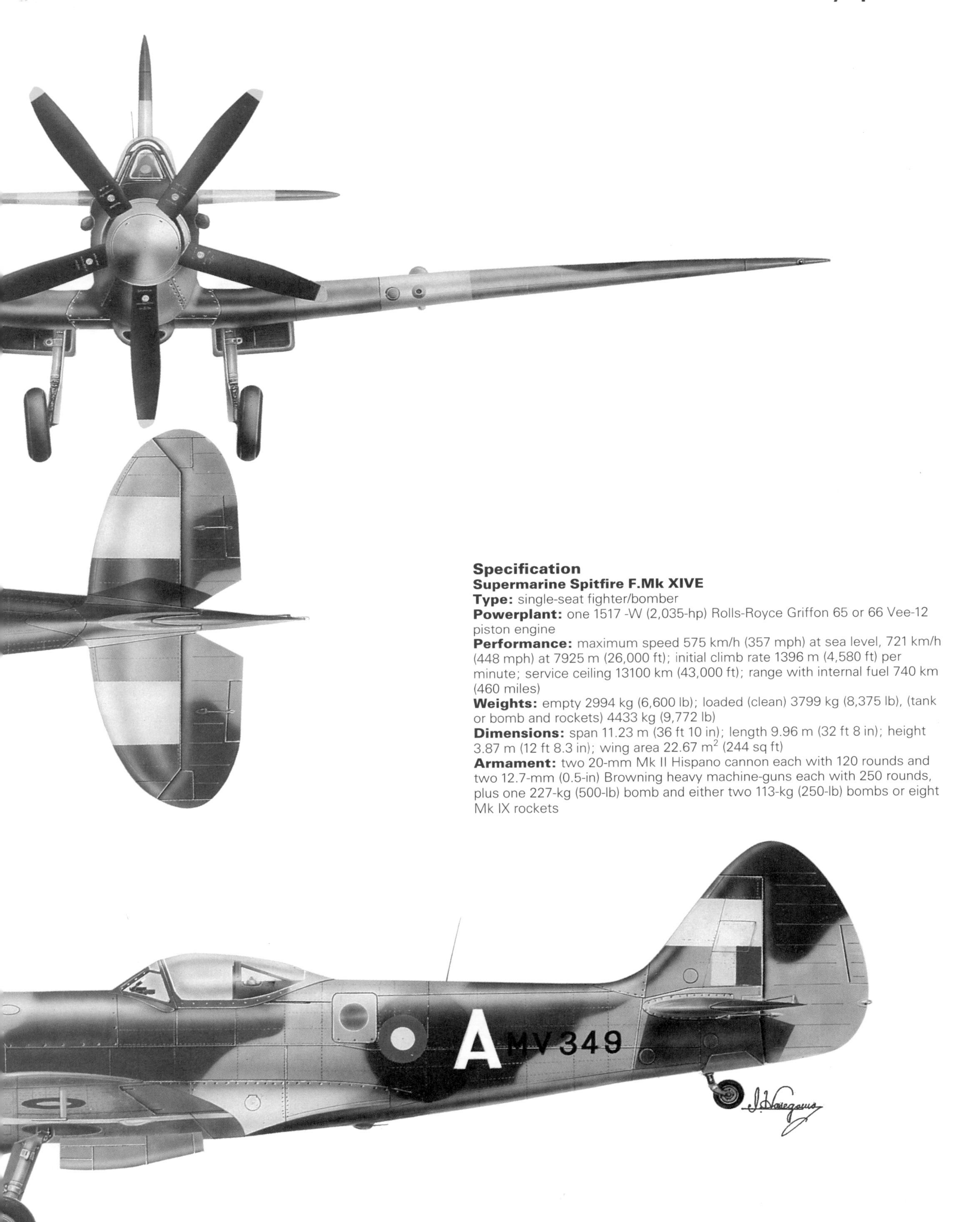

Specification
Supermarine Spitfire F.Mk XIVE
Type: single-seat fighter/bomber
Powerplant: one 1517 -W (2,035-hp) Rolls-Royce Griffon 65 or 66 Vee-12 piston engine
Performance: maximum speed 575 km/h (357 mph) at sea level, 721 km/h (448 mph) at 7925 m (26,000 ft); initial climb rate 1396 m (4,580 ft) per minute; service ceiling 13100 km (43,000 ft); range with internal fuel 740 km (460 miles)
Weights: empty 2994 kg (6,600 lb); loaded (clean) 3799 kg (8,375 lb), (tank or bomb and rockets) 4433 kg (9,772 lb)
Dimensions: span 11.23 m (36 ft 10 in); length 9.96 m (32 ft 8 in); height 3.87 m (12 ft 8.3 in); wing area 22.67 m^2 (244 sq ft)
Armament: two 20-mm Mk II Hispano cannon each with 120 rounds and two 12.7-mm (0.5-in) Browning heavy machine-guns each with 250 rounds, plus one 227-kg (500-lb) bomb and either two 113-kg (250-lb) bombs or eight Mk IX rockets

Suez

In 1952 Egypt's ruler King Farouk was toppled in a military coup and eventually replaced by Colonel Gamal Abdel Nasser. Determined to end the British military presence in his country, he forced their withdrawal by 1956. That same year he nationalised the Anglo-French Suez Canal Company, seizing control of that vital waterway. The British and French decided on a military solution and gathered their forces to launch Operation Muskeeter. The conflict ended in the humbling of the two powers that had hitherto been dominant in the Middle East.

Air Marshal Barnett assured Prime Minister Eden that air attacks alone would cause the collapse of President Nasser's government, but the final plan of Operation Musketeer envisaged massive air strikes on Egyptian Air Force (EAF) airfields on D-day followed by landings to reconquer the Canal Zone from D + 5.

For their part the Israelis hoped to crush Egypt militarily as well as occupy the Gaza Strip and Sharm el Sheikh on the southern tip of Sinai. Their supposed objective was merely a paratroop raid against the western end of the Mitla Pass in Sinai as retaliation for Palestinian guerrilla attacks from the Gaza Strip. On 24 October the Sèvres Agreement was signed by the UK, France and Israel, with 29 October as the planned date for the Israeli 'raid' to trigger an Anglo-French 'ultimatum'. Israel also insisted that her allies destroy the EAF before Israeli armoured units were committed in Sinai. French heavy transport aircraft would give the Israelis logistical support, while two squadrons of French fighters also had to be based in Israel as a defence against Egyptian Ilyushin Il-28 bombers.

Early on 29 October an IAF reconnaissance aircraft spotted an Egyptian road-construction team in the Mitla Pass. Mistaking this for a military unit the Israelis shifted their drop-zone from the western to the eastern end of the Pass, thus posing no 'threat' to the Suez Canal.

The balance of forces

The UK had nine bomber squadrons (120 aircraft), four fighter-bomber squadrons (100 aircraft), one reconnaissance squadron and three aircraft-carriers (200 aircraft) for Operation Musketeer. France had four fighter-bomber wings (100 aircraft), three transport wings and one carrier (50 aircraft). On 23 October three French squadrons arrived in Israel. Their Dassault Mystères would defend Tel Aviv, helped by Republic F-84s which would afterwards support the Israeli army in Sinai. The Nord Noratlases would supply Israel's paratroops in Mitla and central Sinai. Aircraft operating over Egyptian territory were given Israeli markings. Thus, the IAF's 69 jet- and 45 piston-engine fighters could be committed to Sinai, plus its Boeing B-17s and assorted transports. Mystères provided top cover; Gloster Meteors, Dassault Ouragans, North American Mustangs and de Havilland Mosquitoes operated for ground attack; and B-17s carried out night bombing raids.

Deliveries of Soviet equipment to Egypt had begun in October 1955 but a total change of training patterns meant that only two squadrons of Mikoyan-Gurevich MiG-15s (30 aircraft at Kabrit) were operational a year later. A squadron of Il-28s (12 aircraft) was semi-operational at Cairo West. Though being

The crowded park area of a Royal Navy aircraft-carrier with a de Havilland Sea Venom FAW.Mk 21 being catapulted into the air for another mission during the Suez campaign. At the peak, aircraft were taking off or landing every two or three minutes.

***One of six ex-RAF tropicalised Gloster Meteor NF.Mk 13s supplied to Egypt during June-August 1955. During the conflict at least two of these aircraft were destroyed, one by an aircraft from HMS* Bulwark.**

Seemingly an Egyptian air force Vampire, this is in fact a wooden mock-up of a de Havilland Vampire FB.Mk 52 damaged during an IAF attack on the Gaza dispersal strip. Despite the vulnerabilty of the aircraft, many Egyptian pilots preferred the Vampires to the newly-purchased MiG-15s and MiG-17s.

In addition to supplying Israel with Dassault Mystère IVAs, the French Armée de l'Air also deployed the 2ᵉ Escadre from Dijon to Haifa. The unit, with 36 aircraft, remained at Haifa from October to December 1956 and provided fighter cover for Israeli towns. Note the yellow and black Suez identification stripes.

A remnant from Israel's initial purchases of ex-World War II aircraft, the North American P-51D Mustang was still capable of putting up a reasonable fight. In 1956 one was being used to sever Egyptian telephone wires in the Sinai.

phased out, one squadron of de Havilland Vampires (15 aircraft at Fayid) and another of Meteors (12 aircraft also at Fayid) were still operational, with forward strips in Sinai. Supporting them were three transport squadrons (60 aircraft at Almaza and Deversoir). Six other units (84 assorted piston- and jet-engine aircraft) were non-operational, being in the process of conversion or disbandment. The Egyptian army had also withdrawn half its normal strength from Sinai to the Delta to face a British and French build-up in Malta and Cyprus. Much of the air force was also 'facing north' rather than east towards Israel.

The invasion of Sinai

The Suez war began late on the afternoon of 29 October when Israeli forces entered Sinai at two points. Twenty minutes later 16 Douglas C-47s and 10 Meteors crossed the frontier, flying low to avoid radar. Approximately 1,600 paratroopers were then dropped near the eastern end of the Mitla Pass while IAF Mystères patrolled central Sinai to watch for EAF reaction. Cairo received news of the first clashes at 1900 in the evening and within an hour was sending troops across the Suez Canal towards the Mitla Pass. An hour later six French transports dropped heavy equipment to the Israeli paratroops.

In an apparent attempt to kill the Egyptian C-in-C, Field Marshal Amer, unidentified aircraft shot down an Ilyushin Il-14 of the EAF's Presidential flight, which was carrying pressmen from Damascus to Cairo. The field marshal himself was in a second plane that reached Egypt safely. At dawn on 30 October four RAF English Electric Canberras attempted a reconnaissance of Egyptian reaction in the Canal Zone. All were intercepted by MiG-15s, one being damaged, and this so surprised the British government that it decided to delay the bombing of EAF bases until nightfall instead of launching the planned daylight attacks.

Early that same morning the Egyptian destroyer *Ibrahim al Awwal* tried to bombard Haifa harbour but was so damaged by IAF Ouragans that she had to surrender to a couple of Israeli destroyers. At almost the same moment a flight of four EAF Vampires made a reconnaissance of Israeli forces at Mitla and El Thamed to the east. They were followed two hours later by MiG-15s, which destroyed six vehicles and a Piper Cub on the ground. Further attacks by EAF Vampires escorted by MiGs destroyed more vehicles. A standing patrol of IAF Mystères was therefore set up over the Canal Zone. The first air combat came late in the afternoon, when six MiGs held off the six Mystères of this patrol while two Meteors caused further heavy loss to the paras east of Mitla. The air battle rapidly drew in more aircraft and ended with two MiGs being destroyed for a Mystère seriously damaged.

The EAF had been caught by surprise by the Israeli invasion, but nevertheless managed, almost 50 sorties on 30 October. The IAF flew over 100 sorties, the most effective being against Egyptian troops entering the western end of the Mitla Pass. These lost almost all their vehicles but were able to take up strong defensive positions overlooking the pass along the Heitan Defile, while the IAF lost two Mustangs to ground fire.

At 0600 on 31 October the British and French issued their ultimatums demanding that both sides withdraw from the Canal Zone, which the Israelis had nowhere actually reached. As predicted, the Egyptians refused. At dawn four EAF Vampires attempted to attack Israeli positions at Mitla before the IAF standing patrol arrived, and were caught by six Mystères as they began their bombing runs. By pressing on the Vampires again caused serious damage, but two were downed while a third pilot was obliged to bale out before getting home. The fourth Vampire escaped when a patrol of MiG-15s intervened. An attempt by a solitary Il-28 to hit Lod air base failed and the

A Fleet Air Arm Seahawk of No. 802 Sqn recovers on board HMS* Albion *in December 1956. Ample evidence of a difficult target is provided by the remains of the fuel tank under the wing, shot away by triple-A.

An Armstrong Whitworth-built Sea Hawk FB.Mk 3 fighter-bomber operated by No. 802 naval air squadron. This unit was detached from HMS Ark Royal to HMS Albion for operations over the Egyptian mainland. As part of the British carrier force, Sea Hawks mounted daylight attacks on airfields and supply depots.

This Canberra B.Mk 2 from No. 10 Sqn, RAF carries the squadron emblem on the wing tiptank and the Honington wing emblem on the fin. Based at Luqa, Hal Far and Nicosia, the RAF's medium bomber force consisted of English Electric Canberra B.Mk 2s and B.Mk 6s. Flying high-level (40,000-ft) night missions, the aircraft bombed Egyptian airfields.

aircraft dropped its bombs near Ramat Rachel.

Both air forces were heavily engaged in attacks on ground forces at Mitla that afternoon, but neither suffered further loss in this sector. To the east two IAF Ouragans were sent against an isolated flight of EAF aircraft believed to be at Bir Hama (these were in fact at Bir Gifgafa) but were jumped by the MiG-15 top cover for EAF Meteors which had in turn just halted a column of Israeli light tanks near Bir Hasan. Both Ouragans were damaged, one subsequently force-landing in the desert, before IAF Mystères intervened. IAF aircraft then attacked Egyptian armour which was moving south towards Bir Gifgafa, but were intercepted by EAF Meteors, one of which was shot down. The IAF continued to strafe this Egyptian column, but failed to stop it, while the EAF was similarly engaged against Israelis advancing on Bir Hama. An IAF Piper Cub was also shot down by MiGs in this sector.

Reaching the limit

To the north, on 31 October the Israeli army suffered its only real defeat of the campaign, when a series of attacks on Abu Ageila was driven off with serious loss. Things would probably have gone even worse if IAF fighter-bombers had not been able to slow down a column of Egyptian tanks attempting a relief operation from El Arish. So great were the demands now being put on the IAF that French aircraft based in Israel had to intervene against another Egyptian column advancing on Abu Ageila from the Canal Zone. The French continued to help in Sinai on 1 and 2 November. Israeli losses to ground fire were also getting heavy; nevertheless, the IAF was still able to make many more than the 90 or so sorties recorded by the EAF on 31 October.

When the Anglo-French ultimatum expired at 0600 on 31 October, Egyptian air defences were put on full alert in the Nile Delta and Canal Zone. Twenty Il-28s and 20 MiG-15s destined for the Syrian air force had already been flown to Syria via Saudi Arabia by Russian and Czech pilots. Twenty non-operational EAF MiGs, about 15 of them MiG-17s, provided an escort. The EAF's new Il-14 transports were flown directly back to eastern Europe.

Until the last moment the Egyptians thought the British and French were bluffing, so there was neither black-out nor dispersal when the first bombers attacked Almaza shortly after dark. Three waves, mostly of RAF Canberras and Vickers Valiants but with some French participation, came in from Cyprus and Malta to hit Almaza, Inchas, Abu Sueir, Kabrit and Cairo International before midnight. Bombing from 12190 m (40,000 ft) they destroyed or damaged only 14 aircraft. Meanwhile the EAF's operational and non-operational Il-28s went south to Luxor, where it was hoped they would be safe. Lacking an operations room or early warning and communications systems for night fighting, the EAF made only two interception attempts and only once did a Meteor NF.Mk 13 fire on a Valiant.

A pair of reconnaissance Canberras was, however, intercepted by MiGs early on 1 November, one Canberra being damaged. They reported the limited effect of the night assault and so by day the tactics were changed. Land- and carrier-based aircraft, in the form of English Electric Canberras, Venoms, Westland Wyverns, Hawker Sea Hawks, de Havilland Sea Venoms and Gloster Meteors, plus French Republic Thunderstreaks, Vought Corsairs and Grumman Hellcats, attacked every EAF airfield west of Sinai. The MiGs were hurriedly dispersed throughout the Delta but found it hard even to take off as each strip was under almost constant surveillance. On 2 and 3 November Bilbeis Air Academy and the Helwan repair depot were attacked, while on 6 November railway communications, barracks and anti-aircraft sites were added.

On 2 November the French carrier *Arromanches* launched her Corsairs against Alexandria harbour but was in turn attacked by the Egyptian destroyers *El Nasr* and *Tarek*. These were, however, forced to retire beneath a smoke-screen when the aircraft turned on them. These attacks continued on 4 and 5 November as British carrier-based aircraft hit airfields outside Alexandria in a further attempt to divert Egyptian attention away from the intended invasion of Port Said and Port Fuad. Another Canberra was damaged by a MiG near Luxor on 3 November, but Egyptian ground defences put up a more effective resistance, bringing down a Wyvern over Port Said, and a Hellcat and a Mystère over Cairo on 3 November.

The second phase in Sinai

The British and French air offensive against the EAF enabled the Israelis to unleash a full-scale armoured assault. It also led the Egyptians to withdraw from Sinai. This retreat was phased over several nights to minimise the danger of air attack while preparations were made for guerrilla resistance in the Nile Valley and Delta. The garrison at Sharm el Sheikh had, however, to fight on as there was no transport to evacuate them.

Preparing for another launch aboard HMS Albion. In the foreground Sea Hawks taxi out, while four Sea Venom FAW.Mk 21s await clearance. At the rear, an AEW Skyraider from 'B' Flight, No. 849 Sqn, warms up prior to another mission.

The need to transport large numbers of troops to the region placed such a strain on RAF Transport Command's resources that aircraft from other commands were seconded. Here Avro Shackletons from Coastal Command prepare to depart from Britain on the long flight.

Four Vickers Valiant heavy bomber units were based at Luqa, and were tasked with airfield bombardment, though in the event the damage done was slight compared with the size of the raids. This aircraft, a B.Mk 1 from No. 207 Sqn, is seen at Luqa with No. 148 Sqn aircraft in the background.

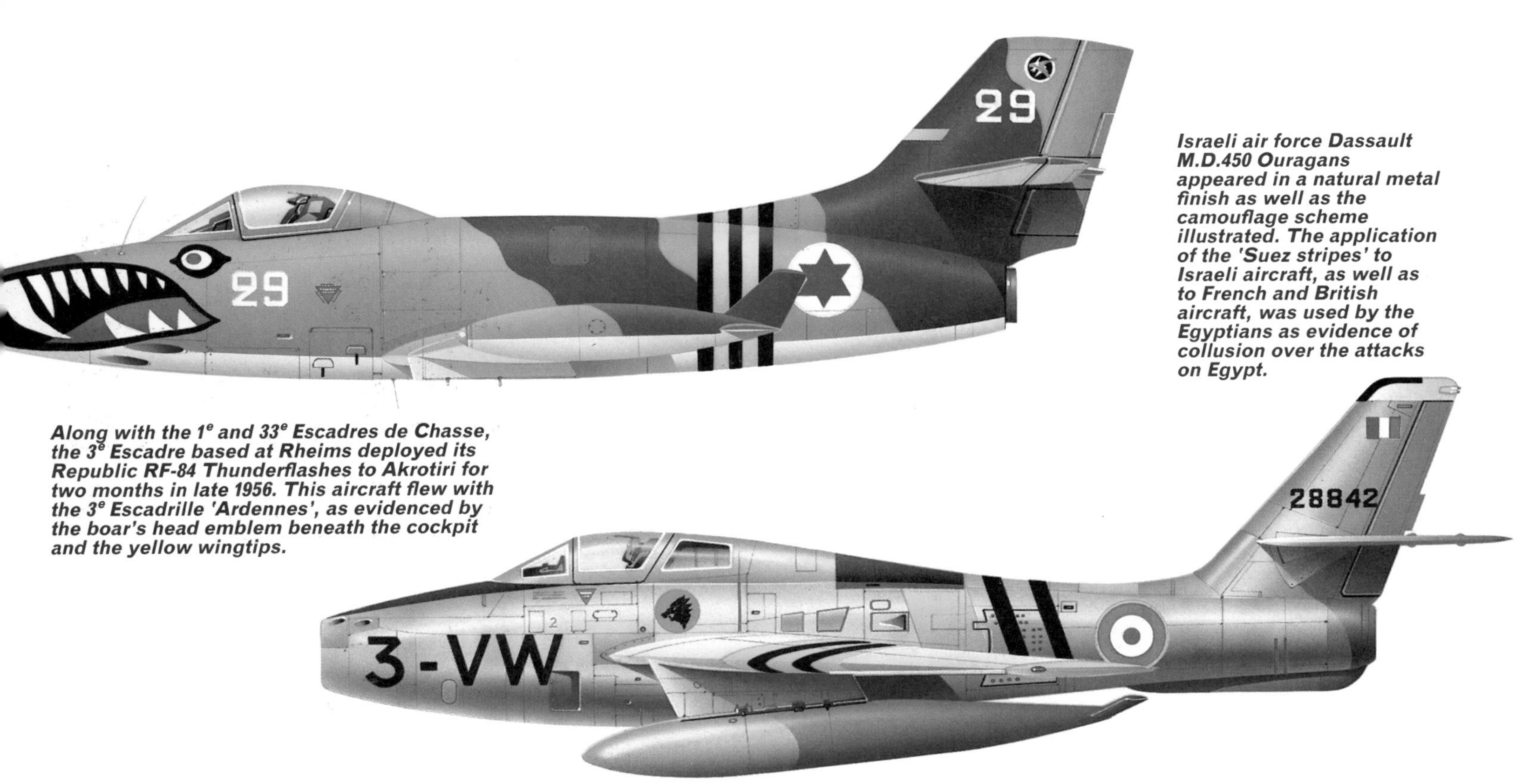

Israeli air force Dassault M.D.450 Ouragans appeared in a natural metal finish as well as the camouflage scheme illustrated. The application of the 'Suez stripes' to Israeli aircraft, as well as to French and British aircraft, was used by the Egyptians as evidence of collusion over the attacks on Egypt.

Along with the 1e and 33e Escadres de Chasse, the 3e Escadre based at Rheims deployed its Republic RF-84 Thunderflashes to Akrotiri for two months in late 1956. This aircraft flew with the 3e Escadrille 'Ardennes', as evidenced by the boar's head emblem beneath the cockpit and the yellow wingtips.

1 November began with the IAF saving the Israeli army from further embarrassment at Abu Ageila, whose garrison had slipped away by night. Ignorant of this, the Israelis advanced into the empty positions from two directions and opened fire on each other. Eight tanks were destroyed before an IAF pilot saw what was going on. Earlier that night a heavy bombardment by B-17s had preceded the Israeli occupation of the Gaza Strip. The Egyptians were now steadily withdrawing towards the Canal, which they crossed on 2 November.

Although there was only rearguard skirmishing on the ground, the IAF and surviving units engaged in a bitter fight above it. Vampires from El Arish withdrew to Bir Gifgafa and Bir Rod Salim, leaving several dummy aircraft and a Mraz Sokol given to President Nasser on completion of the so-called 'Czech Arms Deal' of 1955. These Vampires attacked Israeli paratroops at Mitla later in the morning of 1 November, losing one aircraft to IAF interception. Despite British and French air raids, three Meteor NF.Mk 13s with an escort of MiGs appeared over Sinai in the afternoon. Two other MiGs (said to have been MiG-17s) were subsequently jumped by a pair of Mystères, one being downed. The same two Mystères went on to attack five MiG-15s but were outmanoeuvred; minutes later they were themselves challenged by two MiGs. In the ensuing dogfight an Egyptian was damaged but force-landed safely in the shallow waters of Lake Bardawil. This aircraft was later salvaged by the Israelis.

Down at Sharm el Sheikh a major battle developed from 2 November. Paratroops and their heavy equipment were dropped at El Tor on the western shore of the peninsula while other units advanced down the eastern side. The IAF meanwhile bombed the British frigate HMS *Crane* which, blockading Sharm, was mistaken for an Egyptian ship. On 3 November Mustangs and B-17s destroyed two of the heavy guns overlooking the Straits of Tiran at Ras Nasrani. The rest were destroyed on the night of 3-4 November by their gunners, who then retired into Sharm el Sheikh which, with its harbour and airstrip, could hope to hold out longer. One Mustang was downed and its pilot captured. He, along with wounded and civilians, was then taken to Suez in a couple of Egyptian sailing ships which slipped through the blockade. Preceded by a spotter plane, Israeli troops reached Sharm from Ras Nasrani at 1400 on 4 November. A night attack failed but a second assault backed up by Mustangs dropping napalm broke the Egyptian perimeter. With the arrival of Israeli paras from El Tor the garrison surrendered at 0930 on 5 November.

The invasion of the Canal Zone

By now the British and French assaults had begun. At dawn on 5 November carrier-based aircraft attacked Egyptian defensive positions and at 0820 British paratroops hit Gamil airfield on the outskirts of Port Said. Fifteen minutes later the French dropped just south of Port Fuad. A planned British helicopter-borne raid against Canal bridges was abandoned, but further paradrops reinforced the invaders. Air attacks caused fires in both cities, which burned out of control as the water supply had also been damaged. A temporary truce from 1600 to 2230 won the defenders time to organise guerrilla resistance, but at dawn on 6 November seaborne landings supported by naval bombardment and close air support seized the waterfront while a solitary EAF MiG-15 reportedly strafed the British at Gamil. Two Sea Hawks and a Venom were lost to ground fire, and in the subsequent street fighting air supremacy meant little. It was, however, able to cover a dash down the Suez Canal in the small hours of 7 November. This reached El Kap before the ceasefire which the British and French governments had finally accepted under both domestic and international pressure.

The hectic degree of activity aboard the Royal Navy aircraft-carriers led to several accidents, in this instance involving a Westland Wyvern S.Mk 4 and a Sea Hawk FGA.Mk 6. Aboard HMS* Albion *the Wyverns from Nos 830 and 831 Naval Air Squadrons were operated, while HMS* Eagle *withdrew for refuelling.

The losses

The British and French claimed to have destroyed or damaged 260 aircraft, including 207 combat jets. The EAF, however, claimed that only eight MiG-15s, seven Il-28s, nine North American Harvards, six Curtiss C-46s, four C-47s, three civil Dakotas and a grounded Avro Lancaster were destroyed, with another 62 aircraft damaged. The Ilyushins were among those in the supposed haven of Luxor and were hit by French F-84Fs fitted with extra tanks and based in southern Israel. About 10 MiG-15s and MiG-15UTIs of the Syrian training mission were also destroyed at Abu Sueir.

In Sinai the EAF lost four MiGs, four Vampires, a Meteor and the Mraz Sokol. The IAF admitted the loss of one Mystère, two Ouragans, 10 Mustangs (some of which were later repaired) and two Piper Cubs. A further five damaged aircraft are believed to have crashed on their way home. While the French lost only one aircraft, the British lost four plus a Canberra PR.Mk 3 shot down over the Syrian-Lebanese border.

Hawkeye: Seaborne Sentinel

No matter how impressive the strike power within the carrier air wing, effective over-the-horizon AEW and co-ordination of operations are essential if the force is to maintain its optimum capability. The Grumman Hawkeye shoulders these vital responsibilities, ranging far out from the carrier as the airborne 'eyes of the fleet'.

Though it may seem out of place among the sleek, supersonic jets of modern-day aviation, the Hawkeye, with its deep fuselage, large propellers and ungainly rotodome, is every bit as effective in its intended roles.

Originally gaining operational status aboard the USS *Kitty Hawk* (CVA-63) off the coast of Vietnam in autumn 1965, Grumman's distinctive E-2 Hawkeye recently entered its third decade of service and looks set to retain its present position as the US Navy's primary airborne early warning and control platform until well into the next century.

By today's standards, the aircraft that entered service during the mid-1960s were somewhat primitive although at that time they represented a fantastic improvement over the same manufacturer's 1950s-vintage E-1B Tracer. Since then, the Hawkeye has been the subject of considerable updating, taking full advantage of the microchip age to remain an integral part of modern carrierborne aviation. It says much for the basic soundness of the design that it has been able to incorporate, without undue difficulty and in what is essentially a most compact airframe, the latest developments in AEW technology.

The initial variant of the Hawkeye was the E-2A, production of this model totalling 59 aircraft plus three prototypes, the first of which made its maiden flight on 21 October 1960. This was essentially just an aerodynamic test-bed, and it was not until 19 April 1961 that a full-system aircraft took to the air. Not surprisingly in view of system complexity, research and development took time, and deliveries to fleet units finally got under way in January 1964 when VAW-11 of the Pacific Fleet at North Island, California, began to receive the Hawkeye. Subsequently, the E-2A was also assigned to VAW-12 of the Atlantic Fleet at Norfolk, Virginia, with effect from February 1966.

Mission-related equipment employed by this original model included General Electric APS-96 search radar, its antenna housed in a massive 7.31-m (24-ft) diameter rotodome carried above the centre fuselage section, this being a distinctive and ever-present feature of succeeding variants of the Hawkeye. Less obvious, but no less vital to the AEW task, was the impressive array of computerised processing equipment, most of which was accommodated in the rather cramped confines of the cabin and all of which was necessary in order to present data in a coherent form to the three systems operators. Other members of the five-man crew comprised a pilot and co-pilot, and despite the vast improvements made since the type first flew the Hawkeye still relies on just a five-man crew.

The first major attempt at enhancing capability occurred in the late 1960s, this mainly centering around the on-board computer package. When the Hawkeye made its debut, com-

A Hawkeye is about to engage one of the trap wires traversing the deck of an aircraft carrier. Prominent in this view is the A-frame arrester hook beneath the rear fuselage.

puter technology dictated the adoption of a system which frequently required physical modification, this often being a most complex process and one which tended to limit overall capability. The advent of the far more flexible digital computer permitted system revision by the means of programme changes, and the Navy was not slow to take advantage of this, initiating an update programme which entailed installation of a Litton L-304 general-purpose computer, the resulting aircraft being known as the E-2B and flying for the first time on 20 February 1969. However, rather than purchase new-build Hawkeyes, it was decided to retrofit this system to existing E-2As, 52 aircraft being brought to E-2B standard by the time this programme terminated in December 1971.

Even as the E-2B project was getting under way, work on a rather more sophisticated version of the Hawkeye was also beginning, this eventually resulting in the appearance of a variant known as the E-2C. Arising mainly from the desire to enhance overland target-detection capability, the E-2C introduced a completely new radar, development of which began as early as 1964. Extensive evaluation of the General Electric APS-111 radar aboard an E-2A between June 1965 and October 1967 proved sufficiently encouraging to warrant further development of the Hawkeye, and this continuing evolutionary process eventually culminated in the E-2C, funding being released for a couple of prototypes in March 1968, these being produced by the simple expedient of modifying two former E-2A test specimens.

Increased capacity

The E-2C made its maiden flight on 20 January 1971, initial evaluation of the pair of prototypes revealing significant increases in overall capability. This led directly to a decision to proceed with the E-2C, production of which began in mid-1971. By then the radar had been further improved into the APS-120, and it was this unit which was installed in production examples, the first of which made its initial flight on 23 September 1972.

Deliveries to the Navy began in December of that year, initially to Atlantic Fleet squadrons stationed at Norfolk, Virginia, and the E-2C duly made its operational debut with VAW-123 in September 1974 when it sailed for the Mediterranean aboard the USS *Saratoga* (CV-60). Pacific Fleet units had to wait quite some time before they also began to convert from the considerably less capable E-2B, a process which got under way shortly before the end of the decade.

With an operational career on the Hawkeye dating back to the mid-1960s, VAW-114 'Hormel Hawgs' has a record second to none on this AEW workhorse. A 14-year accident-free period has enhanced the E-2's reputation.

Subsequent updating of the radar system led to the appearance of an improved variant of the E-2C in 1976, this utilising the APS-125 which was somewhat more flexible in that it was able to perform the detection, acquisition and tracking functions automatically while also being more resistant to electronic jamming. Introduced on the 34th production example of the E-2C, the APS-125 radar was retrospectively fitted to earlier aircraft but is itself now in the process of being supplanted, the latest examples of the E-2C incorporating General Electric's APS-138 advanced radar processing system, and it seems likely that this will also be retrofitted to older aircraft.

Key features of the newest radar are greater range: detection, identification and tracking can be accomplished over land and sea at ranges approaching 480 km (300 miles) when operating at an altitude of about 9145 m (30,000 ft), and the system also has an expanded computer 'memory', and is able to accomplish triangulation automatically. Passive detection capability has also been greatly enhanced, the E-2C being able to recognise and classify enemy electronic emissions at ranges well in excess of that of the onboard radar.

Currently operational with a total of 15 front-line US Navy squadrons as well as two Reserve Force units, the Hawkeye has the ability to keep pace with developments in the radar and computer fields, and this has resulted in a tremendous increase in the scope of the missions it performs. The type is truly unique in being the only aircraft ever designed from the outset to undertake the task of airborne early warning and control.

Increasing capability has brought with it a commensurate increase in workload, but the advent of new automated processing systems and other mission-related equipment has in many ways simplified the task of the three system operators by freeing them from the necessity to perform routine activities. Thus they are now able to devote virtually all of their attention to monitoring the developing tactical situation which is presented by means of the Hazeltine APA-172 control indicator group in the cabin of the Hawkeye, where the combat information centre officer, the air control officer and the radar operator work.

Each of the three crew stations is identical, these featuring a 25.4-cm (10-in) diameter main radar display screen and a 12.7-cm (5-in) alphanumeric auxiliary display, the former providing data pertaining to target tracks. Independent controls at each station enable crew members to select information relevant to their respective responsibilities, data which can be presented including target symbols, velocity vectors, disposition of friendly fighter forces, surface task forces and waypoints, it being possible for the E-2C to track automatically more than 250 targets while simulta-

Delivery of four Hawkeyes to Israel during 1981 added to an already formidable air force inventory. There can be no doubt that the quartet has proved invaluable in this nation's conflicts with its neighbours, though publicity is rarely given.

Hawkeye: Seaborne Sentinel

Specification

Grumman E-2A Hawkeye

Type: five-seat shipboard early warning and fighter control aircraft
Powerplant: two 3021-kW (4,050-shp) Allison T56-A-8 turboprops
Performance: maximum speed 639 km/h (397 mph); typical cruising speed 507 km/h (315 mph); patrol speed 402-451 km/h (250-280 mph); service ceiling 9662 m (31,700 ft); endurance 6 hours 6 minutes; ferry range 3065 km (1,905 miles)
Weights: empty 16358 kg (36,063 lb); maximum take-off 22516 kg (49,638 lb)
Dimensions: span 24.56 m (80 ft 7 in). folded 8.94 m (29 ft 4 in); length 17.7 m (56 ft 4 in); height 5:59 m (18 ft 4 in), with radome lowered 5.02 m (16 ft 5½ in); wing area 65.03 m^2 (700 sq ft)

An E-2A Hawkeye painted in standard US Navy grey and white, with its serial 150534 abbreviated on the fin below and NH of carrier air wing CVW-11 of USS **Kitty Hawk** ***(CVA-63). Note the wild boar badge of VAW-114 on the sides of the front fuselage and around the upper rim of the radome. On the starboard side of the fuselage can be seen the relatively small intake associated with avionics cooling on the E-2A/B. Hawkeyes from the*** **Kitty Hawk** ***introduced the type to the Vietnam War in late 1965, when they began to control strike missions, guiding aircraft around high ground and defensive concentrations, and warning them of enemy aircraft in the vicinity.***

N
H
0534
CVW-11
USS KITTY HAWK
NAVY
VAW-114

Space is always at a premium aboard aircraft carriers, and the Hawkeye, like most naval aircraft, has a wing-fold mechanism which dramatically reduces the area taken up by the aircraft both on deck and in the hangars.

neously controlling some 30 airborne interceptions. Data inputs and requests for information may be made either by means of an alphanumeric keyboard or by light-pen, the latter, for instance, being used to 'hook' a specific F-14 Tomcat interceptor to a specific target, information relating to that target then being automatically fed to the Tomcat's AWG-9 weapons control system by means of a data-link.

Processing of data generated by the radar and other E-2C sub-systems is handled by a pair of Litton L-304 computers, these performing the necessary calculations in real time, thus providing crew members with a continuously updated picture of the developing tactical scene. As already noted, data-link facilities permit information to be rapidly transmitted to friendly interceptors or to ground- or sea-based combat control centres.

As far as the Navy is concerned, the primary tasks of the Hawkeye are those of area and on-station search, and when operating at sea it is usual for the E-2C to launch first so as to be aloft when other carrierborne elements get off the carrier. Since the Navy routinely employs a cyclical pattern of operations, normally launching and recovering waves of aircraft at 105-minute intervals, the E-2C's good endurance characteristics usually result in its performing double- or, on occasion, treble-cycle sorties, thus permitting it to spend a considerable amount of time on station.

Operating at an altitude of around 30,000 ft when employed in the on-station search mode, the E-2C normally flies out to a distance of about 370 km (230 miles) from the parent carrier before initiating a constant orbit, gaining altitude steadily as fuel burns off. In both area and on-station search tasks, the flaps are set at 10° deflection to provide the optimum 3° radar scanning attitude. The on-station Hawkeye maintains constant communication with the parent carrier and other aircraft operating in the area.

Mission variety

Although employed mainly to augment the radar coverage of the aircraft-carrier, the Hawkeye can of course readily undertake a variety of other roles, such as exercising control over strike forces and serving as a communications link between strike aircraft and the combat information centre on the parent carrier. Air traffic control, monitoring of the area around the carrier task group for sea and air threats, and management of inflight-refuelling rendezvous are other missions which are often accomplished, while in Vietnam it was by no means unknown for the E-2 to observe enemy air space for signs of North Vietnamese MiG interceptors, this aspect extending to control of McDonnell Douglas F-4 Phantoms and Vought F-8 Crusaders engaged in furnishing combat air patrol cover to strike elements, personnel on the E-2 vectoring CAP aircraft into advantageous positions from which to initiate an attack with either Sparrow or Sidewinder air-to-air missiles. Today, of course, the principal Navy fighter is Grumman's Tomcat and the means of control rather more sophisticated, but the same basic task is still undertaken.

The Hawkeye can also be employed on duties of a less militaristic nature. For instance, the excellent resolution of the radar picture over both land and sea readily lends itself to use in the search and rescue task, while the ability to detect small objects (it has been claimed that the radar can observe cruise missile-sized targets at ranges exceeding 185 km (100 miles)) makes it an ideal tool in curtailing drug trafficking. This is a job which it has undertaken with some success in the recent past, Navy Hawkeye squadrons working in close co-operation with narcotics agents in attempting to stem the flow of such illegal substances from Latin American countries. Another mission undertaken by the E-2C has been that of augmenting radar coverage of Space Shuttle launches from Cape Canaveral.

Production of the E-2C is continuing at a fairly modest rate, the US Navy having taken delivery of 121 of the planned 144 examples by the end of 1988, whilst the Hawkeye has also enjoyed some success on the world export market in recent years.

Israel's Defence Force/Air Force was the first overseas customer, acquiring four E-2Cs in the late 1970s, while Japan has purchased eight, all of these now being in service with plans for five more. In addition, Egypt has received five E-2Cs while Singapore has taken four. Both the US Coast Guard and US Customs Service each have a pair of Hawkeyes for anti-drug work.

With engines wound up to full power and the nosewheel tie-bar securely locked into the deck catapult launch shuttle, a Hawkeye awaits the final 'go' signal from the deck launch officer before being hurtled into the air for another mission.

E-2 Hawkeye in service units and example aircraft

VAW-78
Air Wing assignment: CVWR-20
Shore base: Norfolk, Virginia
Aircraft: E-2C

This Hawkeye wears the colourful and prominent insignia of VAW-78, the Atlantic Coast Naval Reserve AEW squadron.

VAW-88
Air Wing assignment: CVWR-30
Shore base: Miramar, California
Aircraft: (E-2B) 152478/ND-013

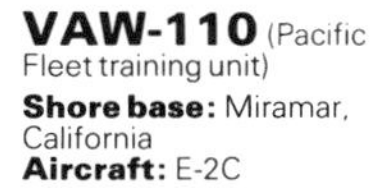

VAW-110 (Pacific Fleet training unit)
Shore base: Miramar, California
Aircraft: E-2C

VAW-112
Air Wing assignment: CVW-2
Shore base: Miramar, California
Aircraft: (E-2C) 161226/NE-603

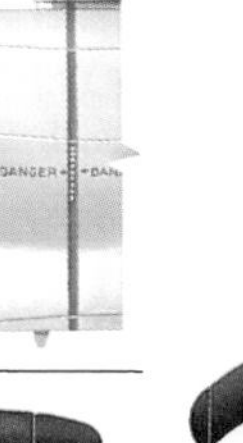

VAW-113
Air Wing assignment: CVW-14
Shore base: Miramar, California
Aircraft: E-2C

VAW-114
Air Wing assignment: CVW-15
Shore base: Miramar, California
Aircraft: (E-2C) 161343/NL-603

VAW-115
Air Wing assignment: CVW-5
Shore base: Atsugi, Japan
Aircraft: E-2C

VAW-116
Air Wing assignment: CVW-9
Shore base: Miramar, California
Aircraft: (E-2C) 160699/NG-603

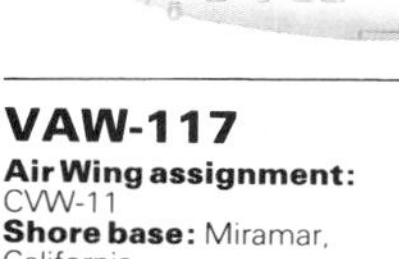

VAW-117
Air Wing assignment: CVW-11
Shore base: Miramar, California
Aircraft: E-2C

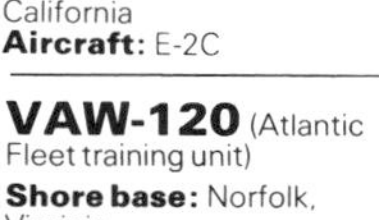

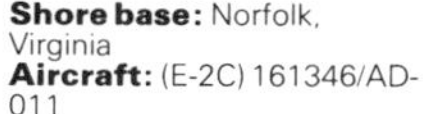

VAW-120 (Atlantic Fleet training unit)
Shore base: Norfolk, Virginia
Aircraft: (E-2C) 161346/AD-011

VAW-121
Air Wing assignment: CVW-7
Shore base: Norfolk, Virginia
Aircraft: E-2C

VAW-122
Air Wing assignment: CVW-6
Shore base: Norfolk, Virginia
Aircraft: E-2C

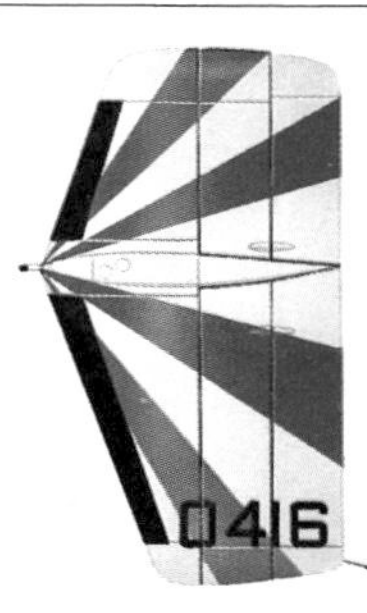

This E-2C bears the markings of VAW-110, the Pacific Fleet training unit based at NAS Miramar, California.

VAW-123
Air Wing assignment: CVW-1
Shore base: Norfolk, Virginia
Aircraft: (E-2C) 161098/AB-601

VAW-126
Air Wing assignment: CVW-3
Shore base: Norfolk, Virginia
Aircraft: (E-2C) 161701/AC-602

Japanese Air Self-Defence Force
601 Hikotai
Base: Misawa AB
Aircraft: (E-2C) 34-3451, 34-3452, 34-3454

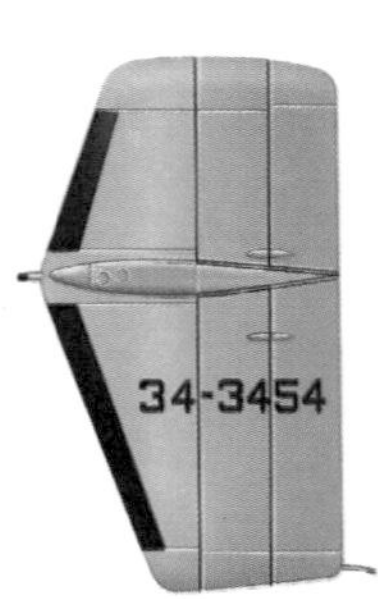

This Hawkeye of VAW-123 carries 'Screwtops', the squadron badge, with the prominent eye seemingly appropriately positioned atop the radar housing.

VAW-127
Air Wing assignment: CVW-13
Shore base: Norfolk, Virginia
Aircraft: (E-2C) 160987/AK-603

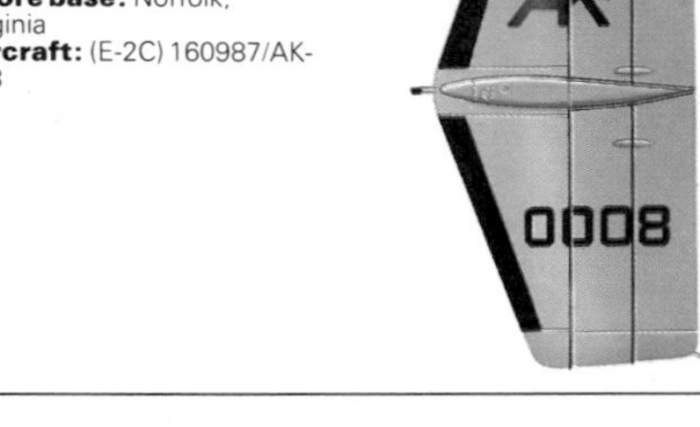

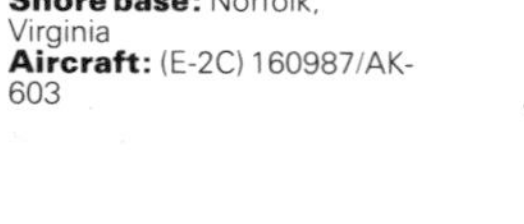

Israel Defence Force/ Air Force
Four E-2Cs were delivered during 1981, '946' having since been positively identified

Republic of Singapore Air Force
Four E-2Cs delivered

Egyptian Air Force
Five E-2Cs delivered by October 1987

VAW-124
Air Wing assignment: CVW-8
Shore base: Norfolk, Virginia
Aircraft: (E-2C) 161552/AJ-600

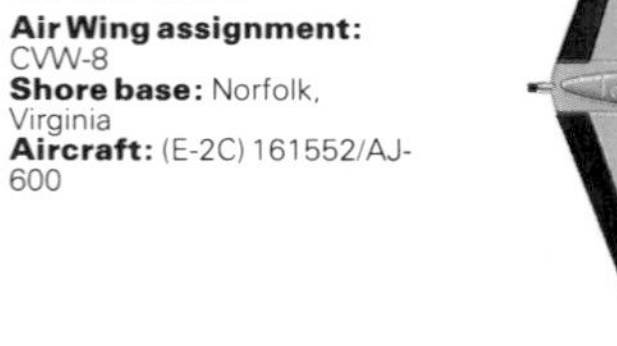

VAW-125
Air Wing assignment: CVW-17
Shore base: Norfolk, Virginia
Aircraft: (E-2C) 161550/AA-600

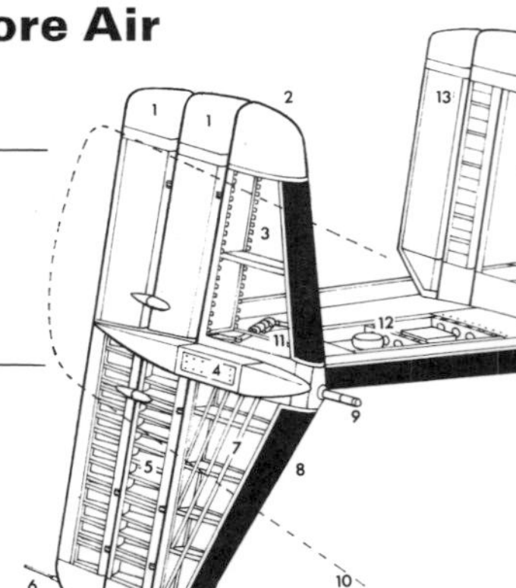

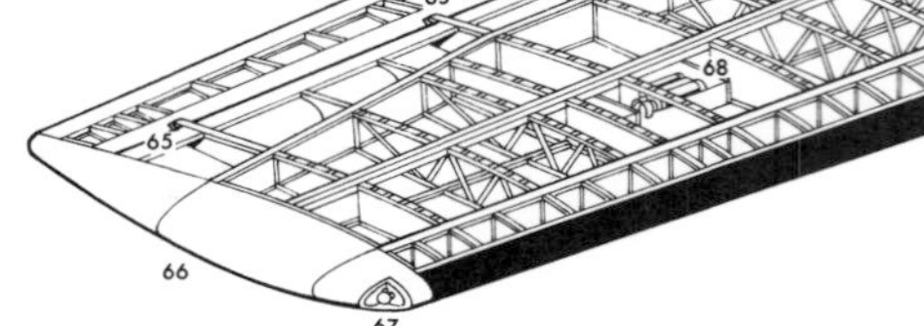

Grumman E-2C Hawkeye cutaway drawing key

1 Two section rudder panels
2 Starboard outboard fin
3 Glassfibre fin construction
4 Passive defence system antenna (PDS)
5 Rudder construction
6 Static discharger
7 Fin construction
8 Leading edge de-icing
9 Wing fold jury strut lock
10 Wing folded position
11 Rudder jack
12 PDS receivers
13 Starboard inboard rudder sections
14 Starboard inboard glass fibre fin
15 Port elevator construction
16 Port inboard fixed fin
17 Port outboard rudder sections
18 Rudder controls
19 Tailplane construction
20 Fuel jettison pipes
21 Rearward PDS antenna
22 Tailplane fixing
23 Rear fuselage construction
24 Tailskid jack
25 Arrester hook
26 Tailskid
27 Arrester hook jack
28 Lower PDS receiver and antenna
29 Rear pressure dome
30 Toilet
31 Rotodome rear mounting struts
32 Rotating radar scanner housing (Rotodome)
33 Rotodome edge de-icing
34 UHF aerial array, AN/APS-125 set
35 Pivot bearing housing
36 IFF aerial array
37 Rotodome motor
38 Hydraulic lifting jack
39 Front mounting support frame
40 Radar transmission line
41 Fuselage frame construction
42 Toilet compartment doorway
43 Antenna coupler
44 Rear cabin window
45 Air controller's seat
46 Radar and instrument panels
47 Combat information officer's seat
48 Combat information radar panel
49 Radar operator's seat
50 Radar panel and instruments
51 Swivelling seat mountings
52 Wing rear fixing
53 Wing fold break-point
54 Spar locking mechanism
55 Wing fold hinge
56 Wing folding hydraulic jack

A Hawkeye of the Japanese Air Self-Defence Force (JASDF), one of eight examples currently in service with this nation.

57 Starboard outboard flap
58 Flap construction
59 Flap guide rails
60 Flap drive motors and shaft
61 Starboard drooping aileron
62 Flap to drooping aileron connection
63 Aileron jack
64 Aileron construction
65 Aileron hinges
66 Starboard wing tip
67 Navigation light
68 Jury strut locking mechanism
69 Outer wing construction
70 Leading edge construction
71 Leading edge de-icing
72 Lattice rib construction
73 Engine exhaust pipe fairing
74 Front spar locking mechanism
75 Main undercarriage leg
76 Undercarriage leg door
77 Single mainwheel
78 Mainwheel door
79 Engine pylon construction
80 Engine mounting strut
81 Allison T56-A-425 engine
82 Oil cooler
83 Oil cooler intake
84 Engine intake
85 Hamilton Standard four-bladed propeller
86 Gearbox drive shaft
87 Propeller mechanism
88 Cooling air intake
89 Engine-to-propeller gearbox
90 Oil tank, usable capacity 9.25 US gal (35 litres) each nacelle
91 Bleed air supply duct
92 Vapour cycle air conditioning plant
93 Wing front fixing
94 Computer bank
95 Wing centre rib joint
96 Inboard wing section fuel tank, capacity 912 US gal (3452 litres) each wing
97 Lattice rib construction
98 Port inboard flap
99 Wing fold hinge
100 Wing fold joint line
101 Sloping hinge rib
102 Port outboard flap
103 Aileron jack
104 Port aileron
105 Port outer wing panel
106 Port wing tip
107 Navigation light
108 Leading edge de-icing
109 Aileron control cable mechanism
110 Engine mounting strut attachment
111 Engine-to-propeller gearbox
112 Propeller spinner fairing
113 Hamilton Standard four-bladed propeller
114 Engine intake
115 Gearbox drive shaft
116 Port engine
117 Fuel system piping
118 Cooling air intake
119 Vapour cycle system radiator
120 Cooling air outlet duct
121 Radar processor
122 IFF processor
123 Radar transmission line
124 Rangefinder amplifier
125 Port side entry doorway
126 Equipment cooling air duct
127 Port side equipment racks
128 Starboard side radio and electronics racks
129 Radar duplexer
130 Electronics boxes
131 Forward fuselage frame construction
132 Lower electronics racks
133 Scrambler boxes
134 Navigation equipment
135 Cockpit air conditioning duct
136 Cockpit doorway
137 Electrical system junction box
138 Air conditioning diffuser
139 Signal equipment
140 Cockpit floor level
141 Co-pilot's seat
142 Parachute stowage
143 Pilot's seat
144 Headrest
145 Cockpit roof window
146 Cockpit roof construction
147 Instrument panel shroud
148 Windscreen wiper
149 Bulged cockpit side window
150 Instrument panel
151 Control column
152 Nose undercarriage strut
153 Nose undercarriage door
154 Rudder pedals
155 Nose construction
156 Pitot head
157 Sloping front bulkhead
158 Navigation code box
159 Nose electrical junction box
160 Rudder pedal linking mechanism
161 Windscreen heater unit
162 Nose undercarriage leg
163 Steering mechanism
164 Twin nosewheels
165 Catapult strop attachment arm
166 Nosewheel leg door
167 Nosewheel emergency air bottle
168 Nose PDS receivers
169 Oxygen tank
170 Landing lamp

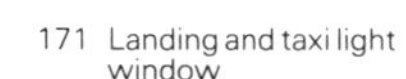

171 Landing and taxi light window
172 Nose PDS antenna array
173 Nose aerial fairing

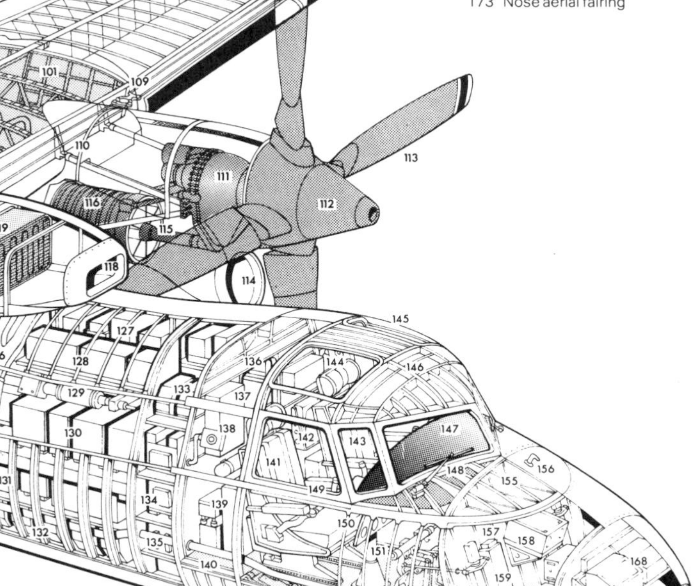

Specification: Grumman E-2C Hawkeye

Powerplant

two 3661-kW (4,910 shp) Allison T56-A-425 turboprop engines driving Hamilton Standard four-blade reversible-pitch propellers

Wings

Span, standard	24.56 m	(80 ft 7 in)
with wings folded	8.94 m	(29 ft 4 in)
Area, standard	65.03 m^2	(700 sq ft)

Fuselage and tail unit

Length overall	17.54 m	(57 ft 6.75 in)
Height overall	5.58 m	(18 ft 3.75 in)
Tailplane span	8.53 m	(28 ft 0 in)
Rotodome diameter	7.32 m	(24 ft 0 in)

Weights

Empty	17265 kg	(38,063 lb)
Maximum take-off	23556 kg	(51,933 lb)
Maximum internal fuel	5624 kg	(12,400 lb)
Maximum take-off with auxiliary fuel	27161 kg	(59,880 lb)

E-2 Hawkeye recognition points

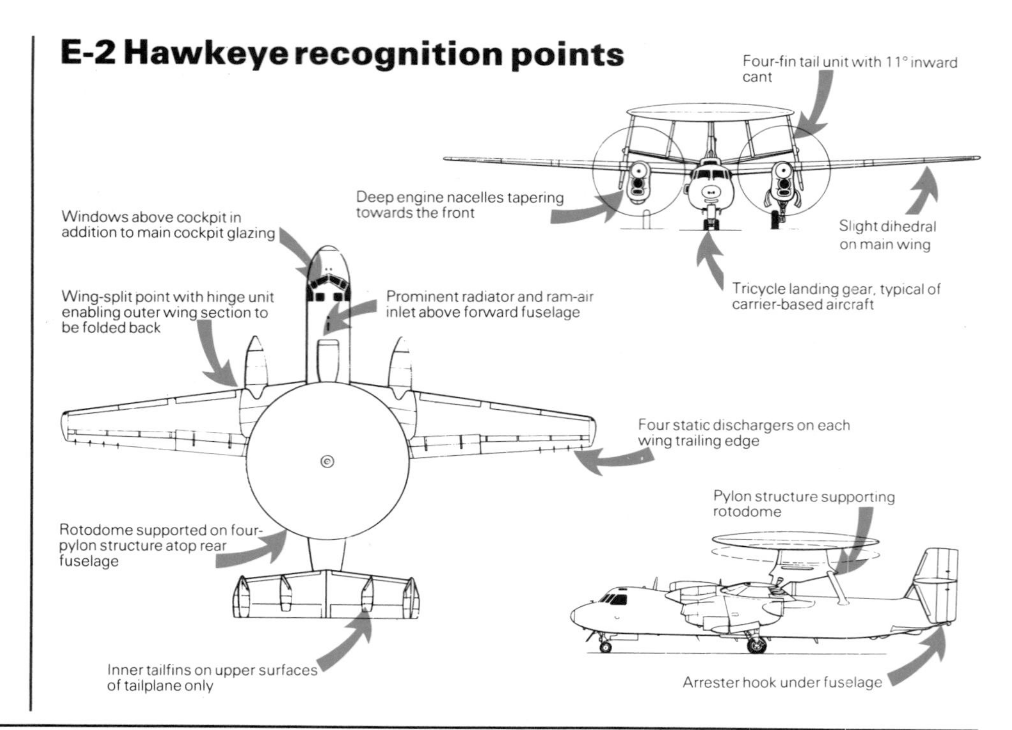

Performance

Maximum level speed	323 kts	(599 km/h; 372 mph)
Maximum cruising speed	311 kts	(576 km/h; 358 mph)
Approach speed	103 kts	(192 km/h; 119 mph)
Stalling speed in landing configuration	75 kts	(138 km/h; 86 mph)
Service ceiling	30,800 ft	(9390 m)
Minimum take-off run	610 m	(2,000 ft)
Minimum landing run	439 m	(1,440 ft)
Ferry range	2583 km	(1,605 miles)
Time on station 320 km (200 miles) from base	3-4 hours	
Unrefuelled endurance	6 hours 6 minutes	

Service ceiling

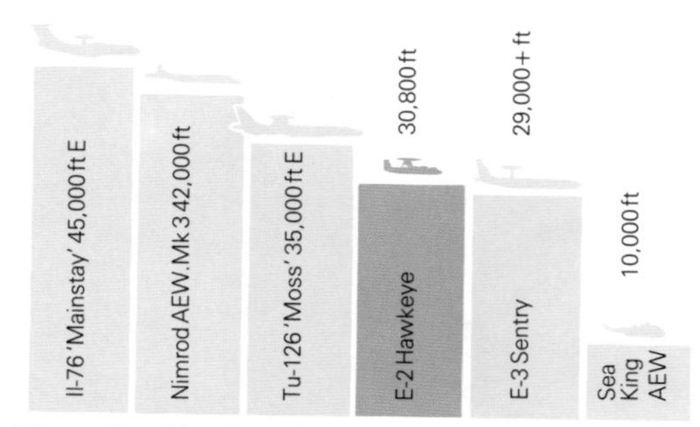

Speed

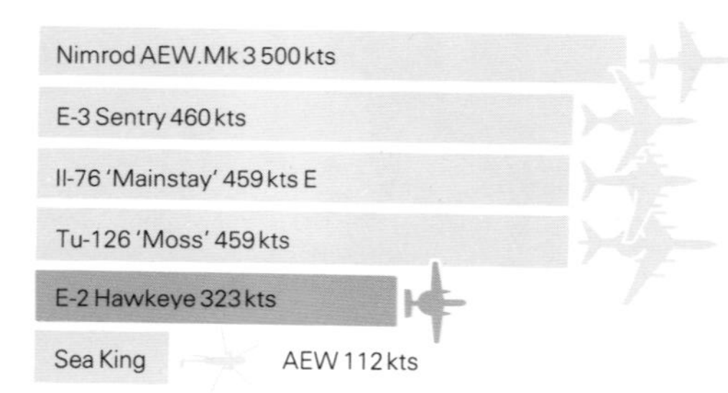

Unrefuelled endurance

Tu-126 'Moss' 20+ hours E

E-3 Sentry 11+ hours

Il-76 'Mainstay' 10+ hours E

Nimrod AEW.Mk 3 10+ hours

E-2 Hawkeye 6 hours 6 mins

Sea King AEW 4 hours

E-2 Hawkeye variants

E-2A: initial production version for the US Navy with APS-96 radar optimized for overwater operation, and T56-A-8/8A engines of 3021 kW (4,050 shp) (total three prototypes and 59 production aircraft)

E-2B: all E-2As were subsequently brought to this improved standard by a series of modifications to improve reliability and by the introduction of a Litton L-304 general-purpose computer giving greater flexibility of operation

E-2C: second production series for the US Navy, with APS-120 radar designed for overland target detection; this became APS-125 with the addition of ARPS (Advanced Radar Processing System), giving automatic detection and targeting of overland targets and improved resistance to jamming; distinguished from earlier variants by revised avionics cooling, requiring enlarged radiator over front fuselage, and by longer nose for ESM (electronic support measures), increasing length to 17.54 m (57 ft 6.75 in); engines uprated to 3,661 kW (4910 shp) T56-A-422, or Dash-425 when fitted with plastic-blade propellers (at least 83 planned for US Navy, 4 delivered to Israel and 4 on order for Japan)

TE-2C: trainer version of E-2C, externally identical

Layout of the Hawkeye cockpit displays many typical multi-engined operating features; full dual controls are fitted, and basic flight instruments are duplicated in front of each pilot station. Radio transmit and trimming buttons are fitted to each control yoke, and there is a central throttle quadrant incorporating brake levers and reversible-pitch levers. The duplicated engine instruments are placed in front of the captain (left-hand seat).

de Havilland Venom

De Havilland was one of Britain's foremost aircraft builders during World War II. The Venom was a product of its wartime experience and yet was a design far from the cutting edge of technology. Despite its lacklustre appearance beside its contemporaries, the Venom and Sea Venom fought at Suez and served as day and night fighters with several air forces. It was licence-produced in France and remained in service well into the 1960s and beyond.

At the end of World War II de Havilland's project staff at Hatfield had virtually completed development of the de Havilland Goblin-engined Vampire Mk I, which was in full-scale production by English Electric at Preston, and was drawing up later versions. The emergence of much more powerful engines led to the Vampire F.Mk 2 and F.Mk 4 with different installations of Rolls-Royce Nene, and more importantly (because de Havilland people were rather pro-de Havilland) the Vampire Mk 8. This was tailored to the company's next and much more powerful engine, originally called the Halford H.2 but soon named the de Havilland Ghost. Little interest was shown by the British government, but the company lost no time in preparing drawings for the Vampire Mk 8, which initially was distinguishable only by its rather larger wing-root inlets to handle the much greater engine airflow.

By this time the vital German test data on swept wings had been fully digested. A little tunnel work was done on swept models, including some with fore- and aft-facing V-shaped tailplanes and one with a diagonal tailplane linking booms of dramatically differing lengths. Eventually it was agreed with the ministry to stick to conventional aerodynamics, and put off the bold swept-wing technology until it was later adopted for the F.3/48 project which became the D.H.110, and many years later the Sea Vixen. Thus the D.H.112 could not hope to compete with its best foreign rivals, though de Havilland had the nerve to call its wing, with 17° taper on the leading edge, 'swept back'. It was an appalling reflection on British fighter production that in its day the D.H.112 was the best aircraft available.

Compared with that of the Vampire, the wing was not only thinner but of slightly greater area, and it was designed to carry a 355-litre (78-Imp gal) tank on each tip plus a 454-kg (1,000-lb) bomb, or another tank or eight rockets on each of two underwing pylons. These pylons were just outboard of the outwards-retracting main landing gear, and as the aircraft was going to be heavier than a Vampire yet have a much thinner wing there were problems in accommodating the mainwheels. Eventually the wheels were made thinner but of considerably greater diameter, with tyres inflated to a greater pressure; in the retracted position they caused bulges above and below the wing, even after Dunlop had worked wonders with a single-disc hydraulic brake, then as novel a feature as tip-tanks on British aircraft. There were remarkably few other changes, the main items being a revised fuel system to cope with up to four external tanks, spring-tab controls and extended boundary-layer deflectors on the fuselage nacelle ahead of the inlets. The four 20-mm guns, wooden nacelle and non-ejection seat were all retained.

First showing at Farnborough

By mid-1949 two aircraft (VV612 and 613) had been removed from a batch of English Electric Vampire FB.Mk 5s, and sent to Hatfield for completion as the prototype D.H.112s, by this time given the name Venom (previously applied to a Vickers fighter of 1937). VV612 made a successful first flight just in time for the SBAC Show at Farnborough, on 2 September 1949. The tailplane was extended outboard of the booms, the flaps and airbrakes were modified, and various other small changes were made, but on the whole the Venom was a colossal improvement on the latest Vampires and better (and faster) than the Meteor F.Mk 8. VV613 was flown on 23 July 1950, and was the first to have wing fences to prevent tip-stall at high angles of attack. Later the tip-tanks were given horizontal fins, and

The NF.Mk 3 variant was the definitive land-based night-fighter version, combining the Westinghouse APS-57 radar with a clear-view jettisonable canopy, powered ailerons and the short-span tailplane, dorsal fins and aft-pointing bullet fairings. The biggest gripe was that there were still no ejection seats. These are from No. 151 Sqn.

Few fighters in history have had such a long and active life as the Venoms of the Swiss Flugwaffe. The EFW consortium made 250 under licence, and the example shown was one of the first 100 built to Mk 1 standard. In 1979 it was serving with 10 Fliegerstaffel, with the nose reshaped for radios and a reconnaissance pod under the wing. Swiss Venoms were finally retired in 1983.

Fastest of all the naval Venoms was the French SE Aquilon 203, seen here serving with Aéronavale Flottille 16F. A single-seater, the 203 had Westinghouse APQ-94 radar, and from late 1958 was armed with the Nord 5103 (later designated AA.20) command-guidance AAM launched from wing pylons. Most served into the 1960s.

tip-stall was further avoided by small fixed slats on the leading edge inboard of the tank, the latter having a strake extending upstream from the wing. In such respects as general manoeuvrability at medium altitudes, rate of climb, ceiling and steadiness as a gun platform, the new fighter was outstanding.

Production was authorised in early 1950, and plans were made for the Venom to become, with the F-84, the standard NATO fighter-bomber. At the Palais de Chaillot a scheme was drawn up for more than 2,000 Venoms, of which 1,185 were to be made in the UK by a consortium made up mainly of de Havilland Chester, Bristol Aircraft and Fairey Aviation at Stockport and Ringway. The main assembly centres on the continent were to be Macchi and Fiat in Italy, with the designation Fiat G.81, and Sud-Aviation in France, both of whom were already building Vampires. In the event things were so slow to get moving, largely because of the crippling rundown of the British industry, that hardly any of this programme became fact.

Rather outclassed

A total of 373 was built in the UK of the first mark, the Venom FB.Mk 1. By this time de Havilland did have productive capacity (and was taking over the production of the Vampire), and the majority of subsequent Venoms was assembled at Chester after delivery of 16 largely hand-built machines from Hatfield. Most of these went to West Raynham, Boscombe Down and other service test and development establishments. The first RAF squadron to receive the new fighter was No. 11 at Wunstorf, in 2nd ATAF, West Germany, under Squadron Leader D. H. Seaton, DFC. The squadron was operational with the Venom FB.Mk 1 by September 1952, and in many respects was pleased with its new mount. The worst faults were a severe (+2*g*) structural manoeuvre limitation, caused by two catastrophic failures of early Venom FB.Mk 1s in England and enforced by broad red stripes across the wings; lack of an ejection seat; lack of cockpit air-conditioning, which caused pilots to become quickly drenched in sweat, losing efficiency; and poor rate of roll (described in an official report as 'poor' without tip-tanks and as 'deplorable' with such tanks fitted and filled). On the whole a Venom could beat a straight-wing Republic F-84 at all heights and hold its own against a Dassault Ouragan, but it was hard-pressed to get an English Electric Canberra in its sights, and of course had no hope of catching an F-86.

So sustained was the outcry about ejection seats that, spurred on by recurring crashes resulting from a further (but different) structural failure, as well as inflight fires and many other problems, Martin-Baker Mk 1F seats were fitted from late 1954 together with Godfrey air-conditioning. The de Havilland company also continued to develop the basic aircraft, and on 29 December 1953 flew a modified Venom FB.Mk 1 (WE381) as the prototype of the Venom FB.Mk 4. This rectified most of the more severe deficiencies, the most important being hydraulically boosted ailerons giving a respectable rate of roll even with tip-tanks. The rudders were also powered, and the tail was aerodynamically improved with aft-facing bullets as well as forward-facing ones at the junction of the vertical and horizontal surfaces, and with considerably larger fins and rudders cropped diagonally at the top. This was what the Venom should have been from the start, but by the mid-1950s the Venom was hardly impressive and only 150 Venom FB.Mk 4s were built, in 1955-57. Together with the Hawker Hunter they swiftly replaced the Venom FB.Mk 1 and served until 1962, seeing much action in Cyprus, Malaya, Suez, Aden and Oman.

de Havilland Sea Venom FAW.Mk 22 cutaway drawing key

1 Radome
2 ARI 5860(AI Mk 22) radar scanner
3 Radome hinge
4 Radar tracking mechanism
5 Nosewheel leg door
6 Approach light
7 Nosewheel forks
8 Anti-shimmy nosewheel
9 Shock absorber leg strut
10 Radar equipment access door
11 Frequency modulator unit
12 Forward electronics equipment bay
13 Laminated (plywood/balsa/plywood sandwich) forward fuselage skinning
14 IFF aerial
15 Front pressure bulkhead
16 Pilot's instrument panel
17 Nosewheel housing
18 Control column
19 Rudder pedals
20 Cockpit floor level
21 Cannon muzzle blast trough
22 Nosewheel door
23 'Pull-out' step
24 Control system linkages
25 Engine throttle lever
26 Emergency hydraulic handpump
27 Direct vision side window panels
28 Reflector gunsight
29 Navigator/radar operator's instrument console
30 Windscreen wiper
31 Armoured windscreen panel
32 Cockpit canopy cover
33 Ejection seat headrests
34 Face blind firing handle
35 Navigator/radar operator's ejection seat (behind and below level of pilot's seat)
36 Cockpit coaming
37 Pilot's Martin-Baker Mk4 ejection seat
38 Radio and electronics equipment bay

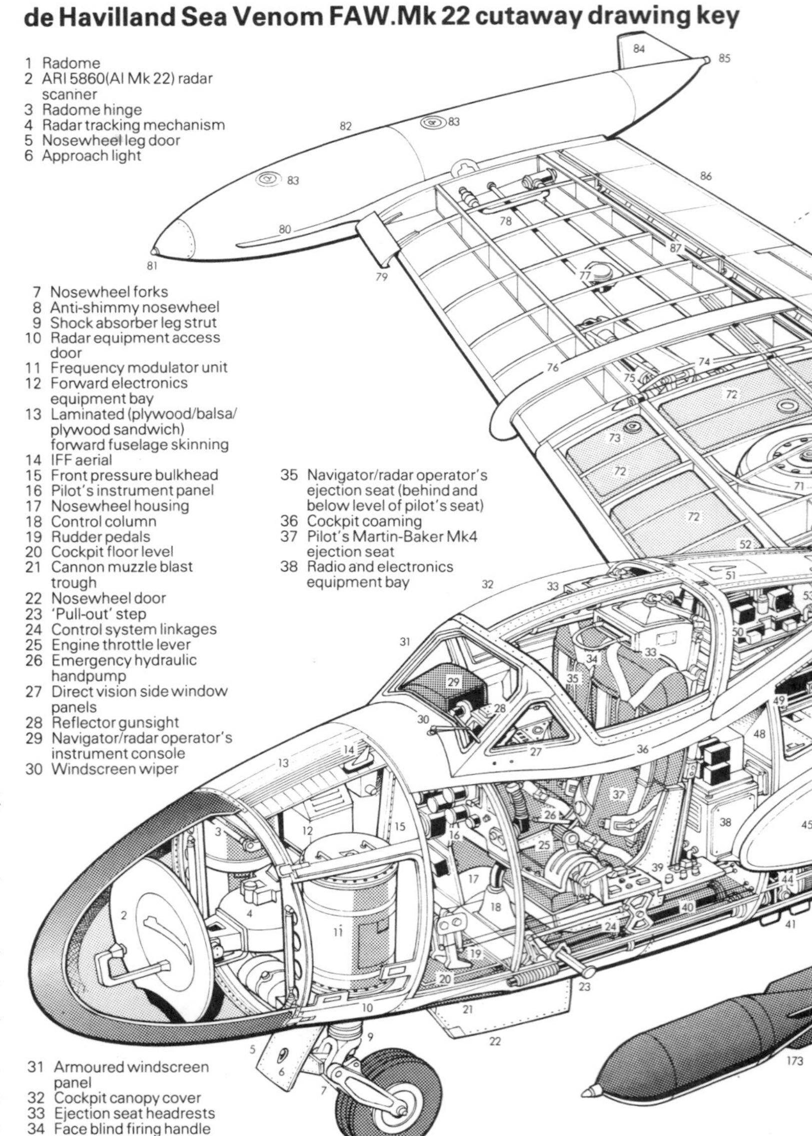

Export customers for the basic fighter-bomber Venom included Iraq (15 Venom FB.Mk 50s), Venezuela (22 Venom FB.Mk 54s) and, by far the most satisfied of all Venom users, Switzerland. In this last country the Venom was adopted during 1952 as the successor to the Vampire, and a group of companies led by the EFW consortium (Federal Aircraft Factory at Emmen, Flug-und Fahrzeugwerke at Altenrhein and Pilatus at Stans) built 100 to approximately Venom FB.Mk 1 standard followed by another 150 to Venom FB.Mk 4 standard, with engines made mainly by Fiat in Italy and the Swiss Sulzer works at Winterthur. These Venoms served 25 years in 11 attack regiments and in 1982 a few were still with the 1st and 2nd regiments as well as the Fliegerschule. They have been largely rebuilt with new systems, extended noses, and better structures.

de Havilland goes it alone

From the start of the D.H.112 programme de Havilland had studied a night-fighter variant, using the same wood nacelle with almost side-by-side seats for the pilot and navigator and AI Mk 10 radar in the nose. This arrangement had worked in the Mosquito, and at company expense was carried across to the Vampire. As the RAF continued to show little interest, de Havilland repeated the story of the D.H.113 Vampire night-fighter and built a prototype Venom night-fighter at its own expense. In 1949 Hatfield began making Venom wings, landing gear and a new tail with enlarged triangular fins, which were mated to a D.H.113 Vampire nacelle and flown on 22 August 1950, with the civil SBAC Class-B markings G-5-3. Though it was extremely sluggish in roll, lacked ejection seats and even retained the disastrous heavily framed canopy with a small lid for access and emergency escape, the aircraft was in most respects better than the night-fighter Meteors and so, with continuing heated arguments about ejection seats, it went into production for the RAF as the Venom NF.Mk 2. The first such aircraft (WL804) flew from Hatfield on 4 March 1952, but the main run of 90 was eventually (1953-55) delivered from Chester. Early examples had the old canopy and tail, but would have been welcome in No.141

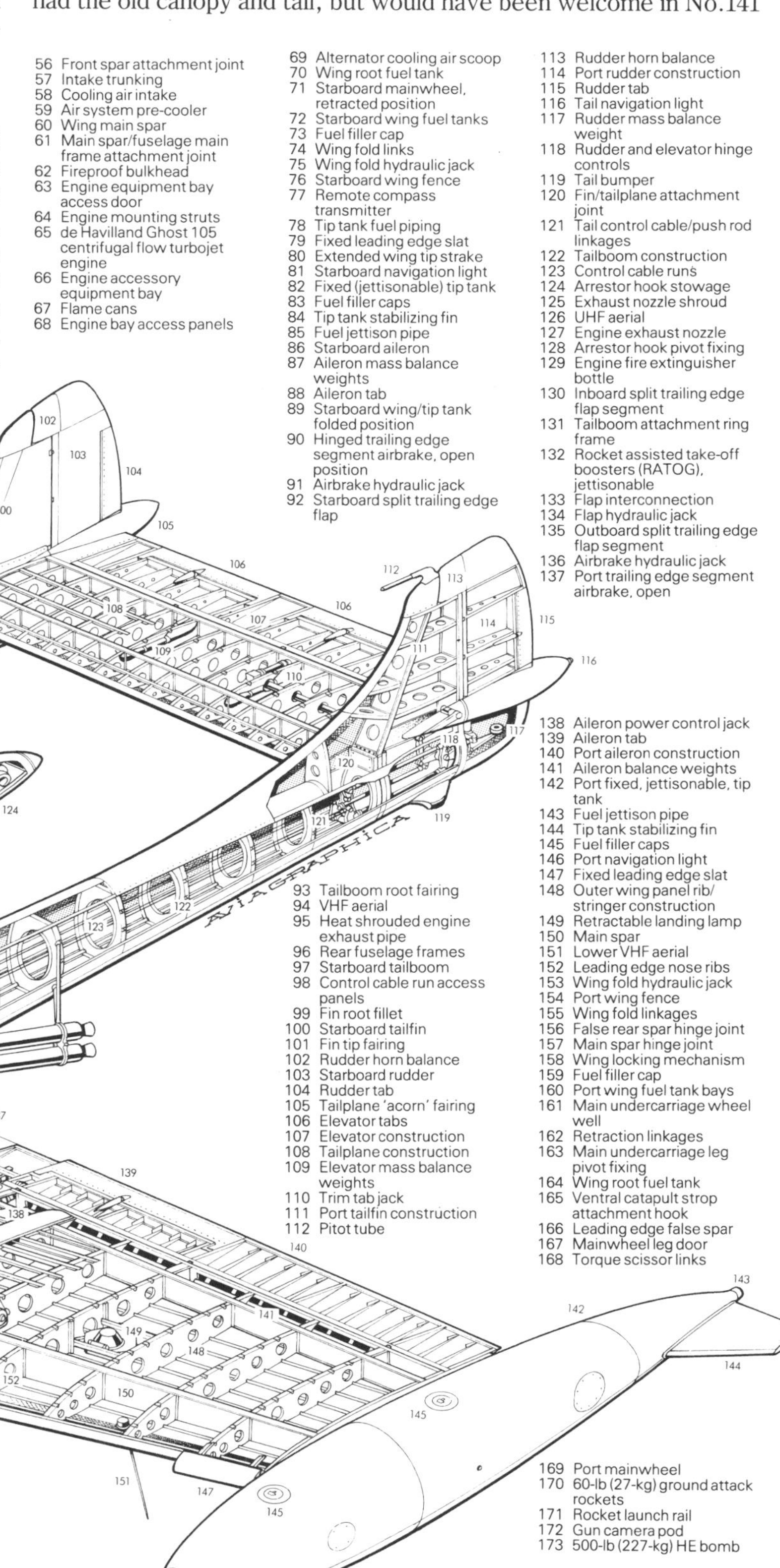

39 Port side console panel
40 Underfloor cannon barrels
41 Spent cartridge case ejector chutes
42 Cannon bay
43 20-mm cannon (four)
44 Ammunition feed chute
45 Boundary layer splitter plate
46 Port engine air intake
47 Ammunition tanks, 150 rounds per gun
48 Cockpit rear pressure bulkhead
49 Equipment bay access panel
50 Electrical system equipment
51 External canopy handle
52 Canopy aft glazing
53 Hydraulic system header tank
54 Fuel filler access
55 Fuselage fuel tank; total system capacity including fixed tip tanks 464-Imp gal (2109 litres)
56 Front spar attachment joint
57 Intake trunking
58 Cooling air intake
59 Air system pre-cooler
60 Wing main spar
61 Main spar/fuselage main frame attachment joint
62 Fireproof bulkhead
63 Engine equipment bay access door
64 Engine mounting struts
65 de Havilland Ghost 105 centrifugal flow turbojet engine
66 Engine accessory equipment bay
67 Flame cans
68 Engine bay access panels
69 Alternator cooling air scoop
70 Wing root fuel tank
71 Starboard mainwheel, retracted position
72 Starboard wing fuel tanks
73 Fuel filler cap
74 Wing fold links
75 Wing fold hydraulic jack
76 Starboard wing fence
77 Remote compass transmitter
78 Tip tank fuel piping
79 Fixed leading edge slat
80 Extended wing tip strake
81 Starboard navigation light
82 Fixed (jettisonable) tip tank
83 Fuel filler caps
84 Tip tank stabilizing fin
85 Fuel jettison pipe
86 Starboard aileron
87 Aileron mass balance weights
88 Aileron tab
89 Starboard wing/tip tank folded position
90 Hinged trailing edge segment airbrake, open position
91 Airbrake hydraulic jack
92 Starboard split trailing edge flap
93 Tailboom root fairing
94 VHF aerial
95 Heat shrouded engine exhaust pipe
96 Rear fuselage frames
97 Starboard tailboom
98 Control cable run access panels
99 Fin root fillet
100 Starboard tailfin
101 Fin tip fairing
102 Rudder horn balance
103 Starboard rudder
104 Rudder tab
105 Tailplane 'acorn' fairing
106 Elevator tabs
107 Elevator construction
108 Tailplane construction
109 Elevator mass balance weights
110 Trim tab jack
111 Port tailfin construction
112 Pitot tube
113 Rudder horn balance
114 Port rudder construction
115 Rudder tab
116 Tail navigation light
117 Rudder mass balance weight
118 Rudder and elevator hinge controls
119 Tail bumper
120 Fin/tailplane attachment joint
121 Tail control cable/push rod linkages
122 Tailboom construction
123 Control cable runs
124 Arrestor hook stowage
125 Exhaust nozzle shroud
126 UHF aerial
127 Engine exhaust nozzle
128 Arrestor hook pivot fixing
129 Engine fire extinguisher bottle
130 Inboard split trailing edge flap segment
131 Tailboom attachment ring frame
132 Rocket assisted take-off boosters (RATOG), jettisonable
133 Flap interconnection
134 Flap hydraulic jack
135 Outboard split trailing edge flap segment
136 Airbrake hydraulic jack
137 Port trailing edge segment airbrake, open
138 Aileron power control jack
139 Aileron tab
140 Port aileron construction
141 Aileron balance weights
142 Port fixed, jettisonable, tip tank
143 Fuel jettison pipe
144 Tip tank stabilizing fin
145 Fuel filler caps
146 Port navigation light
147 Fixed leading edge slat
148 Outer wing panel rib/stringer construction
149 Retractable landing lamp
150 Main spar
151 Lower VHF aerial
152 Leading edge nose ribs
153 Wing fold hydraulic jack
154 Port wing fence
155 Wing fold linkages
156 False rear spar hinge joint
157 Main spar hinge joint
158 Wing locking mechanism
159 Fuel filler cap
160 Port wing fuel tank bays
161 Main undercarriage wheel well
162 Retraction linkages
163 Main undercarriage leg pivot fixing
164 Wing root fuel tank
165 Ventral catapult strop attachment hook
166 Leading edge false spar
167 Mainwheel leg door
168 Torque scissor links
169 Port mainwheel
170 60-lb (27-kg) ground attack rockets
171 Rocket launch rail
172 Gun camera pod
173 500-lb (227-kg) HE bomb

Sqn at Coltishall had it not been for structural failures quite different from those of the single-seater, which caused one grounding and prolonged restriction to below 3050 m (10,000 ft) and below 842 km/h (523 mph).

Well into production, de Havilland introduced a much better canopy, almost identical to that devised by Airspeed for the D.H.115 Vampire Trainer, with clear-vision mouldings and a large upward-hinged central portion giving good access. Airspeed's Vampire Trainer was also the source of the new Venom NF.Mk 2 tail, with graceful curved dorsal fins. There was no official sanction for the commonly used mark number of Venom NF.Mk 2A for the improved aircraft. The type generally suffered from a remarkable list of defects and deficiencies, among which were some of the worst records of unserviceability in the RAF.

A more effective night-fighter

Largely thanks to the US Mutual Defense Assistance Program, which gave the UK the much more modern Westinghouse APS-57 radar (called AI Mk 21 by the RAF), de Havilland received a contract for a further 129 night-fighters, and these, designated Venom NF.Mk 3, incorporated numerous much-needed modifications. Hardly any were on the Mk 3 prototype (WV928), which was a primitive machine apart from the radar, but production Venom NF.Mk 3s had the Ghost 104 of 2245-kg (4,950-lb) thrust, uprated alternators, a stronger radome (pilots were no longer apprehensive at 925 km/h/575 mph) which hinged upwards instead of sliding off for access, hydraulically boosted ailerons, a short-span tailplane and a new vertical tail closely similar to that of the Venom FB.Mk 4 but without forward bullets. Still the company stoutly maintained its inability to fit ejection seats. The Venom NF.Mk 3 batch was assembled at three de Havilland plants, Chester (88), Hatfield (21) and Christchurch (20), the last-named being the former Airspeed works where some of the design of this mark was carried out. A further 62 night-fighter Venoms were built as Venom NF.Mk 51s for Sweden. Production of these began long before any could be made for the RAF, and the first

de Havilland D.H.112 Venom variants

D.H.112: prototype (VV612), originally called Vampire Mk 8
Venom FB.Mk 1: first production version with Ghost Mk 103 engine, tail as Vampire FB.Mk 9 except tailplane sections outboard of booms, no ejection seat
Venom NF.Mk 2: production night-fighter, basically FB.Mk 1 with nacelle of Vampire NF.Mk 10; modified to **Venom NF.Mk 2A** with NF.Mk 3 canopy and tail
Venom NF.Mk 3: improved night-fighter with Ghost Mk 104 of 2245-kg (4,950-lb) rating, new tail with broader fins with dorsal extensions, no tailplane extensions but junction bullets at rear, powered ailerons, US radar, clear-view jettisonable canopy but no ejection seats
Venom FB.Mk 4: improved single-seat fighter-bomber with Mk 4 ejection seat, powered ailerons, broad fins with bullets fore and aft (no dorsal extensions) retaining long-span tailplane
Sea Venom NF.Mk 20: prototype derived from NF.Mk 2 with hook and other changes
Sea Venom FAW.Mk 20: production carrier-based all-weather fighter and attack, folding wings and full naval gear
Sea Venom FAW.Mk 21: improved naval fighter with Ghost Mk 104, US radar, powered ailerons, clear-view jettisonable canopy, bulged above pilot on left, tailplane extensions deleted; later modified to accept Martin-Baker Mk 4A seats
Sea Venom FAW.Mk 22: Ghost Mk 105, Mk 4A seats fitted from start, improved AI.Mk 22 radar, reworked to carry and fire two Blue Jay (later Firestreak) AAMs
Venom FB.Mk 50: basic designation of export versions of FB.Mk 1, supplied to Switzerland (where also built under licence), Iraq and, later, passed to other users; Swiss used Fiat-built Ghost Mk 48
Venom NF.Mk 51: night-fighter based on NF.Mk 2 for Sweden
Sea Venom FAW.Mk 53: carrier-based all-weather fighter for Australia based on FAW.Mk 21
Venom FB.Mk 54: basic designation of export versions of FB.Mk 4, supplied to Venezuela and made in Switzerland
SNCASE Aquilon 20: four prototypes of French carrier-based night-fighter derived from FAW.Mk 20, used as unarmed trainers
Aquilon 201: single-seat land-based night-fighter
Aquilon 202: production naval all-weather fighter, Fiat-built Ghost Mk 48, APQ-65 radar, sliding canopy over two-seat cockpit with ejection seats
Aquilon 203: as Aquilon 202 but APQ-94 radar; from 1956 Nord 5103 (AA.20) AAMs
Aquilon 204: dual unarmed trainers, short-stroke main gears

Specification
de Havilland Venom FB.Mk 4

Type: single-seat fighter bomber
Powerplant: one 2336-kg (5,150-lb) de Havilland Ghost 105 turbojet
Performance: maximum speed 1030 km/h (640 mph) below 6100 m (20,000 ft); initial climb 2200 m (7,230 ft) per minute; service ceiling 14630 m (48,000 ft); range (with underwing tanks) 1730 km (1,075 miles)
Weights: empty 4174 kg (9,202 lb); maximum loaded 6945 kg (15,310 lb)
Dimensions: span (over tip tanks) 12.7 m (41 ft 8 in); length 9.71 m (31 ft 10 in); height 1.88 m (6 ft 2 in); wing area 25.99 m^2 (279.75 sq ft)
Armament: four 20-mm Hispano guns each with 150 rounds; various external loads could include eight 7.62-mm (3-in) rockets with 27.2-kg (60-lb) heads on centre-section launchers, as shown, plus two bombs of 454-kg (1,000-lb) in place of drop tanks

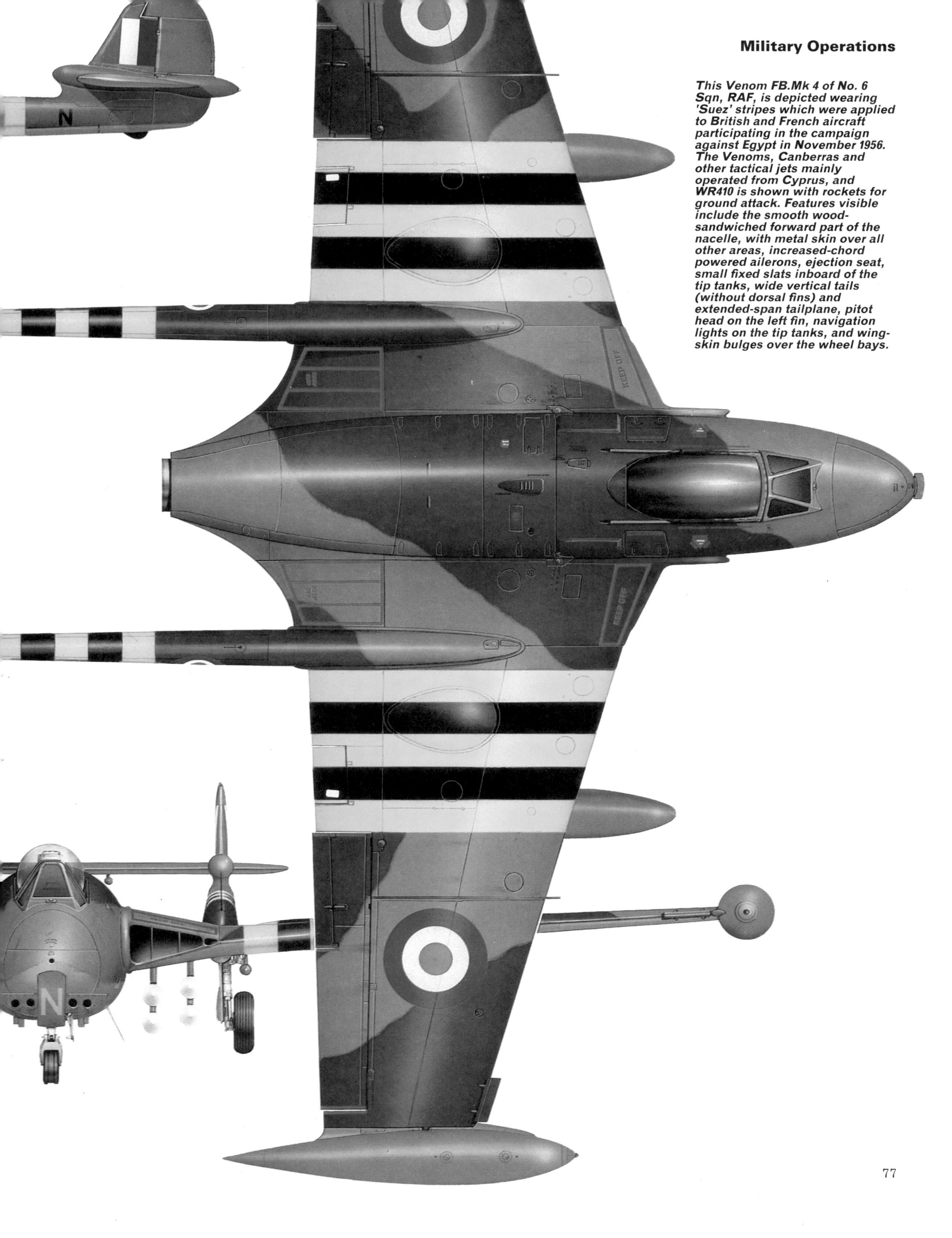

This Venom FB.Mk 4 of No. 6 Sqn, RAF, is depicted wearing 'Suez' stripes which were applied to British and French aircraft participating in the campaign against Egypt in November 1956. The Venoms, Canberras and other tactical jets mainly operated from Cyprus, and WR410 is shown with rockets for ground attack. Features visible include the smooth wood-sandwiched forward part of the nacelle, with metal skin over all other areas, increased-chord powered ailerons, ejection seat, small fixed slats inboard of the tip tanks, wide vertical tails (without dorsal fins) and extended-span tailplane, pitot head on the left fin, navigation lights on the tip tanks, and wing-skin bulges over the wheel bays.

The D.H.112 prototype, originally to have been a Vampire FB.Mk 5 and at first known as the Vampire Mk 8, made its first flight just in time to be demonstrated at the 1949 SBAC show at Farnborough, as seen here. Main differences were the thin wings, new main landing gears and larger nacelle for the Ghost engine.

This flight of early Venom FB.Mk 1 fighters with RAF Germany emphasises dramatically how British fighter design had fallen behind after World War II. Not only was the aircraft fundamentally inferior to the F-86 Sabre and MiG-15, but it did not even have air-conditioning or an ejection seat.

was delivered in December 1952. Designated J33 in Flygvapen service, the Venom NF.Mk 51 had a Swedish SFA-built Ghost RM2A engine; the first 30 had the old tail, but were later modified with kits (sent from the UK) which also added the improved canopy. These machines had a long life with numerous modifications, the last being retired as a civilian target tug in 1969.

Blue water Venom

At the start of the D.H.112 programme in 1948, the company studied carrier-based versions, and in 1949 Admiralty specification N.107 was issued for a replacement for the two-seat Sea Hornet NF.Mk 21. This was really a shockingly retrograde step because it represented a weak disbelief in swept wings and adoption of the Venom instead of the very much more potent D.H.110 (Specification N.14/49). Hatfield accordingly built a prototype (WK376) designated Sea Venom F(AW).Mk 20, flown on 19 April 1951. The original Venom NF.Mk 2 prototype had by this time been purchased as WP227 and it was used for deck-landing trials. The Sea Venom was assigned to Airspeed at Christchurch, but Hatfield also built a second machine, WK379, with long-stroke main legs, catapult hooks, arrester hook and a Venom NF.Mk 3-type tail. The third prototype (WK385) had hydraulically folding wings and AI Mk 10 radar.

Christchurch built 50 production Sea Venom F(AW).Mk 20s, the first flying on 27 March 1953. They had the improved canopy and tail but manual ailerons, and were sluggish performers in roll and shaky in yaw. Next came the Sea Venom F(AW).Mk 21, with AI Mk 21 (Westinghouse) radar, powered rudders and boosted ailerons, Maxaret non-skid brakes and the Ghost Mk 104 engine. A total of 167 was built, plus 39 offset to the Royal Australian Navy as the Sea Venom F(AW).Mk 53. During the run, with just over 100 delivered, a modification was incorporated that for years had been described as not possible: Martin-Baker Mk 4A seats were installed for both crew members! A special rapid-inflation seat pack was added to thrust the occupants out under water, and to give good 'bonedome' clearance to the pilot the top of the canopy was bulged on the left side.

The changes at last made the two-seat Sea Venom a reasonably good aircraft, but there were only 39 aircraft, designated F(AW).Mk 22, left to build, Christchurch delivering these in 1957. As well as the ejection seats from the start, the Sea Venom F(AW).Mk 22 introduced the 2336-kg (5,150-lb) Ghost Mk 105, with new naval features, and the radar was the AI Mk 22. Many Sea Venom F(AW).Mk 22 aircraft were sent to Hatfield in 1958 to be fitted with the Blue Jay (Firestreak) IR-guided air-to-air missile, carried on the deep wing pylons. The related accessory systems and seeker cooling circuits were carried in the nacelle and in the pylons. These were among the first guided AAMs in service, beginning in 1958 with No. 893 Squadron.

The French connection

Though nothing came of the big plan for Italian Venom production (the dramatically more modern F-86K was chosen instead), Sud-Est Aviation in France continued its plans, and with de Havilland collaboration set up a design office to build its own version, with assembly at Marignane, near Marseilles. Named Aquilon (Sea Eagle), the SNCASE variant was originally the Hatfield-outlined Sea Venom Mk 52, based on the Sea Venom F(AW).Mk 20; but this grew into an all-French family, using exclusively Westinghouse radars and Fiat-built Ghost 48 engines. The initial four aircraft were assembled from Hatfield parts and called Aquilon 20, the first flying in midnight blue finish on 20 February 1952. A single land-based Aquilon 201 followed in 1953, with short-stroke main legs. On 25 March 1954 the first of 75 Aquilon 202s took off with long main gears, a neat sliding canopy, full air-conditioning, Martin-Baker N4 seats, Hispano 404 guns and APQ-65 radar. Then came 40 single-seat Aquilon 203s with the pilot on the centreline, APQ-94 radar and Nord 5103 (AA.20) command-guided AAMs. Last of all were 15 Aquilon 204s with dual flight controls, used as unarmed trainers. Aquilons served with Flottilles 11F, 16F, 17F, 2S, 10S, 54S and 59S until 1960-61.

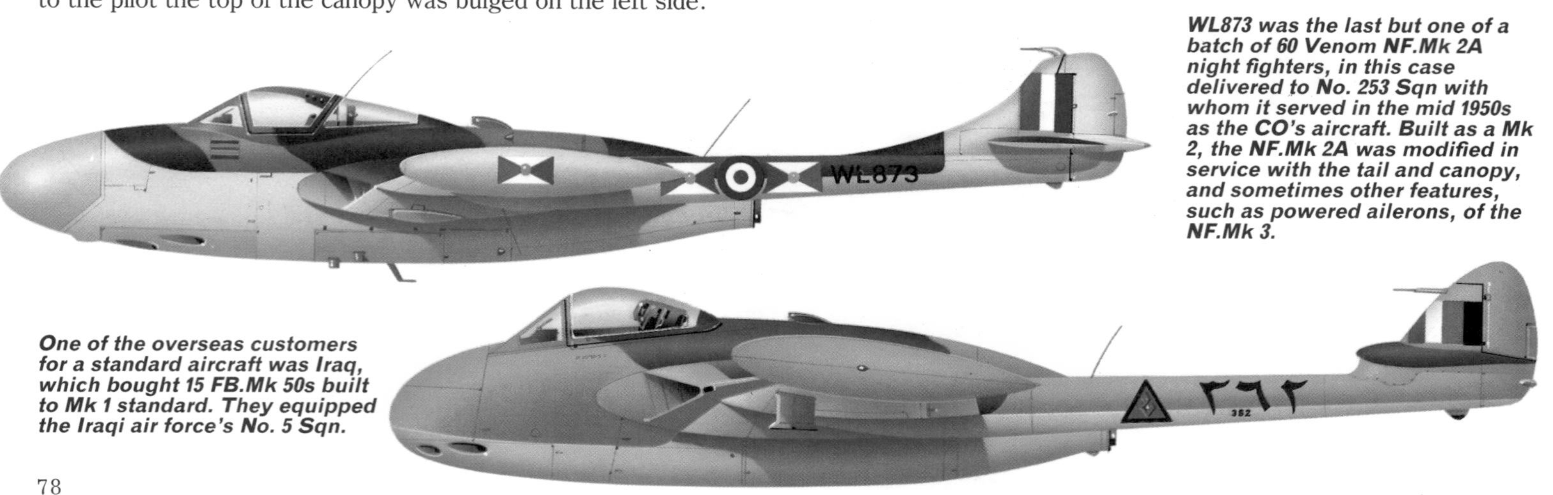

WL873 was the last but one of a batch of 60 Venom NF.Mk 2A night fighters, in this case delivered to No. 253 Sqn with whom it served in the mid 1950s as the CO's aircraft. Built as a Mk 2, the NF.Mk 2A was modified in service with the tail and canopy, and sometimes other features, such as powered ailerons, of the NF.Mk 3.

One of the overseas customers for a standard aircraft was Iraq, which bought 15 FB.Mk 50s built to Mk 1 standard. They equipped the Iraqi air force's No. 5 Sqn.

Air Wing Kuznetsov

Defence cuts accompanying the end of the Cold War have forced the sale of Russia's uncommissioned second supercarrier, scrapping of the incomplete third ship, and abandonment of the fourth, but the first ship, the Kuznetsov, _has been commissioned and is progressing towards operational service._

Soviet naval aviation has a long and proud history. Formed in 1913 as an arm of the Tsarist navy it fought with distinction in World War I, dropping one-third of the bombs delivered by Tsarist and Red air forces. During the early years of the Soviet state, the navy entered a period of decline. Lenin pursued a 'white water' coastal defence strategy, and naval aviation was limited to land-based types and seaplanes operating from tenders.

After the Great Patriotic War, Joseph Stalin toyed with the idea of creating a 'blue water', ocean-going navy to counter US and British naval forces, but died before his ambitious plans could be put into operation. Under Krushchev, the new naval C-in-C, Admiral Gorshkov, was directed to concentrate on the defence of the motherland. Naval aviation lost even its interceptor force, and received only second-hand bombers and obsolete flying-boats for patrol, anti-shipping and maritime reconnaissance duties.

Deployment of the ASW helicopter cruisers *Moskva* and *Leningrad* in the mid-1960s could have provided an increased 'blue water' capability, but were actually used to reinforce the existing, less-ambitious naval strategy, and the pure and simple defence of the motherland role was not challenged until the 1970s, with the construction of the four 'Kiev'-class aircraft carrying cruisers. Like the 'Moskvas', the new carriers were primarily for ASW and the short-ranged and primitive Yak-38 which they carried was of only limited usefulness, and did not allow the ships to operate in conditions of enemy air superiority.

The debate intensified, and many senior Naval officers, most notably Admiral Pushkin, argued for a stronger ocean-going navy with US-style aircraft-carriers. These would, it was argued, allow Soviet naval forces to operate within range of enemy aircraft by establishing local air superiority. The value of such ships in the power projection role was also stressed. Finally the arguments were won, and the keel of the first Soviet supercarrier was laid down in January 1983. Originally plans called for the construction of two 67,000-ton carriers equipped with arrester gear and a novel combination of restrainers and ski-jump, and these

Trailing a plume of black smoke, the first MiG-29K prototype approaches the* Kuznetsov, *carrying a variety of missiles on four of its possible eight underwing pylons. In the foreground is a Kamov Ka-27PS SAR helicopter.

were to have been followed by a class of larger (possibly nuclear-powered) carriers which were, it was rumoured, to have had catapults installed.

The first carrier was launched on 5 December 1985, but predictions that this ship would be named the *Kremlin* (or later the *Leonid Brezhnev*) proved unfounded and the ship rolled down the slipway as the *Tbilisi*, as its sister (the *Riga*) was laid down. The dissolution of the USSR prompted a renaming, since there was little support for naming the Soviet navy's newest flagships after cities in what had become very troublesome centres of resis-

The Su-27K (foreground) and MiG-29K may both be selected for the* Kuznetsov*'s air wing, with the bigger Sukhoi acting as a dedicated long-range interceptor, and the MiG being used as a multi-role strike fighter like the F/A-18.

The Kuznetsov*'s sleek profile is dominated by the ski-jump take-off ramp, hitherto seen only on Western V/STOL carriers. The ship lacks any form of catapult for launching its aircraft, but does have conventional arrester gear.*

Close examination of the Su-27K's cockpit reveals no additional air-to-ground capability by comparison with the land-based 'Flanker'. This lack of versatility may count against the Su-27K if only one fighter type is selected for the Kuznetsov*'s air group.*

An Su-27K prototype with everything folded. The incorporation of tailplane folding is especially novel. Peeping from between the engine nacelles of this aircraft is a huge air-breathing ASM.

tance to Moscow. Thus *Tbilisi* became *Kuznetsov* and *Riga* became *Varyag*. At about the same time, the first big carrier, the 75,000-ton *Ulyanovsk*, was scrapped.

First for 'Flanker'

Flying trials on the *Tbilisi* began before it was formally commissioned as the *Kuznetsov*, (commissioning took place on 21 January 1991). The first fixed-wing aircraft type to land on the ship was the Su-27K, a canard-equipped derivative of the well-known land-based interceptor believed to bear the NATO codename 'Flanker-B2'. Apart from the movable canard foreplanes, which provide extra lift at low speeds and significantly improve take-off, approach and landing performance, the new variant had folding wings and, uniquely, tailplanes. Other changes included a shortened tailcone fairing (to reduce the likelihood of a tailscrape during high nose attitude landings), provision of an arrester hook, and a strengthened undercarriage. Interestingly, the Su-27's single nosewheel has been replaced by twin nosewheels. The Su-27K prototypes are all fitted with retractable inflight-refuelling probes, and production aircraft will also have uprated AL-31F turbofans with between 12 and 15 per cent greater thrust.

At least five Su-27K prototypes are believed to have been produced, differing from one another in detail only. All have had the features listed above, and all have had revised control surfaces. The simple half-span trailing-edge flaps of the original 'Flanker' have been replaced by new, three-section, full-span, trailing-edge flaps. The outboard and middle sections can also operate differentially as ailerons, except on approach, when only the outboard sections are used for roll control.

The Su-27K flown onto the *Kuznetsov* (or *Tbilisi* as it then was) by Victor Pugachev for the historic first fixed-wing non-V/STOL carrier landing on 1 November was closely followed by an example of the navalised MiG-29, flown by Takhtar Aubakirov. This aircraft gained the honour of making the first launch from the new ship. The definitive carrierborne MiG-29 variant is the MiG-29K, also known inside the Mikoyan Design Bureau as the 9-31. This aircraft is closely based on the advanced MiG-29M (9-15), sharing the same basic airframe, engines, avionics and flight control system, but with a strengthened undercar-

Launch entails running up to full power (reheat is not always necessary) against retractable restrainers built into the deck. These are provided at different positions, for long and short take-off runs.

riage, an arrester hook, folding wings, and a number of carrier-specific features. Both the MiG-29M and the MiG-29K feature a dramatic increase in internal fuel capacity, this allowing a significant improvement in range and endurance, which were always the Achilles heel of the original MiG-29. A further increase in range or loiter time for the MiG-29K is made possible by the installation of a retractable in-flight-refuelling probe on the port side of the nose. On the first MiG-29K prototype this was completely covered by a single-piece door, but on the second the leading edge of the probe is uncovered when it is stowed in its recess.

Increased internal fuel capacity is made possible chiefly by the deletion of the complex auxiliary air intakes in the top of the wingroot leading edge. On the original MiG-29 these were used on take-off and landing, while the underslung main intakes were closed off by large doors to prevent the ingestion of foreign objects. The MiG-29M and MiG-29K have had these doors replaced by meshed screens, which fulfil the same function, but which do not require auxiliary intakes. The area previously taken up by these intakes is now part of a 2500-litre (550-Imp gal) fuel tank, this being of welded aluminium lithium construction which saves weight and volume. A second fuel tank, and other parts of the forward fuselage, are of similar construction, and this has provided significant extra internal volume for fuel and avionics (1500 litres/330 Imp gal of extra internal fuel are carried by the MiG-29M and MiG-29K).

Necessary extra power

The MiG-29M and the MiG-29K are powered by a pair of Isotov/Klimov RD-33K engines. These have a new fan and second stage compressor, with variable stators before the first stage. The new engines each give approximately 500 kg (1,100 lb) more reheated thrust, and can generate a further 600 kg (1,325 lb) of thrust for a limited duration, for example on carrier launch or during a 'go-round' or 'bolter'. The intakes have hinged lower lips which can open out when this extra thrust is demanded. The RD-33K engine also offers a slightly longer life and greater time between overhauls than the standard RD-33, and features a digital engine control system.

Like the MiG-29M, the navalised 'Fulcrum' features an analogue fly-by-wire control system, this allowing higher α limits and improved handling characteristics, especially at high angles of attack. This has four pitch channels, and three roll/yaw channels with a mechanical back-up. The extra weight of the analogue system is accepted because of the extra reliability it offers, Mikoyan claims, and digital technology is restricted to the new autostabilisation system. The new flight control system is accompanied by some refinements to the control surfaces themselves. The area below the extended-chord rudders is 'filled in' to present a straight trailing edge, which im-

The MiG-29K 'bolters'. The MiG-29K shares the same airframe and FBW control system as the MiG-29M, and has a substantial increase in internal fuel capacity and air-to-surface capability.

proves rudder effectiveness, for example. The tailplanes are of extended chord, and incorporate a dogtooth leading edge. These bigger tailerons give increased pitch authority, and improve roll rates. Unlike the MiG-29M, however, the MiG-29K does not have increased span ailerons, but does feature extended chord, double-slotted trailing-edge flaps. The latter give considerably better low-speed lift characteristics, allowing lower approach speeds.

To improve vortex flow at high angles of attack both the MiG-29K and the MiG-29M feature a much sharper leading-edge root extension, and both aircraft feature a revised 'boat tail' between the engine nozzles, and have a single enlarged dorsal airbrake in place of the original pair of upper and lower airbrakes. The new airbrake is mounted well forward.

Finally, the MiG-29K and MiG-29M have a slightly recontoured nose radome, which lacks the distinctive concave, double-curvature point of the original radome. This indicates installation of the new NO-10 'Zhuk' ('Beetle') radar, which has a 400 per cent increase in data processing capacity and which offers much improved multi-role capability, including terrain following. It also gives improved air-to-air modes, and can simultaneously track 10 targets, and engage up to four. The radar is also compatible with the new AAM-AE ('Amraamski') active terminal homing AAM. Ground attack capability is also enhanced by the new three-channel infra-red search and track system, which incorporates a laser designator and a TV camera. This has three times the detection range of the original IRST and makes the aircraft compatible with a range of laser- and TV-guided missiles. Ammunition capacity for the internal 30-mm cannon is, however, reduced, from 150 to 100 rounds.

The maiden flight of the first MiG-29K prototype was made by project pilot (and Bureau Deputy Chief Test Pilot) Takhtar Aubakirov, who also made the first 20 MiG-29K launches and recoveries on the *Tbilisi*, as it then was. He was later joined by Chief Test Pilot Valery Menitsky, and by Roman Taskaev (star of various Farnborough and Paris displays). Two prototypes of the MiG-29K have been built, coded 311 and 312, and both have conducted extensive trials from the *Kuznetsov*. A larger number of prototypes was not required, since the new variant's control system, basic aerodynamics and weapons systems had already been tested on the six MiG-29M prototypes. At one stage, the first MiG-29K prototype, emblazoned with camera calibration marks on nose and tail, wore 50 small red stars under the canopy, each with a small black anchor super-

The second of the two MiG-29K prototypes tied down on* Kuznetsov*'s deck. The recontoured radome houses an NO-10 radar, which offers multiple target tracking and engagement capability, and many new air-to-ground modes.

imposed and four with a white '5'. This indicated 66 successful arrested landings. Carrier approaches are flown at 130 kt (240 km/h; 149 mph) and at about 14° α, some 25 kt (46 km/h; 29 mph) slower and 3° higher than a normal approach. Launches are made using the *Kuznetsov's* ski-jump, running up the engines against 'pop-up' restrainers in the deck. The new carrier does not incorporate any form of catapult.

Carrier training

Mikoyan reportedly designed a two-seat operational training version of the MiG-29K, with a raised rear seat to give the instructor a better view forward over the nose. This would have given the new trainer what the Bureau Designer General called a 'hunch-backed' appearance. The MiG-29KU was not proceeded with, however, and at present the situation is that naval MiG-29K pilots will have to train on hook-equipped standard MiG-29s on the dummy deck at Saki airfield in the Crimea, and using the Su-25UTG both at Saki and on the carrier itself. It is believed that some five early 'Fulcrum-As' have been equipped with tailhooks and a carrier landing system to allow them to act as land-based carrier trainers, and some have made dummy approaches to the *Kuznetsov* itself, although their lack of a strengthened undercarriage makes them unsuitable for landing on the deck of a real ship.

The Sukhoi Su-25UTG is a minimum-change version of the two seat Su-25 'Frogfoot'. Five are believed to have been built, and five more may be in production. One of these aircraft became the third fixed-wing aircraft type to land on the *Tbilisi* during the initial trials which began on 1 November 1989. Contrary to some early reports, there are no plans for an operational carrierborne Su-25 version.

Another fixed-wing aircraft type associated with the Soviet carrier programme is the aircraft known as the Su-27IB, also known as the Su-27KU. The correct designation of this aircraft is unknown, since, while Sukhoi personnel publicly use the KU designation, when the aircraft was shown at the closed display for CIS heads of state at Minsk-Maschulische it was clearly labelled as the Su-27IB. A heavily modified derivative of the Su-27, with a new humped-back fuselage and a widened nose accommodating a two-seat, side-by-side cockpit, the Su-27IB/KU has no radar in its broad, flat, 'chined' nose. This is reminiscent of the SR-71's nose contours and has led to the adoption of the nickname 'Platypus'. The aircraft was first seen in a TASS photo of trials on board the *Kuznetsov*, making a dummy approach. The lack of folding wings and arrester hook were puzzling, but early speculation that this was a two-seat carrier trainer seemed to be confirmed by public statements by Design Bureau Chief Mikhail Simonov at the 1992 Farnborough air show. He averred that side-by-side seating had been chosen to give instructor and student the same 'runway' picture on approach. Earlier in 1992, the same aircraft apparently one of two (prototypes), had been shown at Minsk with signboards proclaiming it to be the Su-27IB (fighter-bomber), and festooned with air-to-ground ordnance. Many sources stated that the aircraft was intended as an Su-24 'Fencer' replacement. The truth remains unknown.

The MiG-29 KVP is a converted early-series 'Fulcrum-A' equipped for the training of carrier pilots at land airfields and on dummy decks. The lack of strengthened undercarriage makes actual deck landings unwise except in the calmest conditions. The standard Soviet-style tailhook (right) is rugged and robust, and of square section.

Future plans

It remains uncertain as to which aircraft types will be ordered to equip the *Kuznetsov's* air wing, but most observers believe it will embark a mix of Su-27Ks and MiG-29Ks, the latter serving as an F/A-18-style multi-role strike fighter. Such a view is reinforced by the apparent lack of ground attack capability in the Su-27K, which has been seen carrying various air-to-surface weapons in static displays, but which seems to have no extra avionics or different systems to the standard land-based Su-27, which has only the most basic and 'token' air-to-surface capabilities.

The new carrier may also embark the Yak-44, an E-2C Hawkeye-like AEW aircraft with a rotodome above the fuselage and powered by a pair of turboprop engines. So far seen only in model form, on a model of the carrier displayed at Mosaeroshow '92, the exact

The prototype Su-27KU (or should it be Su-27IB?) makes a dummy approach. This aircraft incorporates side-by-side seating to give pupil and instructor an identical approach picture, but lacks any specific naval features.

As well as restrainers in front of the wheels, large jet blast deflectors are raised behind an aircraft on launch. The Su-27K is equipped with canard foreplanes to improve take-off and landing performance.

This Kamov Ka-29 derivative is believed to have an EW or AEW function. Yakovlev still hope to produce the twin turboprop Yak-44 for AEW, EW and COD duties.

status of the Yak-44 is uncertain. Described as an 'observation, target indication and homing' platform, the aircraft has openly been referred to as an "equivalent to the US Hawkeye" by Victor Chernavin, C-in-C of the CIS navy. The new aircraft is being developed as a result of the abandonment of an AEW & C version of the Antonov An-72/-74 family known to NATO as 'Madcap'.

Kamov's workhorse

The ship will also embark a variety of SAR, utility, assault and possibly ECM versions of the Kamov 'Helix'. The dedicated SAR version of the Ka-27 is the Ka-27PS 'Helix-D', which differs little from the standard ASW Ka-27PL 'Helix-A', which could also be carried. For transport and assault missions, the *Kuznetsov* could embark the Ka-29TB 'Helix-B', which features a new forward fuselage with a widened cockpit. The helicopter is armed with a built-in machine-gun, and can carry a variety of weapons on outriggers. A derivative of this aircraft has been seen operating from *Kuznetsov*, with huge equipment fairings on the fuselage sides and under the cabin. This as-yet unidentified machine is believed to be some kind of electronic warfare platform, or may be some kind of interim AEW type.

The ideal air wing will doubtless be severely compromised by considerations of cost, since only one aircraft-carrier will enter front-line service. *Varyag*, launched on 28 November 1988 and still fitting out, is to be sold, probably to China or India, and *Ulyanovsk* is already so much scrap metal. If economy is the predominant consideration, an air wing of MiG-29Ks would make most sense, since these offer the best multi-role performance. Alternatively, if the V/STOL Yak-141 enters service as a Yak-38 replacement, this aircraft could find itself on both the four 'Kiev'/'Baku'-class carriers and the *Kuznetsov*.

The Yak-141 'Freestyle' seems unlikely to reach production but, if it does, it could be deployed aboard the Kuznetsov as well as the four 'Kiev'/'Baku'-class V/STOL carriers. Despite its supersonic performance, the Yak-141 is severely compromised by its heavy weight.

GRUMMAN F-14 TOMCAT

Whether on routine Fleet defence duties, air-to-air combat engagements or special interception missions, the F-14A Tomcat leads the field, its fearsome missiles ready to eliminate any enemy foolish enough to tangle with it. Here we describe the history of Grumman's deadly 'Turkey'.

A brace of Tomcats pierce the sky away from the familiar overwater operational environment. Capable of covering prodigious tracts of airspace to great effect with its long-range radar, the F-14A leads the interceptor field.

By any yardstick, Grumman's F-14 Tomcat is particularly well qualified to lay claim to being one of the world's most potent interceptors. For a start, its pedigree is quite impeccable, the manufacturer Grumman having been responsible for a remarkable line of carrierborne fighter aircraft which date back to the period before World War II. Notable examples of the many outstanding products which have originated at the Bethpage 'Iron Works' include the stubby but highly effective F6F Hellcat; the sleek and deadly F7F Tigercat; and the company's first jet fighter, the F9F Panther, which compiled an impressive combat record in the Korean War of 1950-3.

Of course potential enemies are, quite rightly, not impressed by heritage. Nevertheless, Grumman's tradition of producing outstanding naval aircraft can only have been enhanced by the Tomcat, for it has already demonstrated that it is an opponent to be treated with a great deal of respect, as a couple of Libyan Sukhoi Su-22 pilots learned to their cost when they engaged a brace of F-14As from US Navy squadron VF-41 over the Gulf of Sidra during August 1981. This brief and highly conclusive encounter resulted in the destruction of both Libyan fighters, these falling victim to the all-aspect AIM-9L Sidewinder heat-seeking air-to-air missile which forms just one part of the Tomcat's impressive arsenal. More recently a pair of Libyan MiG-23s fell to Sparrow and Sidewinder missiles fired by Tomcats.

Fire control system

Alone amongst contemporaries such as the McDonnell Douglas F-15 Eagle, itself by no means a slouch in the air combat arena, the F-14 is expected to deal with threats at short, medium and long ranges, and it accordingly totes a variety of weapons, each optimised for use in a particular set of circumstances. Thus the AIM-9 Sidewinder is the principal short-range weapon, while for combat at medium range the AIM-7F Sparrow is used. Perhaps the most impressive item in the Tomcat's armoury, though, is the Hughes AIM-54 Phoenix, which is a truly long-range weapon, having successfully demonstrated the ability to engage and destroy targets at ranges in excess of 160 km (100 miles). Finally, for really close-in 'dogfight' encounters, the Tomcat carries a single M61A1 Vulcan 20-mm cannon complete with 675 rounds of ammunition.

Inevitably, armament such as this may be impressive but counts for little in the absence of an effective weapons system, and it is in this particular area that the Tomcat scores so heavily, the remarkable Hughes AWG-9 control system possessing the ability to detect targets at ranges greater than 185 km (115 miles). Inherited from the ill-fated General Dynamics/Grumman F-111B project, the AWG-9 was transplanted in late 1968 to the Tomcat along with the Pratt & Whitney TF30 turbofan engine and the AIM-54 Phoenix missile. Indeed, the AWG-9 is perhaps the most outstanding feature of the entire Tomcat package, for it possesses the ability to deal with threats at both high and low levels. Also, when operating in the track-while-scan mode, it can continue to search for intruders while also tracking as many as 24 potential targets and simulta-

As the largest carrier-based fighter ever built, the F-14A takes a lot of stopping when deck-landing. Here, full use is being made of the large split speedbrake and all-moving tailplane (stabiliser) as the aircraft hooks no. 2 deck wire.

One of the latest production examples of the Grumman F-14A Tomcat, shown in the insignia of VF-143 'Pukin' Dogs', part of CVW-7 aboard USS Dwight D. Eisenhower (CVN 69). The aircraft is carrying the standard maximum weapons load of four AIM-54A Phoenix, two AIM-7F Sparrow and two AIM-9L Sidewinder air-to-air missiles, a mix that permits it to counter threats across virtually the entire air-defence spectrum. In addition to the missiles, the F-14A is equipped with an integral Vulcan M61 20-mm cannon for close-in air combat.

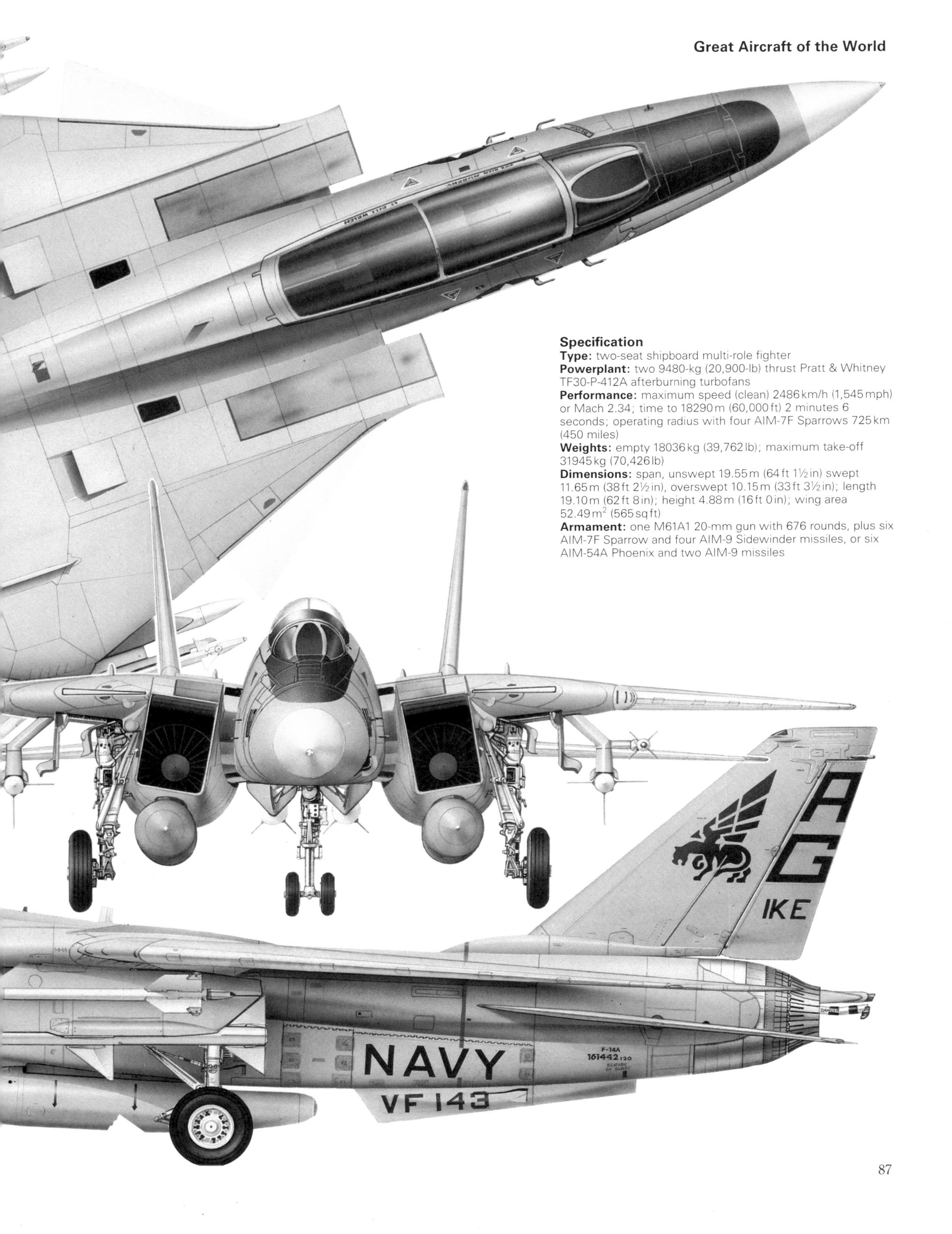

Specification

Type: two-seat shipboard multi-role fighter
Powerplant: two 9480-kg (20,900-lb) thrust Pratt & Whitney TF30-P-412A afterburning turbofans
Performance: maximum speed (clean) 2486 km/h (1,545 mph) or Mach 2.34; time to 18290 m (60,000 ft) 2 minutes 6 seconds; operating radius with four AIM-7F Sparrows 725 km (450 miles)
Weights: empty 18036 kg (39,762 lb); maximum take-off 31945 kg (70,426 lb)
Dimensions: span, unswept 19.55 m (64 ft 1½ in) swept 11.65 m (38 ft 2½ in), overswept 10.15 m (33 ft 3½ in); length 19.10 m (62 ft 8 in); height 4.88 m (16 ft 0 in); wing area 52.49 m^2 (565 sq ft)
Armament: one M61A1 20-mm gun with 676 rounds, plus six AIM-7F Sparrow and four AIM-9 Sidewinder missiles, or six AIM-54A Phoenix and two AIM-9 missiles

neously engaging up to six of them with individual AIM-54 missiles. The normal weapon load in the fleet-defence role seems to be a mixture of Phoenix, Sparrow and Sidewinder missiles, but when engaged in the BarCAP mission, the Tomcat can carry up to six AIM-54As plus a pair of Sidewinders.

Engine problems

Although integration of the AWG-9 system seems to have been accomplished fairly satisfactorily, not every aspect of the Tomcat programme has been quite so successful. Indeed, the TF30 turbofan which powers the Tomcat has been an almost constant source of embarrassment to those immediately associated with this project, and there are few who would claim that the engine-to-airframe match has been 'a marriage made in heaven'. Problems with the TF30 date back to the early years of service with the US Navy, a fault in many aircraft being fan-blade failure. Repeated attempts at eradicating this and other shortcomings resulted in the introduction of new variants of the TF30, but in general this engine has been plagued by poor serviceability, durability and reliability, a situation which eventually resulted in the decision to acquire a new variant of the Tomcat powered by the General Electric F110 engine. Flight testing of a Tomcat fitted with the basically similar F101DFE (Derivative Fighter Engine) was accomplished during 1981-2 and revealed that the performance of the re-engined Tomcat was greatly enhanced throughout the flight envelope. Subsequently, in 1982, full-scale development of the F110 engine began and in 1984 this powerplant was finally selected by the navy for installation in the Tomcat. Offering substantially more power, the F110 will initially be fitted to the F-14A (Plus), and deliveries of new-build aircraft began in April 1988, while several F-14As are to be upgraded to (Plus) standard. Also featuring the F110 engine is the F-14D, which has better digital avionics including the APG-71 radar. Plans calling for 127 new-build F-14Ds and around 400 conversions are under review and likely to be cancelled.

As far as the original F-14A variant is concerned, this has changed little since it entered service with navy training squadron VF-124 at NAS Miramar, California, in late 1972, although, as already noted, attempts to improve engine reliability have resulted in the adoption of new variants of the TF30 turbofan.

In this dramatic plan view of the Tomcat, the fully swept outer wing sections and inner fixed wing carapace are shown to good effect. The fuselage has a noticeably tapered rear aerofoil section through it is well-rounded in cross section.

From the aircrew point of view, though, one particularly valuable new feature is the Northrop AXX-1 TCS, which is a TV system mounted in a pod beneath the nose section to allow visual identification of potential targets to be made at far greater distances than was previously the case. Viewing screens in each cockpit provide both crew members with clear images of fighter-sized targets at distances greatly exceeding 'eyeball' range. Telephoto or wide-angle fields of view can be selected, and the AXX-1 unit also features automatic tracking capability.

The Tomcat's claws have also been sharpened somewhat by virtue of the deployment of new and more effective versions of the primary missile armament. For instance, a new model of the long-range Phoenix AAM, the AIM-54C, is in the process of widespread introduction, this possessing digital avionics, enhanced resistance to countermeasures, a new proximity fuse and greater range, amongst other features. Updating of the medium-range Sparrow and short-range Sidewinder missiles has resulted in the appearance of the AIM-7M and AIM-9M variants of these weapons, and both offer significantly enhanced kill-probability across the air combat spectrum. Looking to the future, the Tomcat is one of the types earmarked to carry the Hughes AIM-120A radar-guided missile, perhaps more widely known as AMRAAM (Advanced Medium-Range Air-to-Air Missile). Expected to enter the operational inventory in 1990, the AIM-120A represents a significant advance over the existing Sparrow medium-range weapon, noteworthy features being greater launch range, increased warhead lethality, reduced miss distance, improved fusing and greater average velocity.

Tomcat in service

As far as the type's service career is concerned, the Tomcat made its operational debut in mid-September 1974 when VF-1 and VF-2 departed from the USA aboard the USS *Enterprise* (CVN-65) at the start of an eight-month deployment to the Western Pacific. The *Enterprise* and her aircraft had been back only a few weeks when the first Atlantic Fleet units, VF-14 and VF-32, put to sea aboard the USS *John F. Kennedy* (CV-67) in June 1975, bound for service with the Mediterranean-based 6th Fleet. Since that time, a further 18 front-line deployable squadrons have converted to the Tomcat, and the type is also in the process of joining the Navy Reserve, VF-301 at Miramar

The supreme fighting qualities of the Tomcat have earned it respect from allies and adversaries alike, VF-41 'Black Aces' proving the point by destroying two Libyan Su-22s in less than a minute on 19 August 1981.

The Tomcat was the first aircraft in which the wings were automatically controlled by a computer system (with manual override), which acts in response to Mach number and angle-of-attack factors. Here the wings are at minimum sweep.

having taken delivery of its first example in late 1984 and sister squadron VF-302 having followed during the course of 1985. In addition, two replacement training squadrons, VF-101 of the Atlantic Fleet and VF-124 of the Pacific Fleet, use the F-14A, although these units do not undertake front-line duty aboard the US Navy's large fleet of aircraft-carriers. By late 1984, 10 years after the F-14A first went to sea, Tomcat squadrons had departed from US ports for extended tours of overseas duty on no fewer than 42 occasions, and the type has replaced older fighters such as the McDonnell Douglas F-4 Phantom in the navy's front-line inventory.

In addition, the Tomcat has also assumed the mantle of being the navy's primary reconnaissance aircraft. The F-14A fulfils navy requirements in this area, approximately 50 aircraft having been configured to carry the TARPS beneath the rear fuselage. This package consists of a CAI KS-87B frame camera for forward-oblique or vertical photography as well as a Fairchild KA-99 panoramic camera and a Honeywell AAD-5 infra-red scanner. TARPS permits the F-14 to obtain high-quality imagery at only a modest penalty in payload capability.

Operational deployment of TARPS-compatible Tomcats began during 1982, and this variant has since been added to the complement of 11 fighter squadrons, thus permitting each F-14-capable carrier air wing to have three TARPS aircraft in one of its two F-14 squadrons. Original plans called for the acquisition of 49 TARPS-configured Tomcats and all of these were manufactured as such by the parent company. More recently, it has been decided to modify three additional examples to this standard in order that Navy Reserve squadron VF-302 can also operate this version.

Iran: sole export customer

Despite the fact that it is capable of countering threats at short, medium and long ranges, the Tomcat has achieved only limited export success, most of the customers in the market for new-generation fighter aircraft opting for uncompromised air-superiority fighters such as the F-15 Eagle. Indeed, only one overseas sale has been achieved, and one rather suspects that the US government would prefer that this had not been the case, for the customer was Iran, the late Shah purchasing a total of 80 Tomcats in 1974-5. Delivered between January 1976 and July 1978, these were mainly intended for use against Mikoyan-Gurevich MiG-25s which were regularly over-flying Iranian territory from the USSR, and part of the deal included the supply of 424 AIM-54A Phoenix missiles, 270 of which were actually handed over before the ousting of the Shah in 1979. Initially equipping four squadrons at Shiraz and Khatami air bases, most (if not all) of the 75 or so surviving Iranian Tomcats are now grounded, the brunt of the aviation contribution in the long and exceedingly bloody war against Iraq having been borne by the F-4E Phantom and the Northrop F-5E Tiger II. The few airworthy Tomcats were largely used as 'Mini-AWACS' platforms, making use of their superb radars to detect and track Iraqi aircraft and then supplying vector information to friendly fighters. This task kept the valuable F-14s away from too much danger. However, at least one Tomcat was claimed shot down by Iraqi pilots during the last months of the fighting in 1988.

Now in its second decade of operation and still supreme, the Tomcat is destined to serve for many years to come. New variants with better performance, state-of-the-art technology and improved armament will meet the high demands of Fleet defence.

Grumman F-14 Tomcat
Performance:

Maximum speed with four Sparrow AAMs, at 49,000 ft (14935 m)			
Mach 2.4 or	1,375 kts	2549 km/h	(1,584 mph)
at sea level Mach 1.2 or	793 kts	1470 km/h	(913 mph)
Maximum cruising speed	500 kts	927 km/h	(576 mph)
Stalling speed	115 kts	213 km/h	(132 mph)
Initial rate of climb per minute		30,000 ft	(9144 m)
Time to 60,000 ft (18290 m), clean			2.1 minutes
Minimum take-off distance		396 m	(1,300 ft)
Minimum landing distance		823 m	(2,700 ft)
Tactical radius, hi-lo-lo-hi interdiction, external fuel and 14 Mk 82 bombs		1167 km	(725 miles)
combat air patrol with six Sparrows and four Sidewinders		1231 km	(765 miles)
Ferry range		3219 km	(2,000 miles)

Service ceiling

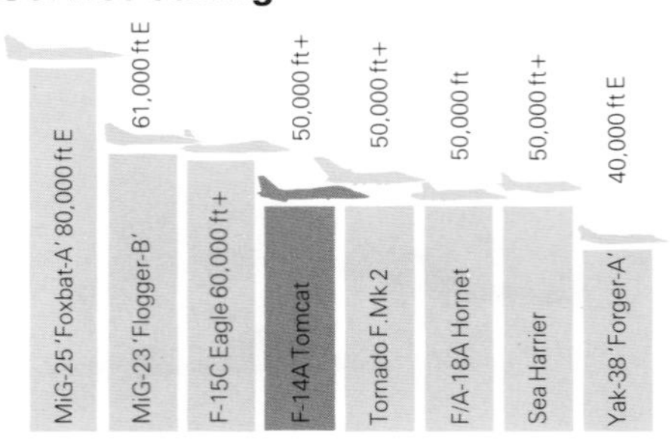

Range with external fuel

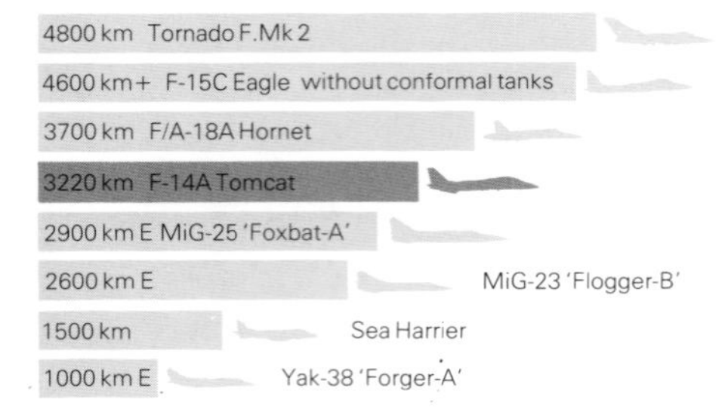

Speed at high altitude

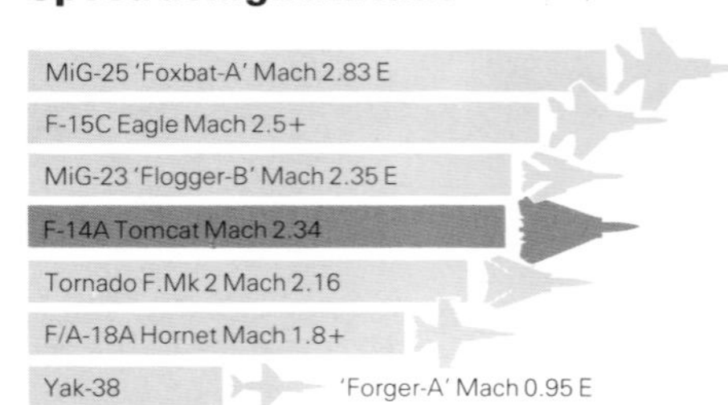

Speed at low altitude

F-14A Tomcat Mach 1.2
F-15C Eagle Mach 1.2
MiG-23 'Flogger-B' Mach 1.2 E
Tornado F.Mk 2 Mach 1.1
F/A-18A Hornet Mach 1
MiG-25 'Foxbat-A' Mach 0.85 E
Sea Harrier Mach 0.85
Yak-38 'Forger-A' Mach 0.8 E

Landing approach speed

Sea Harrier 0 kt
Yak-38 'Forger-A' 5 kt E
Tornado F.Mk 2 115 kt
F-15C Eagle 125 kt
F-14A Tomcat 134 kt
F/A-18 Hornet 134 kt
MiG-23 'Flogger-B' 135 kt E
MiG-25 'Foxbat-A' 146 kt E

Specification:

Grumman F-14A Tomcat (TF30-P-414A engines)

Wings

Span, unswept	19.55 m	(64 ft 1.5 in)
swept	11.65 m	(38 ft 2.5 in)
overswept for carrier stowage	10.15 m	(33 ft 3.5 in)
Area	52.49 m²	(565.0 sq ft)

Fuselage and tail unit

Length overall	19.10 m	(62 ft 8 in)
Height overall	4.88 m	(16 ft 0 in)
Tailplane span	9.97 m	(32 ft 8.5 in)

Landing gear

Wheelbase	7.02 m	(23 ft 0.5 in)
Wheel track	5.00 m	(16 ft 5 in)

Weights

Empty	18191 kg	(40,104 lb)
Take-off, clean	26633 kg	(58,715 lb)
with four Sparrow AAMs	27086 kg	(59,714 lb)
with six Phoenix AAMs	32098 kg	(70,764 lb)
maximum military load	33724 kg	(74,349 lb)
Landing	23510 kg	(51,830 lb)
Fuel, maximum internal	7348 kg	(16,200 lb)
maximum external	1724 kg	(3,800 lb)
Ordnance, maximum external	6577 kg	(14,500 lb)

F-14 Tomcat recognition features

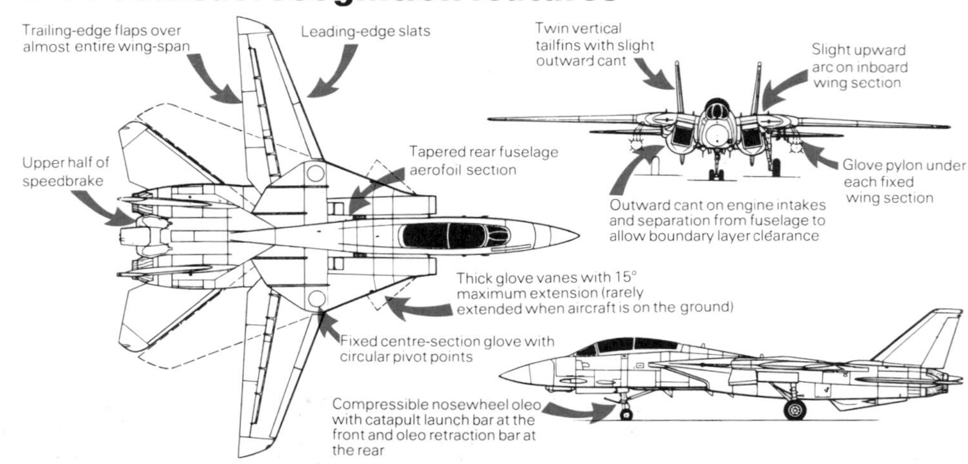

Grumman F-14 Tomcat variants

F-14A: designation of 12 pre-production aircraft for use in the R & D programme and of the major production version, of which the planned procurement covered 485 aircraft
F-14B: designation of two prototypes with Pratt & Whitney F401-P-400 turbofan engines
F-14C: planned development of F-14B with more advanced electronics and new weapons; not built
F-14/TARPS: tactical reconnaissance conversions of F-14As with TARPS (Tactical Air Reconnaissance Pod System) mounted underfuselage between the engine nacelles; pod contains cameras and infra-red sensors
F-14/101DFE: the seventh pre-production aircraft, which had also served as one of the F-14B prototypes, was re-engined with General Electric F101 derivative fighter engines (now designated F110-GE-400) and used in a 25-flight test programme
F-14D: planned production version with F110-GE-400 engines and advanced avionics and weapon systems; an initial 12 aircraft have been requested for evaluation, but planned procurement covers some 300 aircraft with initial deliveries in early 1990

Right: Clearly visible on station no. 5 is the LA-610 TARPS pod, which houses three camera units, an IR line scanner and a data display system as part of an interim reconnaissance package.

Below: A VF-102 F-14 makes full use of the inflight-refuelling capability via the flush-fitting probe extended from its housing within the upper forward fuselage.

VF-1, Miramar, California

Air Wing: CVW-2
Carrier: USS *Kitty Hawk* (CV-63)
Aircraft: 161296/NE-107, 159855/NE-111, 158989/NE-113

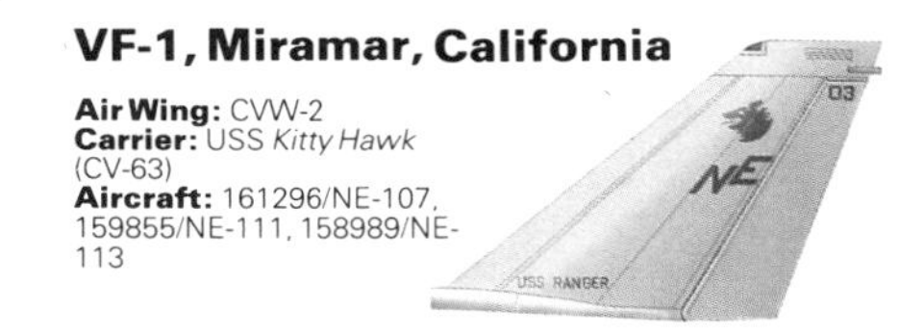

VF-2*, Miramar, California

Air Wing: CVW-2
Carrier: USS *Kitty Hawk* (CV-63)
Aircraft: 161273/NE-201, 161299/NE-210, 158998/NE-213

VF-11, Oceana, Virginia

Air Wing: CVW-3
Carrier: USS *John F. Kennedy* (CV-67)
Aircraft: 159010/AC-100, 159438/AC-111, 161163/AC-112

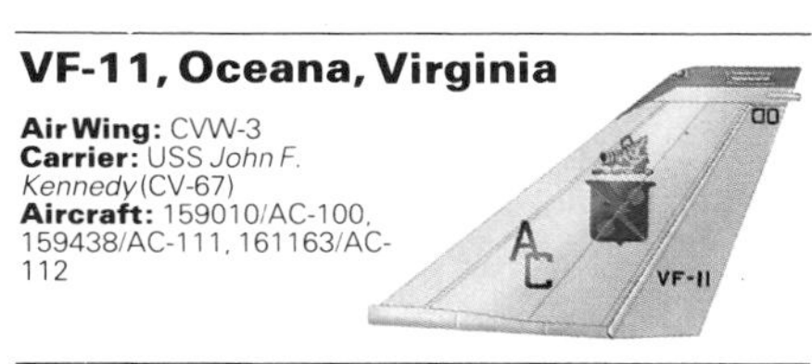

VF-14, Oceana, Virginia

Air Wing: CVW-6
Carrier: USS *Independence* (CV-62)
Aircraft: 159433/AE-103, 159431/AE-106, 159595/AE-112

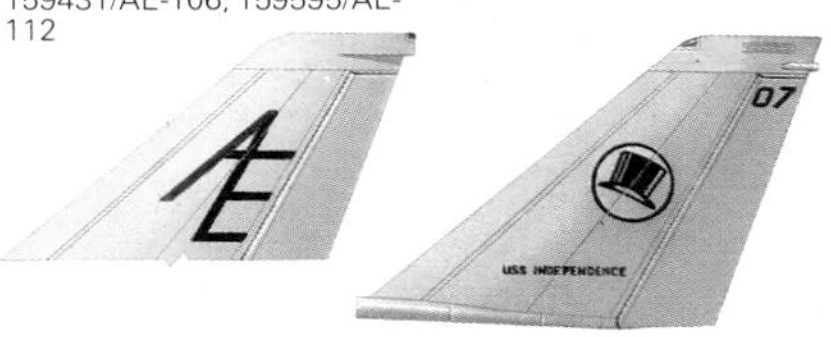

VF-21, Miramar, California

Air Wing: CVW-14
Carrier: USS *Constellation* (CV-64)
Aircraft: 161606/NK-201, 161609/NK-204, 161621/NK-211

VF-24, Miramar, California

Air Wing: CVW-9
Carrier: USS *Ranger* (CV-61)
Aircraft: 159592/NG-200, 160693/NG-204, 160889/NG-214

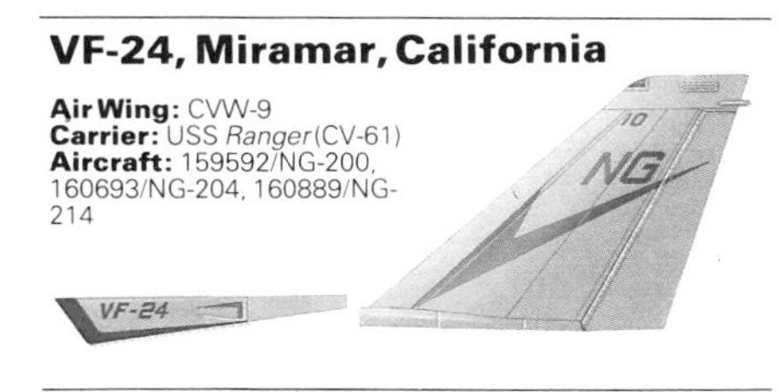

VF-31*, Oceana, Virginia

Air Wing: CVW-3
Carrier: USS *John F. Kennedy* (CV-67)
Aircraft: 159449/AC-204, 159421/AC-207, 159020/AC-210

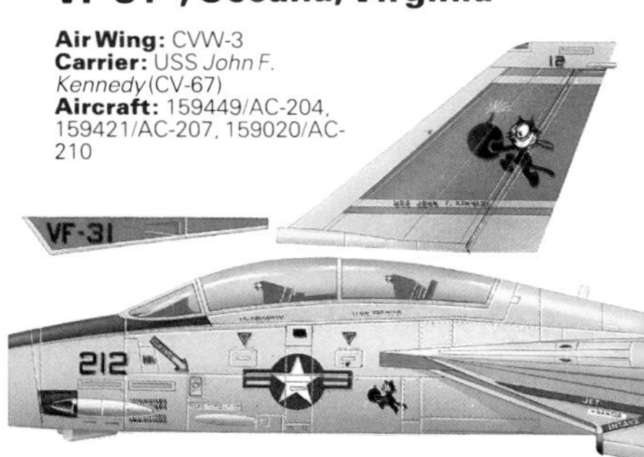

VF-32*, Oceana, Virginia

Air Wing: CVW-6
Carrier: USS *Independence* (CV-62)
Aircraft: 159016/AE-200, 159603/AE-206, 161162/AE-214

VF-33, Oceana, Virginia

Air Wing: CVW-1
Carrier: USS *America* (CV-66)
Aircraft: 159426/AB-202, 159015/AB-206, 159609/AB-211

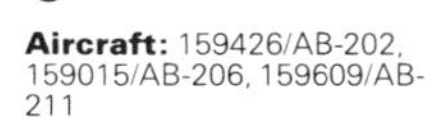

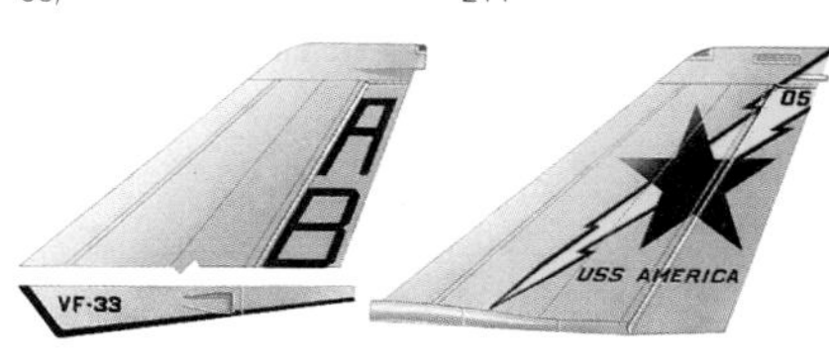

VF-41, Oceana, Virginia

Air Wing: CVW-8
Carrier: USS *Nimitz* (CVN-68)
Aircraft: 160395/AJ-100, 160407/AJ-112, 160399/AJ-113

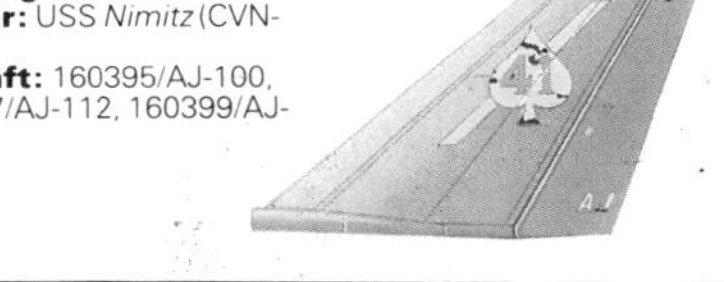

VF-51, Miramar, California

Air Wing: CVW-15
Carrier: USS *Carl Vinson* (CVN-70)
Aircraft: 160657/NL-101, 160685/NL-110, 160694/NL-114

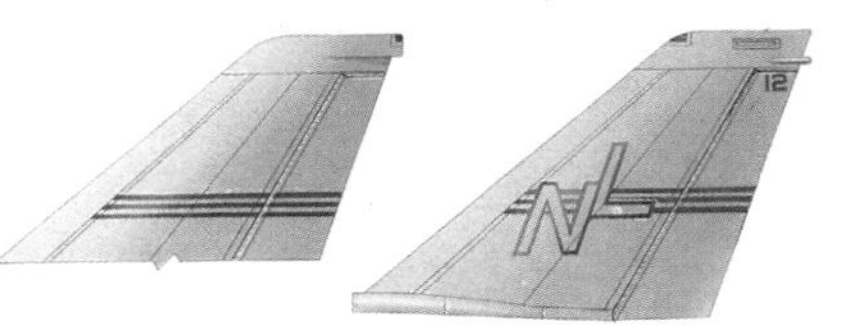

VF-74, Oceana, Virginia

Air Wing: CVW-17
Carrier: USS *Saratoga* (CV-60)
Aircraft: 160896/AA-101, 160905/AA-105, 160918/AA-112

VF-84*, Oceana, Virginia

Air Wing: CVW-8
Carrier: USS *Nimitz* (CVN-68)
Aircraft: 160389/AJ-202, 160405/AJ-204, 160391/AJ-210

VF-101, Oceana, Virginia

Air Wing: RAG
Aircraft: 161136/AD-103, 160902/AD-120, 159018/AD-133

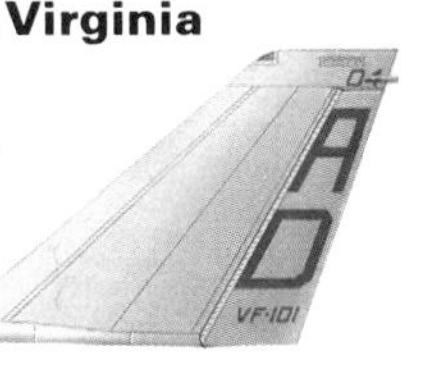

VF-102*, Oceana, Virginia

Air Wing: CVW-1
Carrier: USS *America* (CV-66)
Aircraft: 159458/AB-101, 159006/AB-103, 161285/AB-112

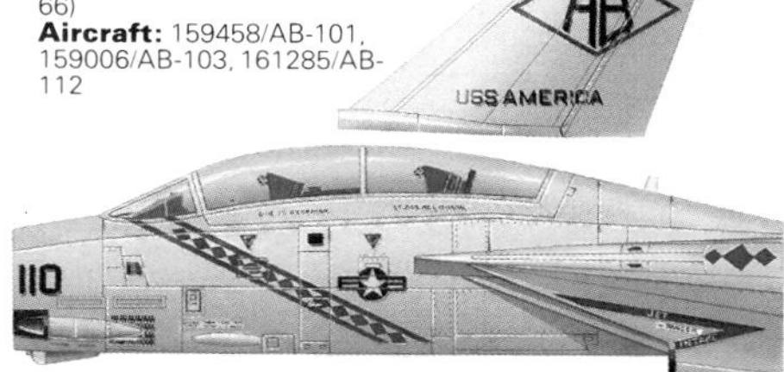

VF-103*, Oceana, Virginia

Air Wing: CVW-17
Carrier: USS *Saratoga* (CV-60)
Aircraft: 160919/AA-200, 160898/AA-204, 161156/AA-211

VF-111*, Miramar, California

Air Wing: CVW-15
Carrier: USS *Carl Vinson* (CVN-70)
Aircraft: 160656/NL-200, 161270/NL-206, 160668/NL-213

VF-114, Miramar, California

Air Wing: CVW-11
Carrier: USS *Enterprise* (CVN-65)
Aircraft: 159825/NH-100, 159852/NH-105, 159872/NH-112

VF-124, Miramar, California

Air Wing: RAG
Aircraft: 161600/NJ-403, 159870/NJ-424, 161153/NJ-473

VF-142, Oceana, Virginia

Air Wing: CVW-7
Carrier: USS *Dwight D. Eisenhower* (CVN-69)
Aircraft: 160427/AG-201, 161435/AG-207, 161441/AG-213

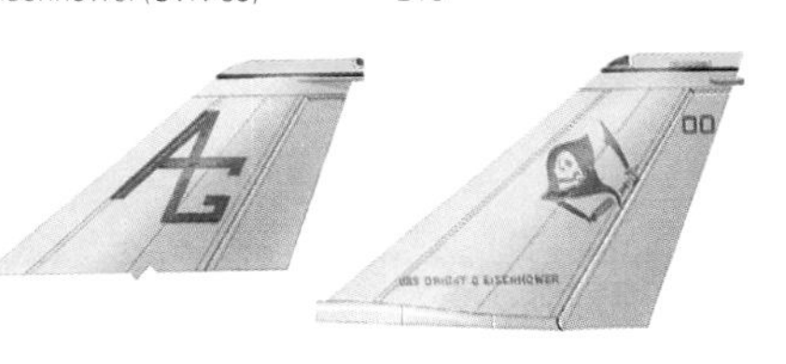

VF-143*, Oceana, Virginia

Air Wing: CVW-7
Carrier: USS *Dwight D. Eisenhower* (CVN-69)
Aircraft: 160428/AG-102, 161281/AG-112, 161282/AG-114

VF-154*, Miramar, California

Air Wing: CVW-14
Carrier: USS *Constellation* (CV-64)
Aircraft: 161610/NK-100, 161620/NK-105, 161626/NK-110

VF-211*, Miramar, California

Air Wing: CVW-9
Carrier: USS *Ranger* (CV-61)
Aircraft: 159624/NG-102, 159608/NG-110, 159634/NG-113

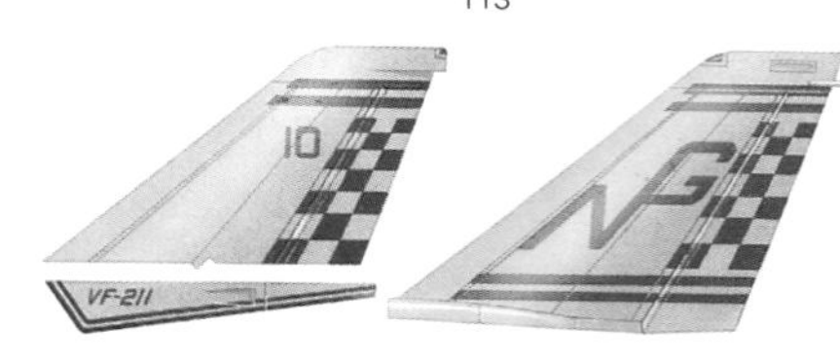

VF-213*, Miramar, California

Air Wing: CVW-11
Carrier: USS *Enterprise* (CVN-65)
Aircraft: 159827/NH-201, 159861/NH-206, 160910/NH-212

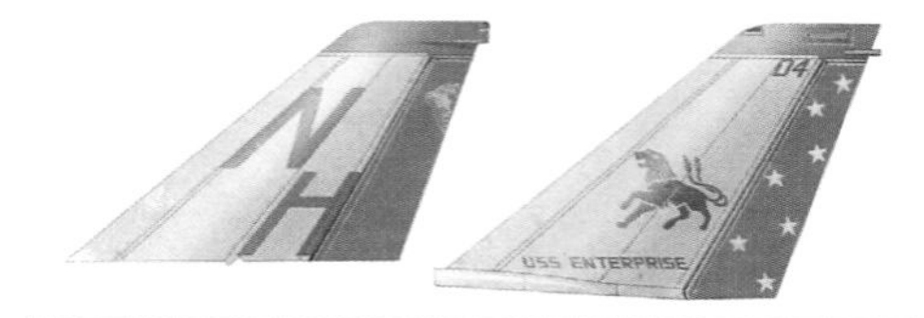

VF-301, Miramar, California

Air Wing: CVWR-39
Aircraft: 158979/ND-100, 158988/ND-105, 159442/ND-113

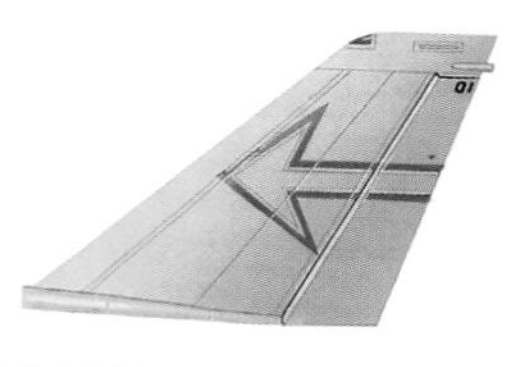

VF-302*, Miramar, California

Air Wing: CVWR-30
Aircraft: 158987 (due in 1985)

(* = TARPS unit)

Note 1: All squadrons resident at Oceana, Virginia, are assigned to Fighter Wing One, which is a subordinate element of the Tactical Wings Atlantic organization

Note 2: With two exceptions, all squadrons resident at Miramar, California, are assigned to Fighter and Airborne Early Warning Wing Pacific, a subordinate element of ComNavAirPac (Commander Naval Air Force Pacific Fleet)

Note 3: VF-301 and VF-302 at Miramar are US Navy Reserve squadrons and do not form part of the Fighter and Airborne Early Warning Wing Pacific although they would almost certainly report to that organization in the event of mobilization

VX-4 (Test & Evaluation Squadron), Point Mugu, California

Aircraft: 159830/XF-44, 161287/XF-46, 161444/XF-47

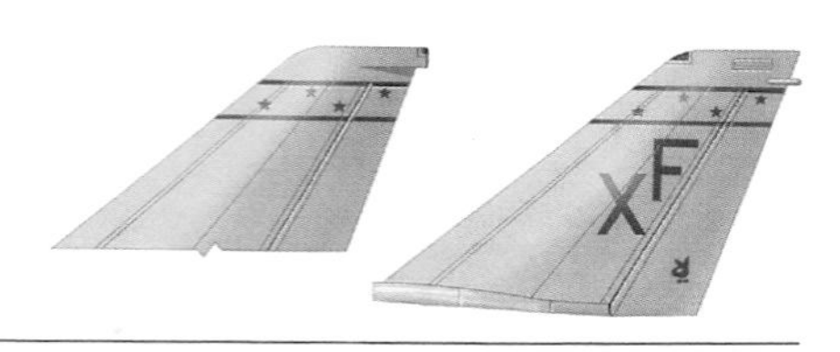

Pacific Missile Test Center, Point Mugu, California

Aircraft: 158615/216, 158623/224, 158625/226

Naval Air Test Center, Patuxent River, Maryland

Aircraft: 158620/7T-202, 158631/7T-206, 160658/7T-207

NASA, Edwards AFB, California

Aircraft: 157991

F-14 cockpit details

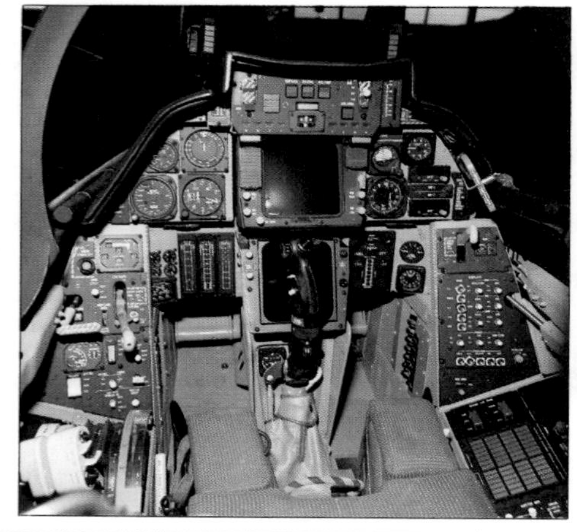

The front cockpit of the F-14 Tomcat is typical of contemporary American layouts, with a sense of order in a relatively small space. Dominating the forward panels is the square vertical display indicator screen, with the air combat manoeuvring panel above. The head-up display unit sits atop the flat portion of the console top rim. To the right of the VDI are dials covering acceleration and bearing distance heading among others, while at left are indicators such as airspeed Mach no. and radar altimeter. Side panels cover launch bar, landing gear and flap control at left, and arrester hook, displays control and elevation lead on the right-hand side.

The rear cockpit, occupied by the Naval Flight Officer, has less instrumentation. The panel at top is the detail data display panel, while the large circular housing incorporates the tactical information display unit. Threat advisory lights, fuel quantity totalizer, canopy jettison handle and bearing distance heading indicators are at top right to the TID. The large panel at far left covers armament operations. Though not visible, the side consoles are quite large and cover a variety of items such as ECM, IFF transponder control, communications and eject command control.

Grumman F-14A Tomcat cutaway drawing key

1 Pitot tube
2 Radar target horn
3 Glass-fibre radome
4 IFF aerial array
5 Hughes AWG-9 flat plate radar scanner
6 Scanner tracking mechanism
7 Ventral ALQ-126 deception jamming antenna
8 Gun muzzle blast trough
9 Radar electronics equipment bay
10 AN/ASN-92 inertial navigation unit
11 Radome hinge
12 Inflight refuelling probe (extended)
13 ADF aerial
14 Windscreen rain removal air duct
15 Temperature probe
16 Cockpit front pressure bulkhead
17 Angle of attack transmitter
18 Formation lighting strip
19 Cannon barrels
20 Nosewheel doors
21 Gun gas vents
22 Rudder pedals
23 Cockpit pressurization valve
24 Navigation radar display
25 Control column
26 Instrument panel shroud
27 Kaiser AN/ANG-12 head-up display
28 Windscreen panels
29 Cockpit canopy cover
30 Face blind seat firing handle
31 Ejection seat headrest
32 Pilot's Martin-Baker GRU-7A ejection seat
33 Starboard side console
34 Engine throttle levers
35 Port side console panel
36 Pitot static head
37 Canopy emergency release handle
38 Fold out step
39 M61A1 Vulcan 20-mm six-barrel rotary cannon
40 Nose undercarriage leg strut
41 Catapult strop link
42 Catapult strop, launch position
43 Twin nosewheels
44 Folding boarding ladder
45 Hughes AIM-54A Phoenix air-to-air missile (six)
46 Fuselage missile pallet
47 Cannon ammunition drum (675 rounds)
48 Rear boarding step
49 Ammunition feed chute
50 Armament control panels
51 Kick-in step
52 Tactical information display hand controller
53 Naval Flight Officer's instrument console
54 NFO's ejection seat
55 Starboard intake lip
56 Ejection seat launch rails
57 Cockpit aft decking
58 Electrical system controller
59 Rear radio and electronics equipment bay
60 Boundary layer bleed air duct
61 Port engine intake lip
62 Electrical system relay controls
63 Glove vane pivot
64 Port air intake
65 Glove vane housing
66 Navigation light
67 Variable area intake ramp doors
68 Cooling system boundary layer duct ram air intake
69 Intake ramp door hydraulic jacks
70 Air system piping
71 Air data computer
72 Heat exchanger
73 Heat exchanger exhaust duct
74 Forward fuselage fuel tanks
75 Canopy hinge point
76 Electrical and control system ducting
77 Control rod runs
78 UHF/TACAN aerial
79 Glove vane hydraulic jack
80 Starboard glove vane, extended
81 Honeycomb panel construction
82 Navigation light
83 Main undercarriage wheel bay
84 Starboard intake duct spill door
85 Wing slat/flap flexible drive shaft
86 Dorsal spine fairing
87 Fuselage top longeron
88 Central flap/slat drive
89 Emergency hydraulic generator
90 Bypass door hydraulic jack
91 Intake bypass door
92 Port intake ducting
93 Wing glove sealing horn
94 Flap/slat telescopic drive shaft
95 Port wing pivot bearing
96 Wing pivot carry-through (electron beam welded titanium box construction)
97 Wing pivot box integral fuel tank
98 Fuselage longeron/pivot box attachment joint
99 UHF data link/IFF aerial
100 Honeycomb skin panelling
101 Wing glove stiffeners/dorsal fences
102 Starboard wing pivot bearing
103 Slat/flap drive shaft gearbox
104 Starboard wing integral fuel tank (total internal fuel capacity 2,364 US gal/8949 litres)
105 Leading edge slat drive shaft
106 Slat guide rails
107 Starboard leading edge slat segments (open)
108 Starboard navigation light
109 Low-voltage formation lighting
110 Wing tip fairing
111 Outboard manoeuvre flap segments (down position)
112 Port roll control spoilers
113 Spoiler hydraulic jacks
114 Inboard, high lift flap (down position)
115 Inboard flap hydraulic jack
116 Manoeuvre flap drive shaft
117 Variable wing sweep screw jack
118 Starboard main undercarriage pivot fixing
119 Starboard engine compressor face
120 Wing glove sealing plates
121 Pratt & Whitney TF30-P-412 afterburning turbofan
122 Rear fuselage fuel tanks
123 Fuselage longeron joint
124 Control system artificial feel units
125 Tailplane control rods
126 Starboard engine bay
127 Wing glove pneumatic seal
128 Fin root fairing
129 Fin spar attachment joints
130 Starboard fin leading edge
131 Starboard all-moving tailplane
132 Starboard wing (fully swept position)
133 AN/ALR-45 tail warning radar antenna
134 Fin aluminium honeycomb skin panel construction
135 Fin-tip aerial fairing
136 Tail navigation light
137 Electronic counter-measures antenna (ECM)
138 Rudder honeycomb construction
139 Rudder hydraulic jack
140 Afterburner ducting
141 Variable area nozzle control jack
142 Airbrake (upper and lower surfaces)
143 Airbrake hydraulic jack
144 Starboard engine exhaust nozzle
145 Anti-collision light
146 Tail formation light
147 ECM aerial
148 Port rudder
149 Beaver tail fairing
150 Fuel jettison pipe
151 ECM antenna
152 Deck arrester hook (stowed position)
153 AN/ALE-29A chaff and flare dispensers
154 Nozzle shroud sealing flaps
155 Port convergent/divergent afterburner exhaust nozzle
156 Tailplane honeycomb construction
157 AN/ALR-45(V) tail warning radar antenna
158 Tailplane boron fibre skin panels
159 Port wing (fully swept position)
160 All-moving tailplane construction
161 Tailplane pivot fixing
162 Jet pipe mounting
163 Fin/tailplane attachment mainframe
164 Cooling air louvres
165 Tailplane hydraulic jack
166 Hydraulic system equipment pack
167 Formation lighting strip
168 Oil cooler air intake
169 Port ventral fin
170 Engine accessory compartment
171 Ventral engine access doors
172 Hydraulic reservoir
173 Bleed air ducting
174 Port engine bay
175 Intake compressor face
176 Wing variable sweep screw jack
177 Main undercarriage leg strut
178 Hydraulic retraction jack
179 Wing skin panel
180 Fuel system piping
181 Rear spar
182 Flap hinge brackets
183 Port roll control spoilers
184 Flap leading edge eyebrow seal fairing
185 Port manoeuvre flap honeycomb construction
186 Wing tip fairing construction
187 Low-voltage formation lighting
188 Port navigation light
189 Wing rib construction
190 Port wing integral fuel tank

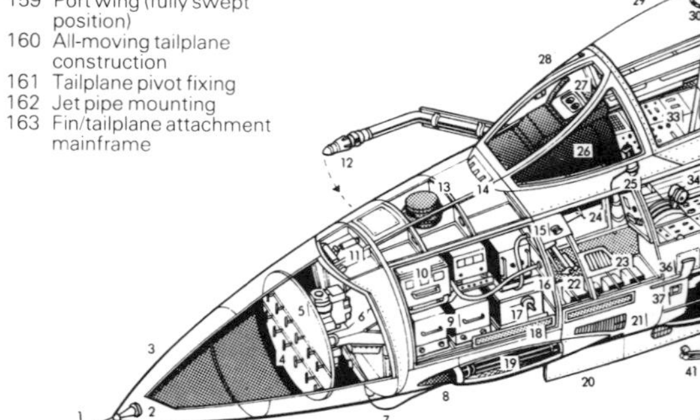

Grumman F-14 Tomcat warload

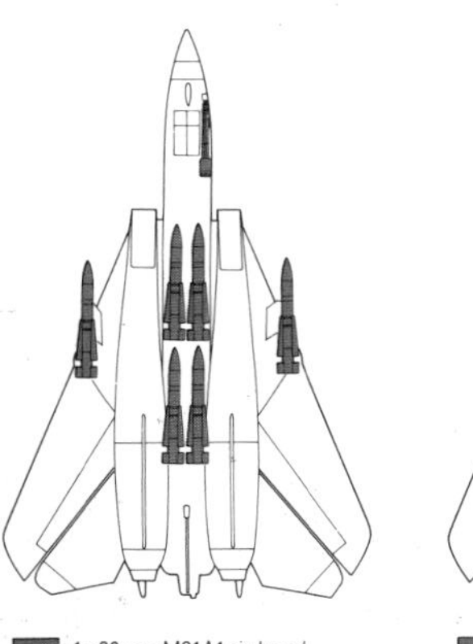

1×20-mm M61A1 six-barrel cannon
6×AIM-54C Phoenix air-to-air missiles

1×20-mm M61A1 six-barrel cannon
4×AIM-54C Phoenix air-to-air missiles on underfuselage pallets
2×AIM-7M Sparrow air-to-air missiles on wing pylons
2×AIM-9M Sidewinder air-to-air missiles on wing pylons

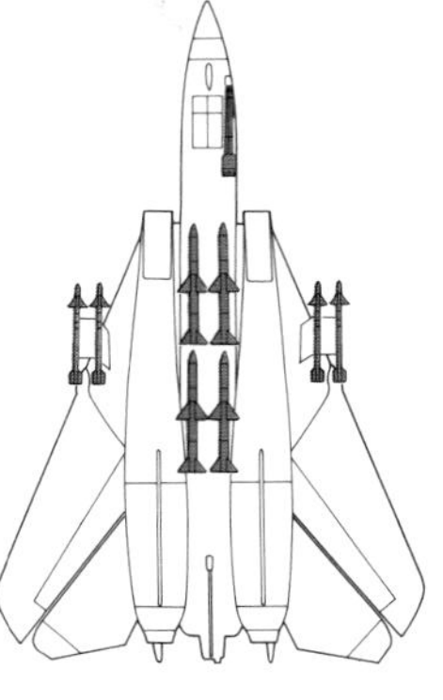

1×20-mm M61A1 six-barrel cannon
4×AIM-7M Sparrow air-to-air missiles recessed under fuselage
4×AIM-9M Sidewinder air-to-air missiles on wing pylons

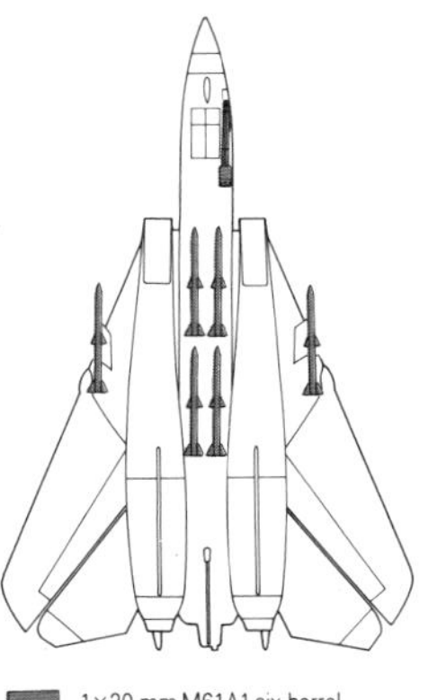

1×20-mm M61A1 six-barrel cannon
6×AIM-120A AMRAAM air-to-air missiles

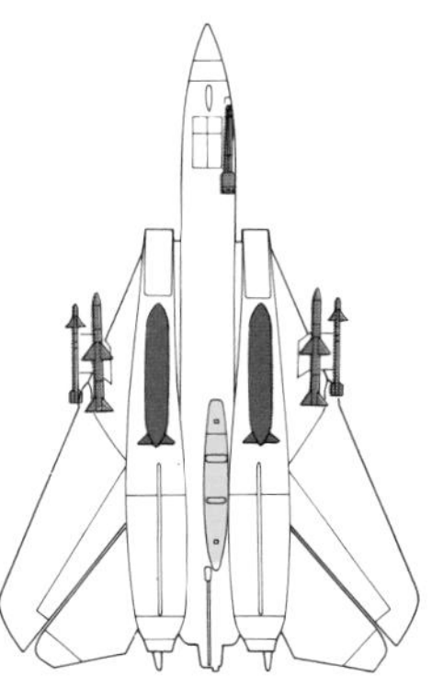

1×20-mm M61A1 six-barrel cannon
2×AIM-7M Sparrow air-to-air missiles on wing pylons
2×AIM-9M Sidewinder air-to-air missiles on wing pylons
TARPS under rear port fuselage
2×1011-litre (267-US gal) auxiliary fuel tanks beneath each intake trunk

Maximum stand-off interception

The Tomcat was designed for the protection of US Navy surface combatant groups by destroying intruding aircraft and cruise missiles at the greatest possible distance from the ships. The AWG-9 weapon-control system can detect airborne targets at ranges of up to 314 km (195 miles) according to their size, and can control up to six simultaneous engagements.

Standard interception

With this typical load all F-14s have greater versatility than any other fighter. Many Tomcats also carry a TCS (Television Camera Set) to permit the crew to make positive identification of targets beyond normal visual range.

Close-range interception

The primary role of the Tomcat is to kill at a distance, but there will always be intruders who pierce the outer screen and must therefore be engaged by Tomcats at close range. In such a dogfight mode the F-14 has an MSP (Mach Sweep Programmer) which automatically varies the wing sweep angle throughout the combat to extract maximum performance from the US fighter.

1990s interception

Tomcats will remain in service for several years yet; the F-14D update is not likely to replace older aircraft. A significant improvement will be the adoption of AMRAAM which will replace Sparrow. The Navy's next interceptor may well be a carrier-capable version of the USAF's F-22/F-23 currently under development.

Reconnaissance mission

In 1980-1 a total of 49 Tomcats was modified to carry the Tactical Air Reconnaissance Pod System (TARPS) package, which carries reconnaissance cameras and a large infra-red linescan system. This is the only shipboard reconnaissance platform currently available to the US Navy.

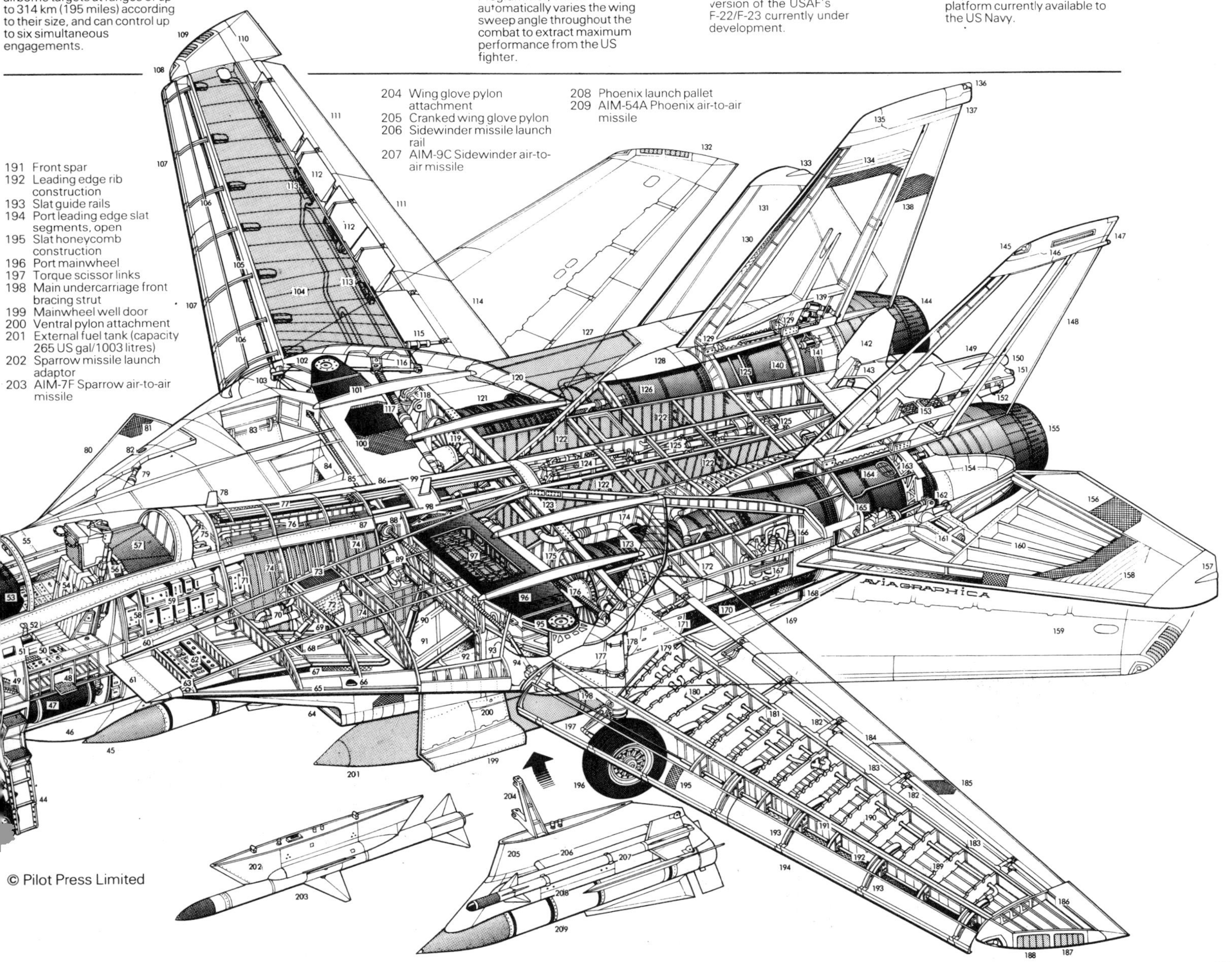

A-6 Intruder: The Navy's Iron Fist

While few could call the Intruder beautiful, the effectiveness of the A-6 in operations cannot be doubted. Capable of carrying a vast array of weapons and delivering a knock-out punch in the worst of weathers, the Intruder is second to none in the naval attack arena, as proven in a long string of campaigns.

Deck activity aboard a US Navy aircraft carrier as an A-6E is towed to its hold position among the other aircraft before flying begins. Normal complement aboard a carrier is 10 A-6Es alongside four KA-6D tankers within one squadron.

Conceived during the mid- to late- 1950s in response to a US Navy requirement for a new jet-powered medium attack aircraft capable of operating with equal facility by both day and night and with the ability to deliver nuclear weaponry, the Grumman A-6 Intruder made its maiden flight in prototype form as long ago as April 1960.

Now, some 30 years later, the final Intruder is due to leave the production line before the end of this year, but if the type seems to lack aesthetic appeal it more than makes up for this shortcoming in operational capability.

Capable of carrying up to 8165 kg (18,000 lb) of ordnance on five external store stations beneath the wing and fuselage, the Intruder has a sophisticated package of radar and computer technology which permits the type to operate virtually 'blind' at low level and to deliver a variety of weapons with near-pinpoint accuracy in virtually all types of weather conditions.

Conventional 'iron' bombs obviously form part of the A-6E's armoury, but the latest examples are also fully capable of operating with the newest generation of 'smart' weapons such as the Harpoon, HARM and Skipper missiles, all adding to the A-6E's already impressive weapons complement. A measure of self-defence capability is provided by the AIM-9 Sidewinder and, as already noted, the Intruder is equally capable of operating with nuclear weapons.

In the years which have passed since it first joined the fleet in February 1963, the basic airframe has changed little and, externally, today's Intruder looks much the same as those that were delivered to the Navy and Marine Corps during the 1960s. If one takes a look under the skin, however, the picture is very different, for the A-6 has demonstrated a remarkable ability to accommodate newer and more sophisticated items of electronic wizardry, and it is this flexibility which has been a primary factor in permitting the Intruder to remain a key element of the Navy's carrierborne sea-going forces and, perhaps more importantly, to figure prominently in Navy planning for the remainder of this century.

Sophisticated design

At the time the Intruder entered service it was without doubt one of the most sophisticated warplanes yet conceived, and its early years of service were not without problems since it took some considerable time for Navy technicians to become familiar with the complexities of Intruder sub-systems and get 'fully up to speed' in the art of maintaining aircraft in peak operational condition. However, when everything was working as advertised, the initial A-6A model was infinitely superior to the Douglas A-1 Skyraider which it largely replaced, being able to operate independently in all but the most appalling weather conditions and with a most respectable weapons payload, as it demonstrated repeatedly during the course of the Vietnam War. Indeed, once the early trials and tribulations were overcome, ardent advocates of Grumman's attack aircraft seriously suggested that Navy aircraft-carriers be loaded with nothing but Intruders, adding that these should be employed either singly or in small groups against targets in both North and South Vietnam when the weather con-

Although a comparatively small strike force, the five US Marine Corps front-line A-6E units have a high degree of interoperation with their Navy counterparts, including carrier deployments for four of the squadrons.

ditions confined everybody to the ground. Clearly, when it came to putting bombs on target, the A-6 put up a first-class performance.

Like most good wines and like many combat aircraft, the Grumman machine has also matured with the passing of the years. Operational experience and increasing familiarity with the special demands of all-weather attack have undoubtedly played a part in this but, as already noted, the type has been significantly updated in the intervening period, improvement in the avionics field playing a major role in helping Intruder to remain the Navy's sole carrierborne medium attack aircraft for the past 20 years. Like the Skyraider, the Intruder has also demonstrated the ability to take on new roles. It is probably fair to say that the Intruder is less versatile than the remarkable 'Spad', but this may well be a function of cost as much as anything else, since the A-6 has never come cheap.

An A-6E TRAM Intruder closes towards the tanker aircraft, with fuel transferred via the prominent boom immediately ahead of the Intruder's windscreen. Underwing pylons can carry a wide variety of ordnance in addition to fuel tanks.

Three models

Thus far, production of new-build Intruders has been confined to just three basic models, namely the A-6A, the EA-6A and the A-6E, the combined total being only just over 660 aircraft. However, modification led to the appearance of three other variants, these being the A-6B, the A-6C and the KA-6D, only the last now being in service alongside the A-6E. In addition, of course, the basic Intruder airframe provided a good starting point for Grumman when the company began work on what eventually appeared as the EA-6B Prowler electronic countermeasures platform.

Production of the original A-6A model eventually totalled 488 before Grumman turned to manufacturing the present A-6E version, but a derivative known as the EA-6A was acquired for operation by the US Marine Corps in the electronic countermeasures task. This too saw extensive combat action in Vietnam with VMCJ-1 from Da Nang. Some 27 EA-6As were produced between 1963 and 1969, 12 being obtained through modification of A-6As whilst the remainder were built as EA-6As. All are instantly identifiable by virtue of the bulbous fairing on the fin top which houses aerials, additional specialised electronic equipment (pod-mounted jammers and emitters) being carried beneath the fuselage and wing. Replaced in Marine Corps service by the rather more capable EA-6B during the latter half of the 1970s, the EA-6A is nevertheless still very active, most notably with electronic warfare squadrons of the Navy and Marine Corps Reserve, whilst about half-a-dozen operate with Navy squadron VAQ-33 in what might best be described as the ECM 'aggressor' role.

Modification of the A-6A for specialised roles did not cease with the EA-6A, however, for a further 19 aircraft were eventually brought to A-6B configuration in order to undertake the hazardous and demanding SAM-suppression role. There were three different variations on the A-6B theme, all employing anti-radiation missiles such as the Standard-ARM.

A dozen more A-6As metamorphosed to A-6C standard, being fitted with prominent ventral fairings containing FLIR and LLLTV sensors as part of the TRIM package, and these also saw action in Southeast Asia, being employed to interdict the celebrated Ho Chi Minh Trail. Like the A-6A, these two subtypes no longer feature in the operational inventory.

Fuel for the fleet

Yet another model to arise from modification was the KA-6D tanker and this is still very active, each deployable Navy squadron usually going to sea with four KA-6Ds. Some 51 aircraft were initially converted to KA-6D configuration in 1970-71, attrition and the ageing process having resulted in further small batches of Intruder (a total of about 20) being fitted with the hose-and-reel equipment required for the inflight-refuelling mission so as to 'top up' the number in fleet service.

The current production attack model is the A-6E, development of which began in the summer of 1967. This variant flew for the first time in prototype form during February 1970 and attained operational status with VA-85 aboard the USS *Forrestal* in September 1972. Introducing a drastically revised avionics fit, the A-6E has been further enhanced since then, production switching to the so-called A-6E(TRAM) in the late 1970s, this incorporating a FLIR sensor and laser designator and spot seeker equipment in a prominent turret beneath the nose radome. The sensor package is, not surprisingly, wholly integrated with the Intruder to detect, identify and attack a variety of targets with much improved accuracy, employing either conventional or laser-guided weaponry, the latter being able to home on laser energy provided by the A-6E itself, by

An integral part of the modern carrier air wing, the Intruder squadrons are assigned a variety of mission profiles including minelaying, close-support and precision attack. Here an A-6E TRAM awaits launch via the steam catapult.

Representing the early generation of Intruders is this A-6A of VA-35 'Black Panthers', armed with a standard load of 18 iron bombs on fuselage and wing MERs (Multiple Ejector Racks). Such aircraft as these brought a new dimension to the war in Southeast Asia, being able to use their sophisticated bombing radar to undertake accurate strikes in weather which other aircraft would have difficulty even flying in. To maximise the precision capabilities of the Intruder, they often flew with other types such as A-4 Skyhawks, providing bomb release commands to the less well-equipped aircraft.

10
152940
USS ENTERPRISE
NAVY
VA-35
ABA

A-6 Intruder in service units and example aircraft

US Navy Atlantic Fleet

VA-34
Shore base: NAS Oceana, Virginia
Role: medium attack
Equipment: A-6E
Tail letters: 'AB'
Aircraft: 157002 '502', 161660 '503', 151548 '511'

VA-55
Shore base: NAS Oceana, Virginia
Role: medium attack
Equipment: A-6E and KA-6D
Tail letters: 'AK'
Aircraft: (A-6E) 155718 '504', 161084 '512'; (KA-6D) 155583 '513'

VA-176
Shore base: NAS Oceana, Virginia
Role: medium attack
Equipment: A-6E and KA-6D
Tail letters: 'AE'
Aircraft: (A-6E) 159178 '500', 157025 '511'; (KA-6D) 154133 '515'

VA-35
Shore base: NAS Oceana, Virginia
Role: medium attack
Equipment: A-6E and KA-6D
Tail letters: 'AJ'
Aircraft: (A-6E) 161668 '504', 159317 '511'; (KA-6D) 151789 '517'

VA-65
Shore base: NAS Oceana, Virginia
Role: medium attack
Equipment: A-6E and KA-6D
Tail letters: 'AG'
Aircraft: (A-6E) 151804 '500', 155589 '510'; (KA-6D) 149942 '514'

The famous fin markings of VA-35 'Black Panthers' have seen many years of service on the Intruder, this aircraft displaying an interim low-visibility scheme with all markings appearing in black.

VA-42
Shore base: NAS Oceana, Virginia
Role: Atlantic Fleet replacement training squadron
Equipment: A-6E
Tail letters: 'AD'
Aircraft: 149955 '500', 161086 '511', 155711 '522'

VA-75
Shore base: NAS Oceana, Virginia
Role: medium attack
Equipment: A-6E and KA-6D
Tail letters: 'AC'
Aircraft: (A-6E) 160431 '501', 158531 '504'; (KA-6D) 152934 '513'

VA-85
Shore base: NAS Oceana, Virginia
Role: medium attack
Equipment: A-6E
Tail letters: 'AC'
Aircraft: 159896 '540', 159900 '544', 161665 '552'

Pacific Fleet

VA-52
Shore base: NAS Whidbey Island, Washington
Role: medium attack
Equipment: A-6E and KA-6D
Tail letters: 'NL'
Aircraft: (A-6E) 161674 '502', 160423 '512'; (KA-6D) 151568 '513'

VA-165
Shore base: NAS Whidbey Island, Washington
Role: medium attack
Equipment: A-6E and KA-6D
Tail letters: 'NG'
Aircraft: (A-6E) 159176 '50', 1604245 '510'; (KA-6D) 151570 '516'

VA-196
Shore base: NAS Whidbey Island, Washington
Role: medium attack
Equipment: A-6E and KA-6D
Tail letters: 'NK'
Aircraft: (A-6E) 158528 '501', 152596 '506'; (KA-6D) 151787 '517'

Illustrating the role of the KA-6D tankers in each squadron are two aircraft from VA-165, a component of CVW-9 aboard USS Kitty Hawk.

VA-95
Shore base: NAS Whidbey Island, Washington
Role: medium attack
Equipment: A-6E
Tail letters: 'NH'
Aircraft: 161090 '502', 161666 '504'

VA-128
Shore base: NAS Whidbey Island, Washington
Role: Pacific Fleet replacement training squadron
Equipment: A-6E
Tail letters: 'NJ'
Aircraft: 155673 '800', 159578 '808', 159310 '821'

VA-115
Shore base: NAS Whidbey Island, Washington
Role: medium attack
Equipment: A-6E and KA-6D
Tail letters: 'NF'
Aircraft: (A-6E) 161109 '503', 159571 '510'; (KA-6D) 149485 '513'

VA-145
Shore base: NAS Whidbey Island, Washington
Role: medium attack
Equipment: A-6E and KA-6D
Tail letters: 'NE'
Aircraft: (A-6E) 154129 '501', 152954 '504'; (KA-6D) 152896 '515'

US Marine Corps

VMA(AW)-121
Base: MCAS El Toro, California
Role: all-weather attack
Equipment: A-6E
Tail letters: 'VK'
Aircraft: 159902 '00', 155689 '07', 155669 '10'

VMA(AW)-332
Base: MCAS Cherry Point, North Carolina
Role: all-weather attack
Equipment: A-6E
Tail letters: 'EA'
Aircraft: 160429 '00', 152936 '11', 152923 '17'

VMAT(AW)-202
Base: MCAS Cherry Point, North Carolina
Role: Marine Corps A-6 training squadron
Equipment: A-6E
Tail letters: 'KC'
Aircraft: 155667 '00', 157013 '09', 155592 '14'

(Note: one USMC Intruder squadron is normally forward-deployed to Iwakuni, Japan on a rotational basis.)

Currently divided between California and North Carolina, the Marine Corps' A-6 force will remain in service probably into the 21st century.

VMA(AW)-224
Base: MCAS Cherry Point, North Carolina
Role: all-weather attack
Equipment: A-6E
Tail letters: 'WK'
Aircraft: 157010 '02', 159904 '07', 155681 '10'

VMA(AW)-533
Base: MCAS El Toro, California
Role: all-weather attack
Equipment: A-6E and KA-6D
Tail letters: 'AA'
Aircraft: (A-6E) 158051 '500', 159316 '505'; (KA-6D) 152913 '522'

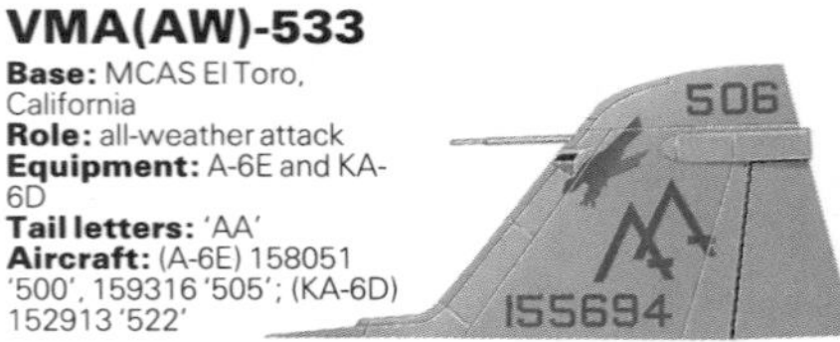

VMA(AW)-242
Base: MCAS El Toro, California
Role: all-weather attack
Equipment: A-6E
Tail letters: 'DT'
Aircraft: 155716 '02', 155708 '05', 155621 '10'

another aircraft fitted with a laser designator or by a ground-based operator. The Intruder can also illuminate targets for laser-guided ordnance carried and released by other aircraft.

CILOP programme

In addition to having manufactured new-build examples of the A-6E, Grumman has also undertaken an extensive CILOP programme, no fewer than 240 A-6As, A-6Bs and A-6Cs being updated to A-6E standard during the course of the 1970s, and many of these aircraft have since returned to Calverton for further retrospective modification to bring them up to the latest configuration. Such work looks set to continue in the immediate future since many of the Navy's sizeable fleet of Intruders will require re-winging as a result of fatigue-induced cracks. This last prompted the service briefly to ground the A-6 for inspection during the first half of 1985, Boeing subsequently being awarded a contract to supply new graphite-epoxy wings for installation on the Intruder.

With regard to operational employment, the US Navy presently has a total of 13 deployable squadrons equipped with the Intruder, each of these normally going to sea with about 10 examples of the primary A-6E attack variant plus four KA-6D tankers. Normally, a Carrier Air Wing (CVW) includes one Intruder-equipped squadron in its line-up, although during 1983-84 CVW-3 embarked aboard the USS *John F. Kennedy* for a tour of duty in the Mediterranean and Indian Ocean with two A-6 squadrons, the second of these taking the place of the two Vought A-7E Corsair squadrons which would normally be present.

In addition to the front-line deployable squadrons, the Navy also has two further units which do not operate at sea, these being assigned to the training role from the two major shore bases, one at Oceana, Virginia, and the other at Whidbey Island, Washington.

Marine squadrons

The Marine Corps also has a single training squadron (at Cherry Point, North Carolina) as well as five front-line all-weather attack squadrons, the latter being nominally based at El Toro, California, or at Cherry Point, and equipped solely with the A-6E. In practice, however, it is usual for one Marine Intruder squadron to be forward deployed to the 1st Marine Air Wing at Iwakuni in Japan, whilst it is not unknown for USMC A-6 units to join Navy CVWs on a temporary basis for tours of duty aboard aircraft-carriers, the most recent instance of this occurring in 1984 when VMA(AW)-533 operated as part of CVW-17 aboard the USS *Saratoga*. When embarked as part of a CVW, Marine units add the usual quartet of KA-6Ds to their complement, this being the only circumstance in which this service operates this model of the Intruder.

The only front-line squadron which now operates electronic Intruders is VAQ-33 at Key West, Florida, this having a handful of EA-6As, a sub-type which also serves with three Reserve squadrons in the ECM role from the Naval Air Stations at Norfolk, Virginia, and Whidbey Island, Washington.

Finally, small numbers of the A-6E also serve with a few test agencies. The most notable of these units is probably VX-5 at China Lake, California, which serves as one element of the Navy's OTAEF, which is equipped with examples of all current front-line types engaged in various aspects of the attack mission.

In July 1984 Grumman received a go-ahead to start development of an improved A-6E, designated the A-6F Intruder II, featuring advanced high-resolution synthetic aperture radar, stand-off air-to-surface and beyond visual range air-to-air missile capability, a new 'glass' cockpit and digital avionics and last, but by no means least, a new engine. To achieve lower operating costs, Grumman proposed a non-afterburning version of the General Electric F404 turbofan. The first of five A-6F prototypes flew on 25 August 1987. However, the programme was terminated in 1989 after three of the five had flown. As a cheaper alternative, Grumman then proposed the A-6G, with the same improvements but retaining the original J52 powerplant, in an effort to cut development costs. However, after a US Navy evaluation this too was cancelled in 1989, in favour of the Systems Weapons Improvement Program later applied to the bulk of the Intruder fleet.

Immediately recognisable by the large fairing atop the tail fin, the two-seat Grumman EA-6A tactical ECM derivative of the A-6 was designed to detect, classify and suppress enemy electronic activity in support of strike forces.

Glossary

ARM Anti-Radiation Missile
CILOP Conversion In Lieu Of Procurement
CRT Cathode-Ray Tube
ECM Electronic CounterMeasures
FLIR Forward-Looking Infra-Red
HARM High-speed Anti-Radiation Missile
LLLTV Low-Light-Level TV
OTAEF Operational Test And Evaluation Force
SAM Surface-to-Air Missile
TRAM Target Recognition and Attack Multisensor
TRIM Trails, Roads, Interdiction Multisensor

An appropriate 'flexing of the muscles' pose by a truly rugged workhorse of contemporary naval aviation. It is such a fitting testimony to the excellence of design and mission effectiveness that there is no true successor in sight.

Other operators

VAQ-33
Base: NAS Key West, Florida
Role: naval ECM
Equipment: EA-6A
Tail letters: 'GD'
Aircraft: 147685 '109', 156990 '111'

VAQ-209
Base: NAS Norfolk, Virginia
Role: naval ECM
Equipment: EA-6A
Tail letters: 'AF'
Aircraft: 156987 '700', 151598 '704'

VAQ-309
Base: NAS Whidbey Island, Washington
Role: naval ECM
Equipment: EA-6A
Tail letters: 'ND'
Aircraft: 156989 '612', 156991 '614'

VMAQ-4
Base: NAS Whidbey Island, Washington
Role: marine corps ECM
Equipment: EA-6A
Tail letters: 'RM'
Aircraft: 151600 '00', 149475 '02'

VX-5
Base: NAS China Lake, California
Role: evaluation and development
Equipment: A-6E
Tail letters: 'XE'
Aircraft: 155707 '20', 154124 '24'

PMTC
Base: NAS Point Mugu, California
Role: test and evaluation
Equipment: A-6E
Tail letters: none
Aircraft: 154162 '52', 159311 '54'

NWC
Base: NAS China Lake, California
Role: weapons development
Equipment: A-6E
Tail letters: none
Aircraft: 159569 '601', 151565 '603'

NATC/SATD
Base: NAS Patuxent River, Maryland
Role: evaluation and test
Equipment: A-6E
Tail letters: '7T'
Aircraft: 159567 '500', 154131 '502'

Below: Development and testing of new avionics and weaponry for the A-6 is an ongoing scheme. This Naval Weapons Centre aircraft is testing HARM (High-speed Anti-Radiation Missile).

Grumman A-6 Intruder variants

A-6A: initial production model for service with USN/USMC; total of 488 built but none remain in front-line service, the majority having been converted to KA-6D or A-6E configuration

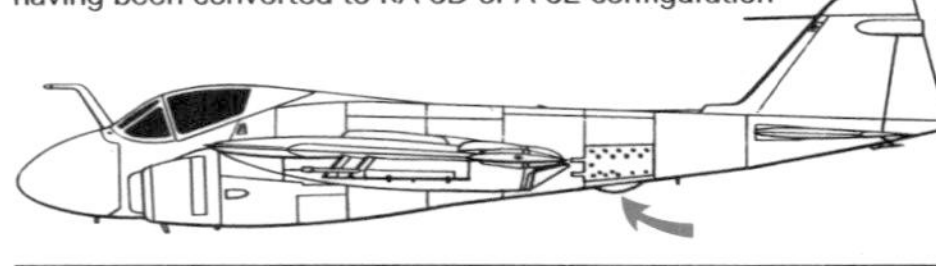

A-6B: specialised variant optimised for SAM-suppression duty, utilising Standard-ARM anti-radiation missile; total of 19 A-6As modified to A-6B configuration but no longer in service, survivors having been further updated to A-6E version

A-6C: specialised variant with TRIM package comprising LLLTV and FLIR sensors in prominent ventral pod; total of 12 A-6As completed to this standard and employed to interdict Ho Chi Minh trail by night; survivors subsequently remanufactured to A-6E configuration

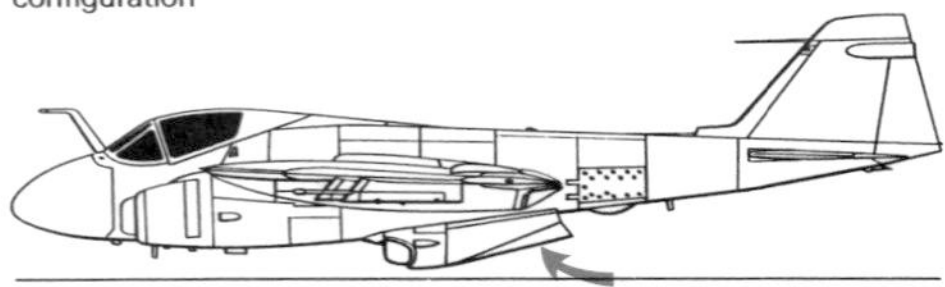

KA-6D: inflight-refuelling tanker version featuring hose and drogue assembly in space previously occupied by aft avionics 'bird-cage' on A-6A; about 70 KA-6Ds have been produced by conversion of A-6A model; presently in service with USN, each operational Intruder squadron normally deploying with four KA-6Ds as well as primary A-6E attack version

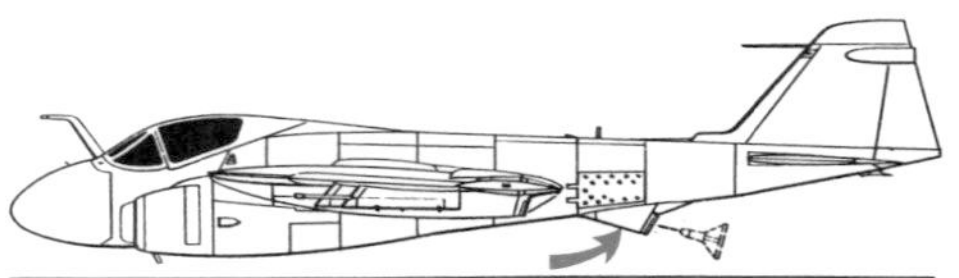

A-6E: current production and service version of Intruder, featuring updated avionics fit; entered operational inventory in 1971 and has been further updated since then, with latest configuration being the **A-6E TRAM** incorporating the Target Recognition Attack Multi-sensor package in nose-mounted steerable turret; has been produced in new-build and remanufactured form, older A-6As being brought to this standard as part of US Navy's CILOP philosophy; presently equips 15 USN and six USMC medium attack squadrons

A-6F Intruder II: A-6E with upgraded avionics proposed for USN/USMC in 1984 but powered by General Electric F404 turbofan; first of five prototypes (162183) flew on 25 August 1987 but programme terminated on economy grounds in 1989

A-6G: alternative A-6E upgrade with A-6F avionics but powered by standard J52 engine to keep costs down; project evaluated by US Navy but cancelled in January 1989 in favour of A-6E SWIP programme covering nearly 350 aircraft in service or on order

EA-6A: specialised ECM variant to replace EF-10B Skyknight with USMC; production in new-build and converted form, quantities completed being 15 and 12 respectively; replaced by EA-6B Prowler in front-line inventory but still equips one ECM 'Aggressor' unit as well as three second-line Reserve Force squadrons

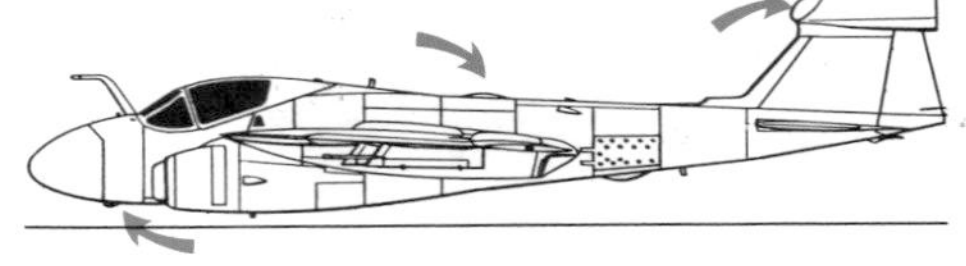

Grumman A-6E (Upgrade) Intruder cutaway drawing

1 Radome
2 Radome open position
3 Norden AN/APQ-148 multi-mode radar scanner
4 Scanner tracking mechanism
5 Intermediate frequency unit
6 ILS aerials
7 TRAM rotating turret mounting
8 Target Recognition and Attack Multisensor turret (TRAM)
9 Taxiing lamp
10 Deck approach lights
11 Nosewheel leg door
12 Hydraulic nosewheel steering unit
13 Catapult tow bar
14 Twin nosewheels, aft retracting
15 Retraction/breaker strut
16 Shock absorber leg strut
17 Torque scissor links
18 Radome latch
19 Hinged avionics equipment pallet, port and starboard
20 Radar scanner mounting
21 Radome hydraulic jack
22 Inflight-refuelling probe
23 ALQ-165 ECM system forward spiral antenna
24 Refuelling probe spotlight
25 Windscreen rain repellant air duct
26 Front pressure bulkhead
27 Nosewheel bay mounted pressure refuelling connection
28 Boundary layer splitter plate
29 Port engine air intake
30 Nosewheel bay electronic equipment racks
31 VHF aerial
32 UHF aerial
33 Intake duct framing
34 Temperature probe
35 Canopy emergency release handle
36 TACAN aerial
37 Folding boarding ladder
38 Integral boarding steps
39 Angle-of-attack transmitter
40 Boundary layer spill duct
41 Cockpit floor level
42 Rudder pedals
43 Engine throttle levers
44 Control column
45 Instrument panel shroud
46 Pilot's optical sighting unit/head-up display
47 Windscreen panels
48 Aft sliding cockpit canopy cover
49 Forward-Looking Infra-red (FLIR) viewing scope
50 Navigator/bombardier's Martin-Baker GRU-7 ejection seat
51 Ejection seat headrests
52 Seat reclining mechanism
53 Centre console
54 Pilot's GRU-7 ejection seat
55 Safety/parachute harness
56 Port side console panel
57 Electrical system equipment
58 Destruct initiator
59 Leading edge stall warning buffet strip
60 Engine intake compressor face
61 Engine bay venting air scoop
62 Accessory equipment gearbox
63 Pratt & Whitney J52-P-8B non-afterburning turbofan engine
64 Mainwheel door
65 Leading edge antenna fairing, port and starboard
66 ALQ-165 high, mid and low band ECM aerials
67 Mainwheel well
68 Hydraulic system reservoir
69 Cockpit rear pressure bulkhead
70 Cooling air spill louvres
71 Electrical equipment bay
72 Electronics and avionics equipment bay
73 Forward fuselage bag-type fuel tank
74 Weapons monitoring module
75 Sliding canopy rail
76 Canopy hydraulic jack
77 Canopy aft fairing
78 Starboard wing inboard integral fuel tank, total fuel capacity 8873-litres (1951 Imp gal/2344 US gal)
79 Fuel system piping
80 Inboard wing fence
81 Leading edge slat drive shaft
82 Slat guide rails
83 Slat screw jacks
84 AGM-65 Maverick air-to-surface missiles
85 Triple missile carrier/launcher
86 Starboard wing stores pylons
87 AIM-9P Sidewinder 'self-defence' air-to-air missile

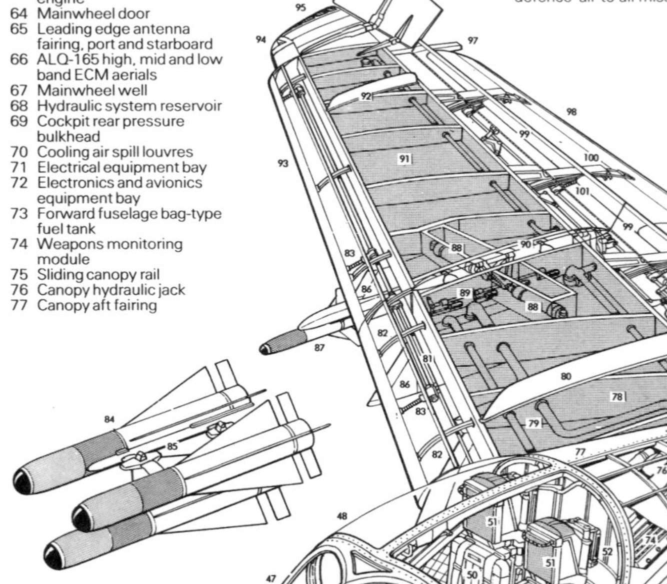

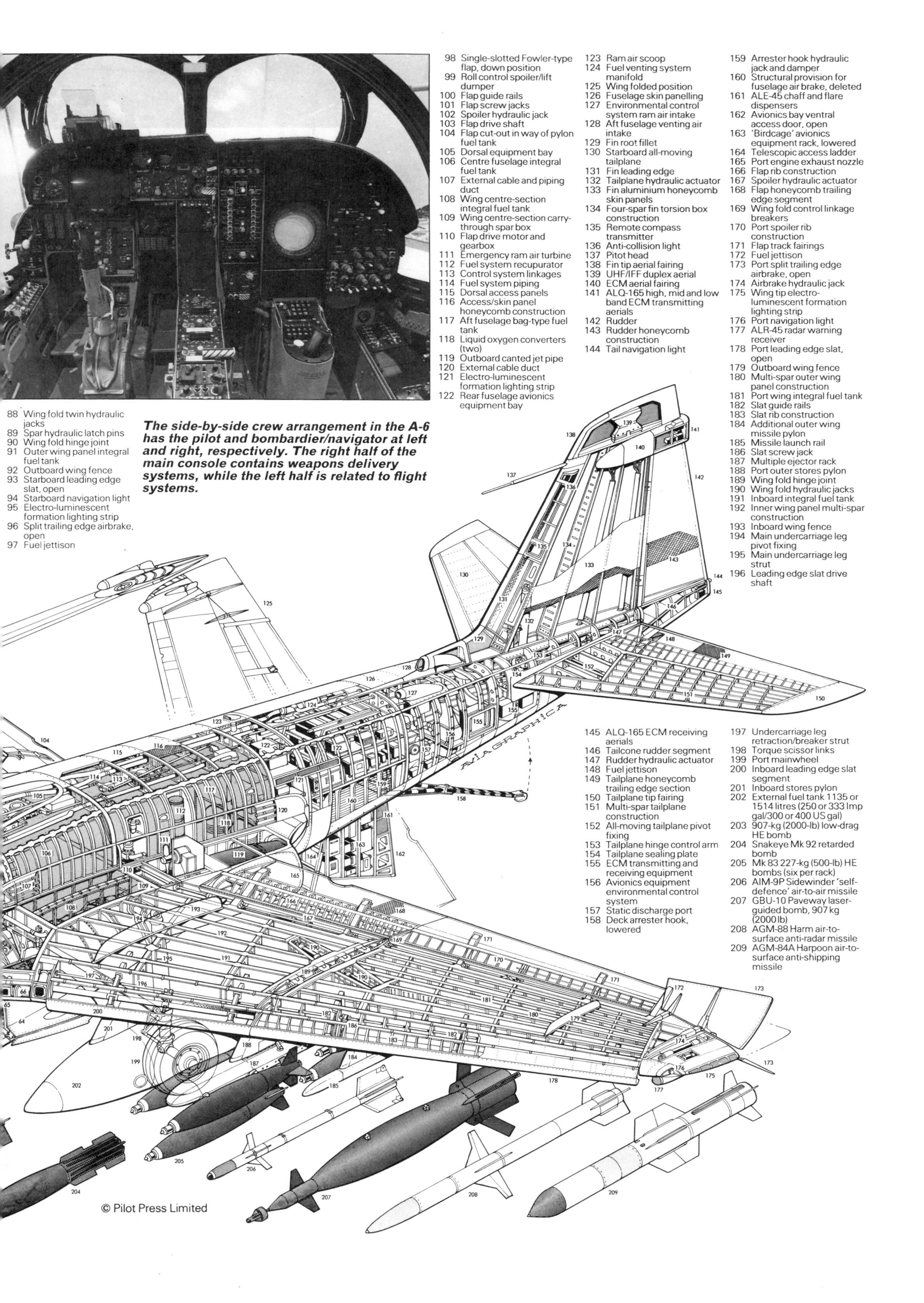

The side-by-side crew arrangement in the A-6 has the pilot and bombardier/navigator at left and right, respectively. The right half of the main console contains weapons delivery systems, while the left half is related to flight systems.

88 Wing fold twin hydraulic jacks
89 Spar hydraulic latch pins
90 Wing fold hinge joint
91 Outer wing panel integral fuel tank
92 Outboard wing fence
93 Starboard leading edge slat, open
94 Starboard navigation light
95 Electro-luminescent formation lighting strip
96 Split trailing edge airbrake, open
97 Fuel jettison
98 Single-slotted Fowler-type flap, down position
99 Roll control spoiler/lift dumper
100 Flap guide rails
101 Flap screw jacks
102 Spoiler hydraulic jack
103 Flap drive shaft
104 Flap cut-out in way of pylon fuel tank
105 Dorsal equipment bay
106 Centre fuselage integral fuel tank
107 External cable and piping duct
108 Wing centre-section integral fuel tank
109 Wing centre-section carry-through spar box
110 Flap drive motor and gearbox
111 Emergency ram air turbine
112 Fuel system recupurator
113 Control system linkages
114 Fuel system piping
115 Dorsal access panels
116 Access/skin panel honeycomb construction
117 Aft fuselage bag-type fuel tank
118 Liquid oxygen converters (two)
119 Outboard canted jet pipe
120 External cable duct
121 Electro-luminescent formation lighting strip
122 Rear fuselage avionics equipment bay
123 Ram air scoop
124 Fuel venting system manifold
125 Wing folded position
126 Fuselage skin panelling
127 Environmental control system ram air intake
128 Aft fuselage venting air intake
129 Fin root fillet
130 Starboard all-moving tailplane
131 Fin leading edge
132 Tailplane hydraulic actuator
133 Fin aluminium honeycomb skin panels
134 Four-spar fin torsion box construction
135 Remote compass transmitter
136 Anti-collision light
137 Pitot head
138 Fin tip aerial fairing
139 UHF/IFF duplex aerial
140 ECM aerial fairing
141 ALQ-165 high, mid and low band ECM transmitting aerials
142 Rudder
143 Rudder honeycomb construction
144 Tail navigation light
145 ALQ-165 ECM receiving aerials
146 Tailcone rudder segment
147 Rudder hydraulic actuator
148 Fuel jettison
149 Tailplane honeycomb trailing edge section
150 Tailplane tip fairing
151 Multi-spar tailplane construction
152 All-moving tailplane pivot fixing
153 Tailplane hinge control arm
154 Tailplane sealing plate
155 ECM transmitting and receiving equipment
156 Avionics equipment environmental control system
157 Static discharge port
158 Deck arrester hook, lowered
159 Arrester hook hydraulic jack and damper
160 Structural provision for fuselage air brake, deleted
161 ALE-45 chaff and flare dispensers
162 Avionics bay ventral access door, open
163 'Birdcage' avionics equipment rack, lowered
164 Telescopic access ladder
165 Port engine exhaust nozzle
166 Flap rib construction
167 Spoiler hydraulic actuator
168 Flap honeycomb trailing edge segment
169 Wing fold control linkage breakers
170 Port spoiler rib construction
171 Flap track fairings
172 Fuel jettison
173 Port split trailing edge airbrake, open
174 Airbrake hydraulic jack
175 Wing tip electro-luminescent formation lighting strip
176 Port navigation light
177 ALR-45 radar warning receiver
178 Port leading edge slat, open
179 Outboard wing fence
180 Multi-spar outer wing panel construction
181 Port wing integral fuel tank
182 Slat guide rails
183 Slat rib construction
184 Additional outer wing missile pylon
185 Missile launch rail
186 Slat screw jack
187 Multiple ejector rack
188 Port outer stores pylon
189 Wing fold hinge joint
190 Wing fold hydraulic jacks
191 Inboard integral fuel tank
192 Inner wing panel multi-spar construction
193 Inboard wing fence
194 Main undercarriage leg pivot fixing
195 Main undercarriage leg strut
196 Leading edge slat drive shaft
197 Undercarriage leg retraction/breaker strut
198 Torque scissor links
199 Port mainwheel
200 Inboard leading edge slat segment
201 Inboard stores pylon
202 External fuel tank 1135 or 1514 litres (250 or 333 Imp gal/300 or 400 US gal)
203 907-kg (2000-lb) low-drag HE bomb
204 Snakeye Mk 92 retarded bomb
205 Mk 83 227-kg (500-lb) HE bombs (six per rack)
206 AIM-9P Sidewinder 'self-defence' air-to-air missile
207 GBU-10 Paveway laser-guided bomb, 907 kg (2000 lb)
208 AGM-88 Harm air-to-surface anti-radar missile
209 AGM-84A Harpoon air-to-surface anti-shipping missile

Grumman TBF Avenger

For over 60 years Grumman has provided some of the world's best carrier-based aircraft, typified by generous wings, amiable handling and such strength that the company is colloquially known as 'The Iron Works'. No aircraft better exemplifies Grumman than the Avenger, chief torpedo-bomber of the Pacific war in 1942-45.

On its first combat mission six new TBF-1s thundered off into the Battle of Midway on 4 June 1942. Only one came back, and that had the pilot flying a shattered aircraft on the trimmers, one crewman injured and the other dead. This seemed almost a repetition of what had been happening with the previous-generation Douglas TBD-1 Devastator, which was simply not survivable in World War II. In fact, nothing could have been more wrong, and the Avenger was to be one of the great war-winners of World War II.

When Douglas had produced the TBD in 1935 it had been as modern as the hour, with all-metal stressed-skin construction, enclosed cockpits and retractable gear. As early as October 1939, however, it was clear that 671 kW (900 hp) was inadequate for the ship-based torpedo-bomber mission, and in that month the US Navy began organising plans for an industry competition for a replacement aircraft. The key to such aircraft lay in the existence of such powerful engines as the Pratt & Whitney R-2800 and the Wright R-2600 and R-3350. Grumman was well-placed to win what was certain to be a major programme.

The US Navy's requirements were no push-over, however, and the numerical requirements for mission radius with particular weapon loads could only just be met. In an intensive five weeks at the turn of the year 1941 the engineering team under chief experimental engineer Bob Hall roughed out the shape that was later to be called the Pregnant Beast, or more kindly, The Turkey. That portly fuselage, giant angular wing and distinctive tail could only have come from Grumman, but what might not have been expected were the internal weapons bay and the gun turret. Project engineer R. Koch was first to decide on an internal bay, partly because this fitted in with the lower rear defensive gun position. There was no problem with the pilot, who sat in lofty state in a roomy and comfortable cockpit above the leading edge, where his view was perfect. The other two crew were less obvious.

A door on the right side aft of the wing gave access to the rear fuselage, packed with equipment, flares, parachutes and ammunition. At the lower level, the bombardier was provided with a folding seat, from which he could either man the lower rear machine-gun, a Browning of 7.62-mm (0.3-in) calibre, or face forward and aim the aircraft for medium-altitude level bombing. During development in 1942 radar was introduced to the US Navy, and the Westinghouse ASB radar became standard equipment on some versions. Another common fit was the APG-4 'Sniffer' low-level auto-bombing radar which used a dipole Yagi array toed out at 40° under each outer wing. The radar viewing scope was ahead of the bombardier, whose compartment thus became somewhat crowded. The radar scope was in fact directly under the turret, and this latter was an innovation where the US Navy was concerned (though a turret had been fitted to a few other single-engined attack types such as the Soviet BB-1/Su-2).

The Avenger takes shape

The US Navy had specified a turret, to mount a single 12.7-mm (0.5-in) gun, and Grumman handled the development itself. Though almost everything on the TBF was hydraulic, it eventually found itself with an electrically driven turret, chiefly because the job was assigned to Oscar Olsen whose entire background (mainly with

This rare colour photograph of one of the first Avengers – believed to be the first production TBF-1 in January 1942 – shows the original national insignia with a red central disc and red/white striped rudder, both discontinued in May 1942. At this time colours were sea green/grey.

One of the first Avengers to enter service, this TBF-1 went into action – disastrously, as it happened – with torpedo squadron VT-8 aboard USS Hornet on 4 June 1942, during the Battle of Midway. Most TBFs at this time had upper surfaces in sea green.

General Electric) had been electrical. He was aware of the problems caused by flight manoeuvres which could impose totally different loads on different parts of the turret mount ring. The best answer appeared to Olsen to be the Amplidyne form of control, which can govern both the torque and speed of an electric motor with great precision. He was thus able to equip the turret with synchronised motors which, no matter what the attitude of the turret or aircraft might be, always gave fingertip gun-pointing accuracy.

By contrast, most of the other movable items were hydraulic, including the massive main landing gears (which could take a bone-crushing arrival at 4.88 m/16 ft per second vertical velocity onto a hard deck), the folding outer wings, the big split flaps and the double-fold bomb doors. Roy Grumman himself had hit on the wing fold only a year earlier, and this feature was first applied to production models of the F4F Wildcat then just coming off the line. He saw the height problem caused by the conventional upward-hinged wings, and so experimented with two partly unfolded paperclips stuck into the sides of a draughtsman's soap-eraser. Eventually he got the two clips at just the right skewed angle so that the 'wings' folded neatly alongside the 'body'. In the folded position the upper surfaces faced outwards. For the big TBF power folding was essential; no crew of men could have handled such wings, loaded with radar, tanks and rockets, on a pitching deck. The only other item driven electrically was the giant sting arrester hook, normally housed inside the rear fuselage but extended on rails when needed by a cable and pulley track.

As well as the two rear guns a 7.62-mm (0.3-in) gun was mounted high on the right side of the nose, firing through the propeller disc. It was always considered good practice to give the pilot a gun, not only to improve morale but for sound offensive reasons. Though the bombardier could aim bombs from altitude it was the pilot who managed torpedo attacks, using the illuminated torpedo sight on the left side of the coaming. Ahead he had merely a ring-and-bead sight for the gun, though this could also be used for dive-bombing, the bombardier then being a mere passenger. The main gears could be extended as airbrakes to hold dives to about 482 km/h (300 mph), though the controls became exceedingly heavy and a great deal of effort and fast re-trimming was needed both in the dive and the pull-out.

The first of two XTBF-1 prototypes, BuNo. 2539, made a highly successful first flight on 1 August 1941. The pilot, as with most experimental Grumman aircraft at the time, was none other than the chief experimental engineer himself, Bob Hall. He had only recently been fished from the ocean after deciding the XP-50 was no longer a safe place to stay, and he found the XTBF-1 a welcome contrast, seemingly as safe as houses with the trusty 14-cylinder Cyclone rumbling lustily ahead of his feet. Grumman was fast becoming overloaded with work and was well into the construction of Plant 2, a complete new factory twice as big as the first. Here would be built the 286 TBFs ordered 'off the drawing board' back in December 1940. Then, as often happens, trouble came out of the blue. On 28 November 1941 the XTBF-1 was flying in the hands of Bob Cook and engineer Gordon Israel. Near Brentwood, about 16 km (10 miles) east of the Bethpage plant, they found the bomb bay was burning fiercely. (The only cause anyone could think of was an electrical fault.) Cook and Israel hit the silk, and the flaming torpedo bomber dived into some woods.

America at war

This did not damage the programme, and by this time the US Navy had changed its order for 286 to an open-ended contract which was to last until 31 December 1943, 2,291 aircraft later (and with even bigger numbers built by others). On an unseasonably hot Sunday morning, 7 December 1941, all was bustle at Bethpage as, amid colourful ceremony, the vast new Plant 2 was dedicated. Spotlighted in the middle was the gleaming new second prototype XTBF-1, which was to be the priority product. Suddenly the company vice-

The unit and occasion are not known, but the TBFs appear to be posing for the photographer. Possibly operating from USS Coral Sea, they are making a practice torpedo attack, though the Mk 13-2 torpedo is real enough. Note the double-fold weapon-bay doors, opened hydraulically.

These TBF-1s of the US Marine Corps were pictured in February 1944 when some, including that in the foreground, had seen over 18 months of action. The squadron was at this time based at Bougainville, operating against both Japanese shipping and surface targets in the Solomons area.

Probably taken in about 1955, this photograph shows one of the final TBM-3S2 anti-submarine versions (no. 53437, built in late 1943 as a TBM-3 and converted in the early 1950s). The Royal Canadian Navy unit was probably No. 881 Sqn, but to suggest the location as Dartmouth NS would be a pure guess.

president, Clint Towl, was called to the telephone by the public address system. He picked up the instrument to be told 'The Japs have attacked Pearl Harbor, we're at war.' Towl prohibited any announcement and had the refreshment line plugged, so that, led by the children, the public began to go home; then, when the last of the thousands had gone through the gate, the plant was locked and searched for any saboteurs. It was to be a secure place for the next four years; and the TBF was appropriately named Avenger.

From defeat to victory

By this time Plant 2 was already full of production TBF-1s, and the number one off the line, BuNo. 00373, flew on 3 January 1942. So few engineering changes had been needed that by the end of six months another 145 had been delivered, with half of US Navy Squadron VT-8 already nearing the end of its conversion course at NAS Norfolk, Virginia. From here the six new TBFs were flown, with 1022-litre (270-US gal) tanks in the bomb bays, right across the USA and over the 10-hour ocean sector to Pearl Harbor. Here their ship, USS *Hornet,* had already departed, so they rumbled on all the way to Midway island. It was here that all six aircraft were shot to pieces, as noted at the opening of this account; it was perhaps the only occasion on which the TBF came off second-best. From that time on, it was to be the destroyer not only of the Japanese navy but also of Hitler's U-boats.

With the normal internal load of a Mk 13-2 torpedo or four 227-kg (500-lb) bombs, and full internal fuel of 1268 litres (335 US gal) in three wing tanks, the TBF-1 could attack targets up to 418 km (260 miles) distant. It was always pleasant to fly, though spinning was prohibited. When flown with determination by a strong pilot it could

For many ex-military Grumman Avengers, life was to continue for a few years as part of numerous water-bomber fleets to fight forest fires in the USA and Canada. In the former country, single-engined aircraft are now banned from such tasks.

Grumman TBM-1C Avenger cutaway drawing key:

1 Starboard elevator
2 Fabric covered aileron construction
3 Elevator trim tab
4 Elevator horn balance
5 Tailplane construction
6 Rudder tab
7 Trim tab control jack
8 Tail navigation light
9 Fabric covered rudder construction
10 Aerial cable rear mounting
11 Fin construction
12 Port elevator
13 Port tailplane
14 Elevator hinge controls
15 Tailplane support frames
16 Deck arrester hook (lowered)
17 Arrester hook guide rails
18 Rudder hinge control
19 Rear fuselage frames
20 Flush-riveted aluminium skin covering
21 Fin root fairing
22 Tailplane control cables
23 Arrester hook retraction drive motor
24 Lifting tube
25 Rear fuselage frame and stringer construction
26 Tailwheel shock absorber strut
27 Catapult 'hold-back' shackle
28 Retractable tailwheel
29 Crew compartment rear bulkhead
30 Search flares
31 Parachute flare launch tube
32 Ventral gun turret
33 Ammunition magazine
34 Browning 0.3-in (7.62-mm) machine-gun
35 Machine-gun mounting
36 Gun camera switch box
37 Crew door
38 Parachute stowage
39 Rear fuselage production break point
40 Spare coil stowage rack
41 Bombardier's side window
42 Upper turret spare ammunition magazines
43 Bombardier's folding seat
44 Gun turret mounting ring
45 Gun elevating mechanism
46 Ammunition feed chute
47 Browning 0.5-in (12.7-mm) machine-gun
48 Upper rotating gun turret
49 Bullet proof windscreen
50 Gunner's armoured seat back
51 Aerial cable
52 Port wing folded position
53 Canopy aft glazing
54 Emergency life raft stowage
55 Hydraulic reservoir
56 Radio communications equipment
57 ASB weapons aiming controller
58 Bomb release levers
59 Cabin heater duct
60 Aft end of bomb bay
61 Fixed wing root construction
62 Wing fold joint line
63 Browning 0.5-in (12.7-mm) fixed machine-gun
64 Ammunition feed chute
65 Ammunition magazine (320 rounds)
66 Trailing edge flap shroud construction
67 Lattice wing ribs
68 Starboard, fabric covered aileron construction
69 Aileron hinge control
70 Aileron trim tab
71 Starboard wing tip
72 Starboard navigation light
73 Leading edge ribs
74 Fixed leading edge slot
75 ASB aerial
76 RT-5/APS-4 search radar pod
77 Radar mounting sway braces
78 Rocket launching pylons
79 Jettisonable fuel tank (58 US gal/219.5 litre capacity)
80 Main undercarriage wheel well
81 Sloping main spar
82 Wing fold hinge axis
83 Twin hydraulic folding jacks
84 Machine-gun blast tube
85 Starboard main fuel tank (90 US gal/340.7 litre capacity)
86 Centre section main spar
87 Oxygen bottle
88 Autopilot controls
89 Rear cockpit entry hatch
90 ASB equipment rack
91 Aerial mast
92 Roll-over crash pylon
93 Second cockpit control column provision
94 Propeller de-icing fluid tank
95 Seat-back armour
96 Headrest
97 Safety harness
98 Pilot's seat
99 Emergency hydraulic handpump
100 Centre main fuel tank (145 US gal/549 litre capacity)
101 Fuel tank filler cap
102 Main undercarriage retraction jack
103 Wing fold locking cylinder
104 Machine-gun muzzle
105 Centre section leading edge construction
106 Front fuselage frames
107 Rudder pedals
108 Back of instrument panel
109 Control column
110 Pilot's sliding entry hatch
111 Illuminated torpedo sight
112 Instrument panel shroud
113 Windscreen panels
114 Ring-and-bead gunsight
115 Gun camera
116 Port split trailing edge flaps
117 Remote compass transmitter
118 Aileron control rods
119 Aileron hinge control
120 Fabric covered port aileron
121 Aileron trim tab
122 Formation light
123 Pitot tube
124 Port navigation light
125 Fixed leading edge slot
126 Wing 'tie-down' shackle
127 ASB aerial mounting
128 Retractable landing lamp
129 Red, white and green approach lights
130 Port ASB aerial
131 Ground attack rockets (5-in/12.7-cm)
132 Oil tank filler cap
133 Engine oil tank (13 US gal/49 litre capacity)
134 Engine compartment bulkhead
135 Engine mounting struts
136 Cowling air exit flap
137 Twin carburettors
138 Carburettor air trunking
139 Wright R-2600-8 Cyclone 14-cylinder two-row radial engine
140 Carburettor air intake
141 Propeller governor
142 Reduction gearbox
143 Hamilton Standard three-bladed variable-pitch propeller
144 Engine cooling intake
145 Engine cowlings
146 Cowling air flap control lever
147 Lower cowling air flap
148 Batteries
149 Starboard exhaust pipe
150 Oil cooler
151 Oil cooler air exit flap
152 Bomb release shackle
153 Four 500-lb (226.8-kg) bombs
154 Bomb bay door construction
155 Bomb doors (open)
156 Port mainwheel
157 Bomb bay jettisonable fuel tank (270 US gal/1,022 litres capacity)
158 Main undercarriage leg door
159 Retraction strut
160 Shock absorber leg strut
161 Torque scissor links
162 Hydraulic brake pipe
163 Starboard mainwheel
164 Removable wheel disc cover
165 Torpedo stabilizing vanes
166 Mk 13-2 torpedo

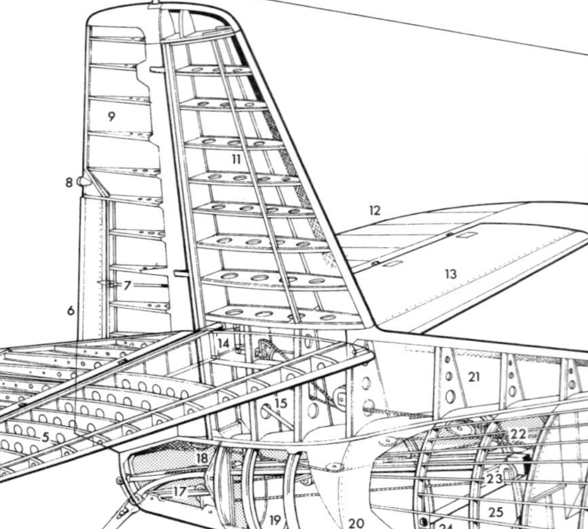

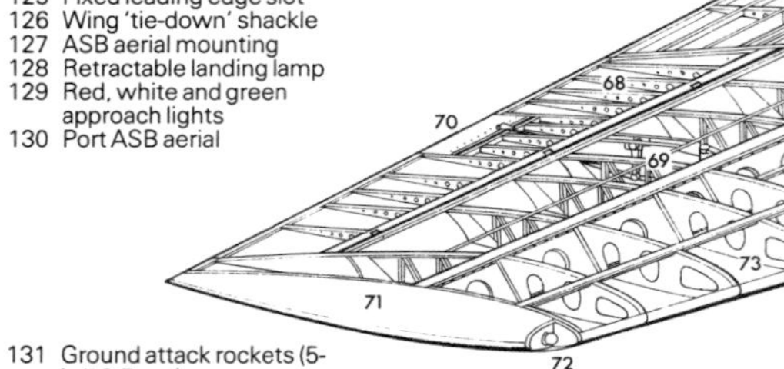

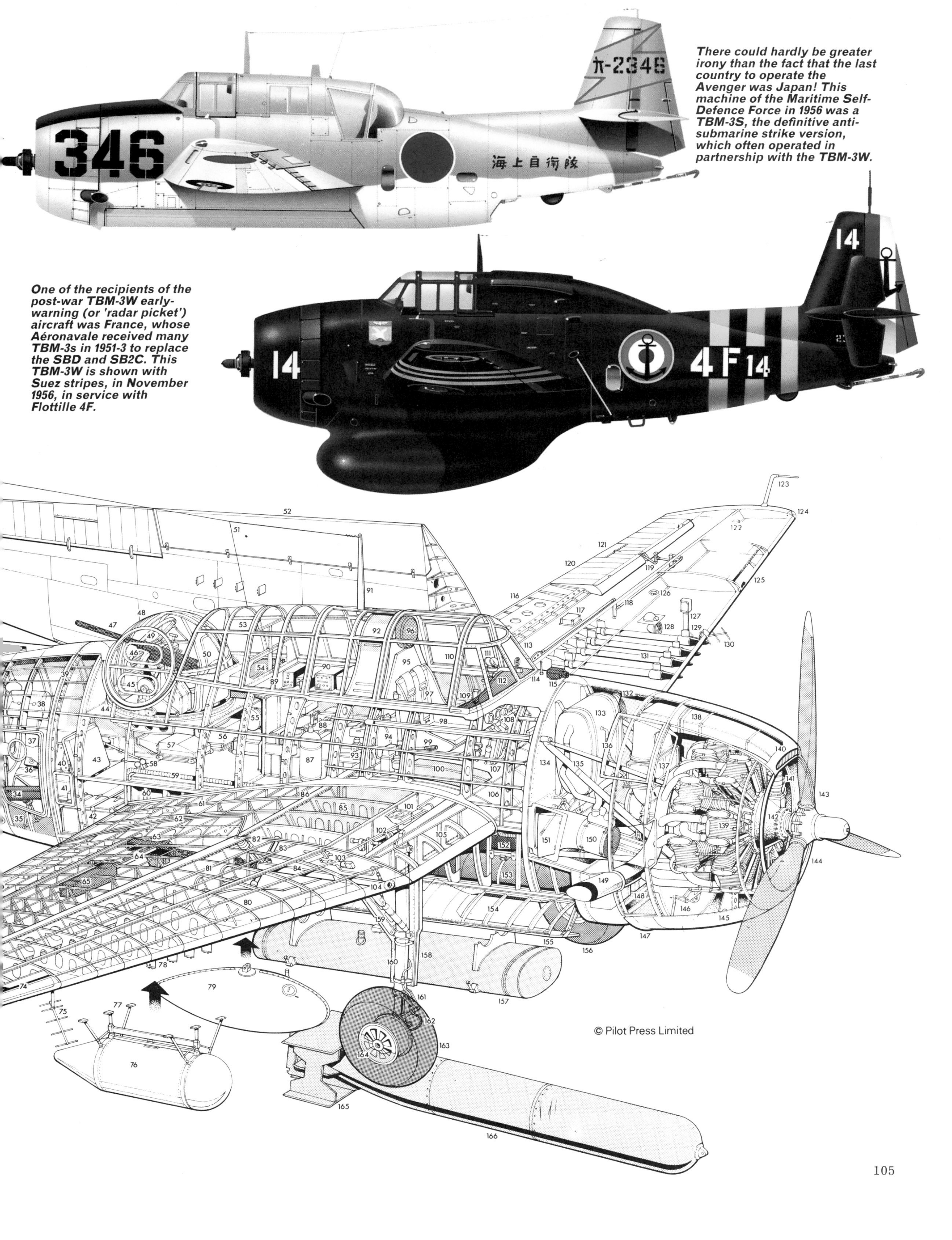

There could hardly be greater irony than the fact that the last country to operate the Avenger was Japan! This machine of the Maritime Self-Defence Force in 1956 was a TBM-3S, the definitive anti-submarine strike version, which often operated in partnership with the TBM-3W.

One of the recipients of the post-war TBM-3W early-warning (or 'radar picket') aircraft was France, whose Aéronavale received many TBM-3s in 1951-3 to replace the SBD and SB2C. This TBM-3W is shown with Suez stripes, in November 1956, in service with Flottille 4F.

This drawing depicts one of the first TBF-1s to come off the line at Bethpage in early 1942. Only about 200 were delivered with the national insignia as shown, a red border with white rectangles being added in June 1943. The colour scheme of sea blue fading through grey to a white underside was introduced in 1943, all earlier TBFs having the original scheme of sea green above and light grey below. Other points of interest include the kinked steel main legs, fixed slots ahead of the fabric-covered ailerons, and crew door in the side of the rear fuselage.

Specification

Grumman TBF-1 Avenger

Type: three-seat carrier-based torpedo-bomber

Powerplant: one 1268-kW (1,700-hp) Wright R-2600-8 Cyclone 14-cylinder two-row radial piston engine

Performance: maximum speed 436 km/h (271 mph); typical long-range cruise 233 km/h (145 mph); range on internal fuel 1778 km (1,105 miles)

Weights: empty (TBF-1C) 4788 kg (10,555 lb); maximum loaded 7876 kg (17,364 lb)

Dimensions: span 16.51 m (54 ft 2 in); length 12.2 m (40 ft 0.2 in); height 4.19 m (13 ft 9 in); wing area 45.52 m^2 (490 sq ft)

Armament: one 7.62-mm (0.3-in) gun firing ahead (in TBF-1C, two 12.7-mm/0.5-in), one 12.7-mm (0.5-in) in turret and one 7.62-mm (0.3-in) in lower rear position; internal bay for one 577-mm (22.7-in) torpedo or up to 907 kg (2,000 lb) of other stores.

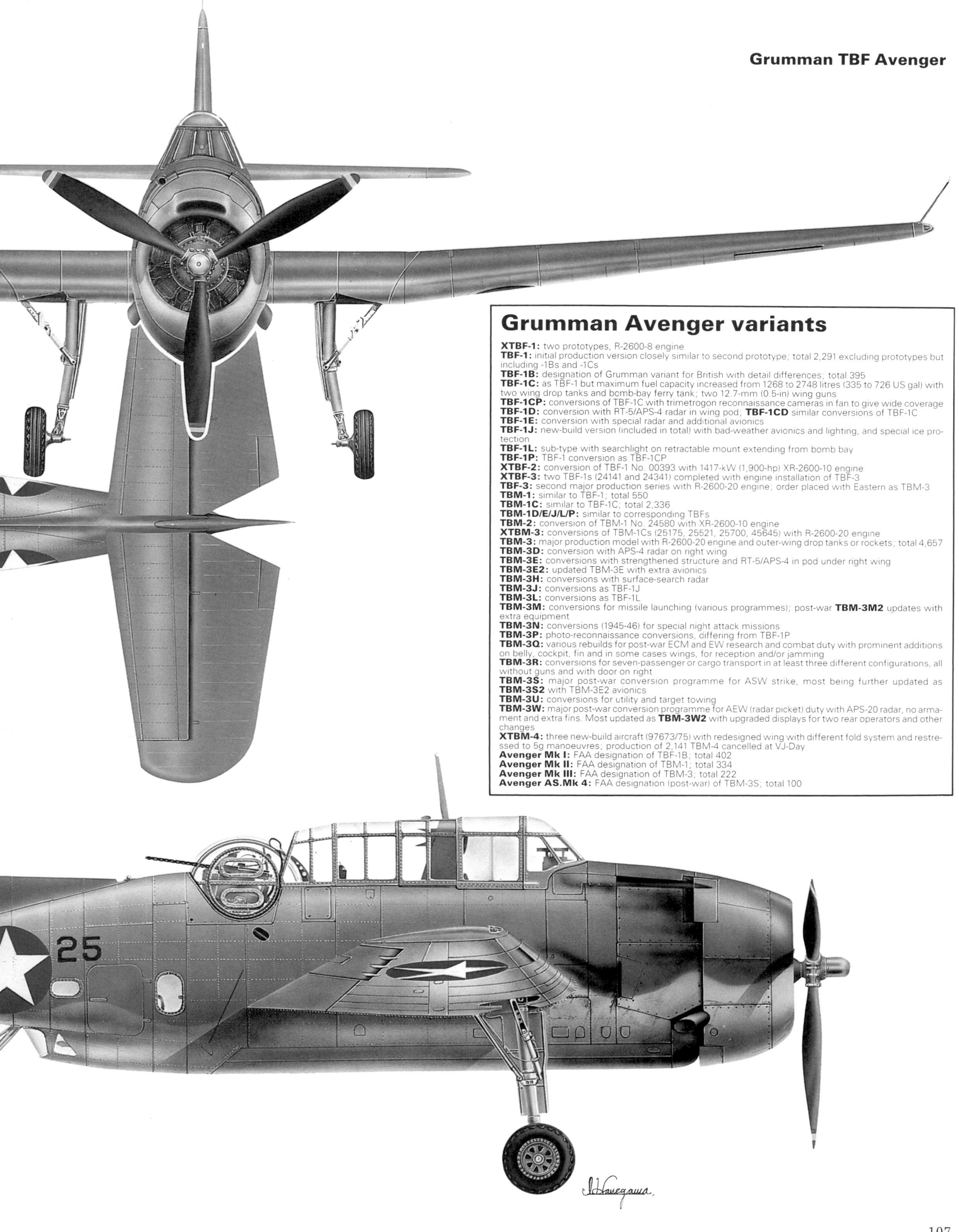

Grumman Avenger variants

XTBF-1: two prototypes, R-2600-8 engine
TBF-1: initial production version closely similar to second prototype; total 2,291 excluding prototypes but including -1Bs and -1Cs
TBF-1B: designation of Grumman variant for British with detail differences; total 395
TBF-1C: as TBF-1 but maximum fuel capacity increased from 1268 to 2748 litres (335 to 726 US gal) with two wing drop tanks and bomb-bay ferry tank; two 12.7-mm (0.5-in) wing guns
TBF-1CP: conversions of TBF-1C with trimetrogon reconnaissance cameras in fan to give wide coverage
TBF-1D: conversion with RT-5/APS-4 radar in wing pod; **TBF-1CD** similar conversions of TBF-1C
TBF-1E: conversion with special radar and additional avionics
TBF-1J: new-build version (included in total) with bad-weather avionics and lighting, and special ice protection
TBF-1L: sub-type with searchlight on retractable mount extending from bomb bay
TBF-1P: TBF-1 conversion as TBF-1CP
XTBF-2: conversion of TBF-1 No. 00393 with 1417-kW (1,900-hp) XR-2600-10 engine
XTBF-3: two TBF-1s (24141 and 24341) completed with engine installation of TBF-3
TBF-3: second major production series with R-2600-20 engine; order placed with Eastern as TBM-3
TBM-1: similar to TBF-1; total 550
TBM-1C: similar to TBF-1C; total 2,336
TBM-1D/E/J/L/P: similar to corresponding TBFs
TBM-2: conversion of TBM-1 No. 24580 with XR-2600-10 engine
XTBM-3: conversions of TBM-1Cs (25175, 25521, 25700, 45645) with R-2600-20 engine
TBM-3: major production model with R-2600-20 engine and outer-wing drop tanks or rockets; total 4,657
TBM-3D: conversion with APS-4 radar on right wing
TBM-3E: conversions with strengthened structure and RT-5/APS-4 in pod under right wing
TBM-3E2: updated TBM-3E with extra avionics
TBM-3H: conversions with surface-search radar
TBM-3J: conversions as TBF-1J
TBM-3L: conversions as TBF-1L
TBM-3M: conversions for missile launching (various programmes); post-war **TBM-3M2** updates with extra equipment
TBM-3N: conversions (1945-46) for special night attack missions
TBM-3P: photo-reconnaissance conversions, differing from TBF-1P
TBM-3Q: various rebuilds for post-war ECM and EW research and combat duty with prominent additions on belly, cockpit, fin and in some cases wings, for reception and/or jamming
TBM-3R: conversions for seven-passenger or cargo transport in at least three different configurations, all without guns and with door on right
TBM-3S: major post-war conversion programme for ASW strike, most being further updated as **TBM-3S2** with TBM-3E2 avionics
TBM-3U: conversions for utility and target towing
TBM-3W: major post-war conversion programme for AEW (radar picket) duty with APS-20 radar, no armament and extra fins. Most updated as **TBM-3W2** with upgraded displays for two rear operators and other changes
XTBM-4: three new-build aircraft (97673/75) with redesigned wing with different fold system and restressed to 5g manoeuvres; production of 2,141 TBM-4 cancelled at VJ-Day
Avenger Mk I: FAA designation of TBF-1B; total 402
Avenger Mk II: FAA designation of TBM-1; total 334
Avenger Mk III: FAA designation of TBM-3; total 222
Avenger AS.Mk 4: FAA designation (post-war) of TBM-3S; total 100

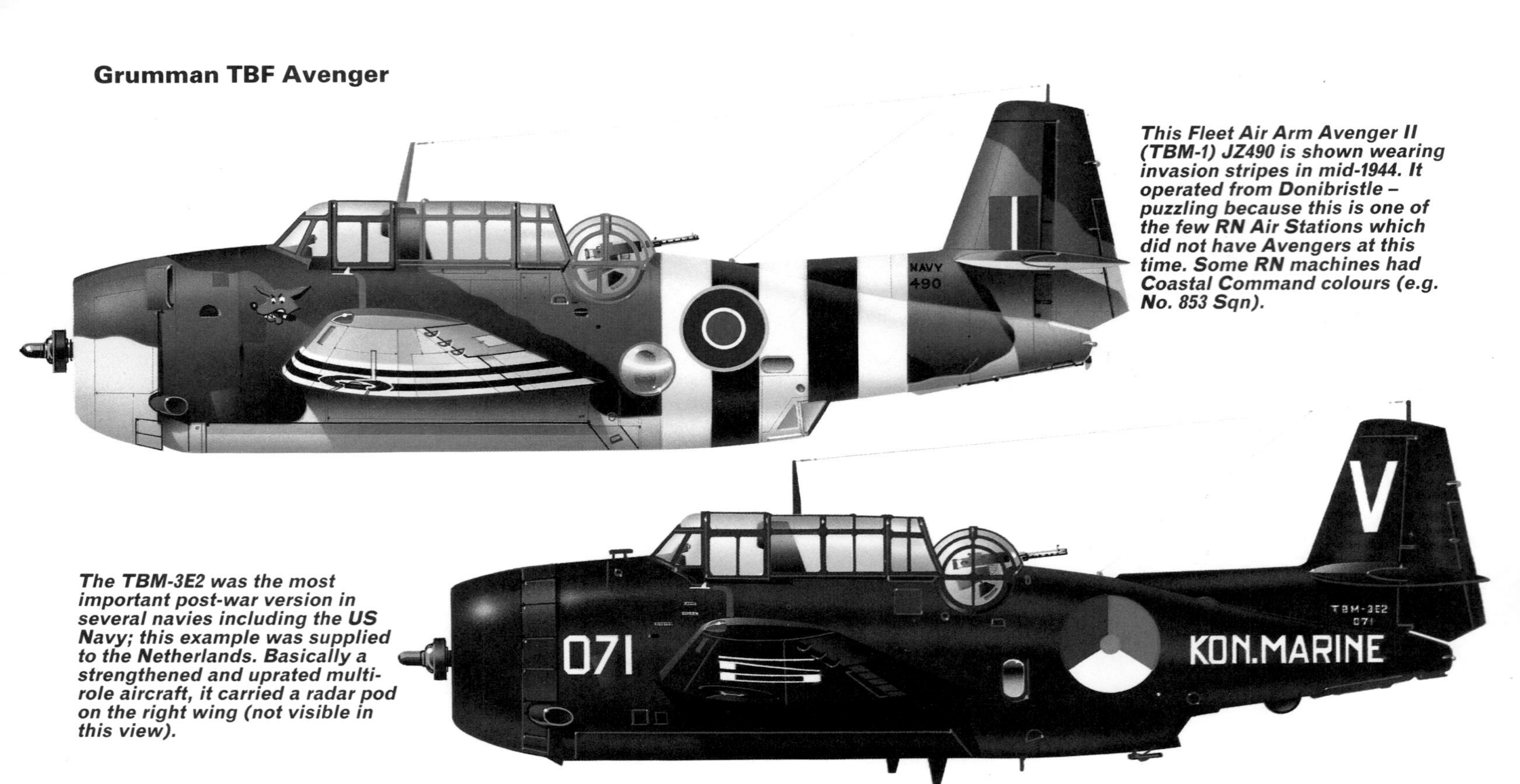

This Fleet Air Arm Avenger II (TBM-1) JZ490 is shown wearing invasion stripes in mid-1944. It operated from Donibristle – puzzling because this is one of the few RN Air Stations which did not have Avengers at this time. Some RN machines had Coastal Command colours (e.g. No. 853 Sqn).

The TBM-3E2 was the most important post-war version in several navies including the US Navy; this example was supplied to the Netherlands. Basically a strengthened and uprated multi-role aircraft, it carried a radar pod on the right wing (not visible in this view).

almost turn like a fighter, and quite early in production it was decided to increase the forward-firing armament, the TBF-1C having the 7.62-mm (0.3-in) nose gun replaced by two of 12.7-mm (0.5-in) calibre in the outer wings, each with 600 rounds. These are included in the Grumman total of 2,291, no breakdown being possible. This total also includes 395 TBF-1Bs, which were fitted with British radio and several other different equipment items for the Fleet Air Arm.

Altogether the FAA received no fewer than 921 Avengers (the original British name Tarpon being dropped), which equipped first-line squadrons Nos 820, 828, 832, 845, 846 and 848 to 857 inclusive, as well as second-line Nos 703, 706, 707, 711, 721, 733, 736, 738, 756, 759, 763, 767, 768, 778, 783-787, 797 and 798.

In December 1941 the urgent need for TBFs made it essential to find a second-source producer. General Motors had five plants on the east coast (Tarrytown, Linden, Bloomfield, Trenton and Baltimore), which were without work. Quickly they were organised into a powerful team called Eastern Aircraft Division, and they tooled up to build not only Wildcat fighters under the designation FM but also Avengers, the latter being designated TBM. The various versions are all listed separately. By December 1943 the 1,000th Eastern TBM had been delivered, and the final total by VJ-Day from this builder was no fewer than 7,546. Most were of the TBM-3 type, with more power and an external arrester hook, often with no turret and in all cases with provision for outer-wing rockets or drop tanks. The Dash-1D (TBF and TBM) and TBM-3D, and also the TBM-3E, had the RT-5/APS-4 search radar, operating at 3-cm wavelength, in a pod well outboard on the right wing.

Thus by the end of the war 9,836 Avengers had been produced, including small numbers of many special variants of which perhaps the most significant was the Project Cadillac test-bed, first of the TBM-3W series, which in November 1946 became the first aircraft to fly the APS-20 surveillance radar in a giant 'Guppy' radome. After 1945 the dominant model was the TBM-3E, used both with and without a turret, and supplied under the Mutual Assistance Program to many friendly navies, including those of Canada, France, the Netherlands and, later, Japan (the country against which most Avengers had fought!). In 1953 the poor state of the British Fleet Air Arm resulted in the supply of 100 of the TBM-3S anti-submarine model as the Avenger AS.Mk 4, these retaining their midnight-blue livery and serving until 1957 with both the RN and RNVR. In the US Navy the Dash-3S served in hunter/killer pairs with the Dash-3W and -3W2 with 'Guppy' radars and triple fins until June 1954, several utility models going on for years longer.

A fine picture of an Avenger Mk I (originally Tarpon I) of the Fleet Air Arm. JZ165 was one of the last of 402 of this mark to be delivered, and it operated with No. 852 Sqn as aircraft 2P on operations in northern Europe, mainly from the escort carrier HMS Trumpeter.

A TBM-3E of the US Marine Corps letting go 227-kg (500-lb) bombs on a target in mainland Japan in June 1945. This was one of the definitive versions of the Avenger, with radar in a pod mounted under the wing.

US Navy Pacific Air Fleet

Currently replacing the Vought A-7 Corsair II in the light attack role, the McDonnell Douglas F-18 Hornet is primarily based at NAS Lemoore for duties with the Pacific Air Fleet. This versatile design is also tasked with strike fighter duties within the composition of each Navy Carrier Air Wing.

The giant US Navy organisation conveniently splits itself in half to maintain its worldwide commitments; the Atlantic Fleet covering that ocean and the Mediterranean, while the Pacific covers the giant tracts of sea to the west of the United States. Here we look at the latter's airpower.

Although the aircraft-operating elements of the US Navy's Pacific Fleet actually constitute only a fairly small part of the contemporary Navy organisation in general, they do represent a most potent force in their own right and one with extremely wide-ranging responsibilities. Indeed, so vast is the area covered that Pacific Fleet fixed- and/or rotary-wing units may be found virtually anywhere in the Pacific, flying from aircraft-carriers and surface combatants or from one of the dozen or so air bases that the Navy regularly uses.

Overall control of aviation units is entrusted to the Commander Naval Air Force, Pacific Fleet (ComNavAirPac), with headquarters at North Island, California. Located adjacent to San Diego (a town which has long enjoyed close ties with the Navy), the naval complex is extremely large and includes a fully-fledged Naval Air Station with adjacent berthing facilities for aircraft carriers as well as a major dockyard, while just a few miles to the north lies NAS Miramar, home for a large number of fighter and airborne early warning units and one of the key west-coast centres of naval aviation.

Such is the size of the ComNavAirPac organisation it is clearly impossible for this one agency to exercise effective control over all its various assets. Consequently, the Navy has adopted the so-called 'community concept' whereby individual squadrons are grouped together under the direct control of a number of major subordinate commands, these providing a link between operating units and the more rarified levels of the chain.

For the most part, the squadrons assigned to a particular 'Community' operate similar equipment and are engaged on similar tasks; an example of this being provided by the Light Attack Wing Pacific (LAtWingPac) at NAS Lemoore in California. Although this furnishes administrative support to the Vought A-7E Corsair- and McDonnell Douglas F/A-18A Hornet-equipped attack (VA) and strike fighter (VFA) squadrons of the Pacific Fleet, operational control is generally retained by organisations known as Carrier Air Wings (CVWs). Individual squadrons only look to LAtWingPac for operational and administrative control on the rare occasions when not assigned to a CVW, such as occurs during the course of transition to new equipment.

Another LAtWingPac responsibility is training, non-deployable squadrons like VA-122 (A-7) and VFA-125 (F/A-18) serving as a source of replacement air and ground crews for the front-line operational echelons which operate these types. In addition, dedicated 'aggressor' units are attached to some of the functional CVW commands, these being epitomised by VFA-127 which operates McDonnell Douglas TA-4 Skyhawks and Northrop F-5Es from NAS Lemoore.

Long-range patrol missions are the domain of the Lockheed P-3 Orion force, which equips two Patrol Wings at NAS Moffett Field, California, and NAS Barbers Point, Hawaii. This example serves with VP-91 at the former base, one of seven patrol squadrons to operate from this west coast base. Given their long-range capabilities, several bases in the Far East act as P-3 mission support points.

Since its introduction into front-line service with the Pacific Air Fleet in the early 1970s, the Grumman F-14A Tomcat has proved a supreme fighter asset. Normal allocation in each Carrier Air Wing is two Tomcat-equipped squadrons. This example serving with VF-1 'Wolf Pack' as part of CVW-9 aboard USS Kitty Hawk.

Control at sea

At sea, however, overall responsibility for operational and administrative control of the various units embarked aboard a specific aircraft carrier is firmly in the hands of the CVW commander. A typical CVW is assembled around a hard core of five squadrons, comprising two VFs with Grumman F-14 Tomcats or two VFAs with F/A-18 Hornets, two light VAs with A-7 Corsairs or two VFAs with F/A-18 Hornets, and one medium VA with Grumman A-6/KA-6 Intruders.

Other elements which are usually to be found within a CVW consist of one fixed-wing ASW squadron (VS) with Lockheed S-3 Vikings, one helicopter ASW squadron (HS) with Sikorsky SH-3 Sea Kings, one electronic warfare (EW) squadron (VAQ) with Grumman EA-6B Prowlers, and one airborne early warning (AEW) squadron (VAW) with Grumman E-2 Hawkeyes, a typical large carrier having a total complement of about 85 aircraft. Individual squadron skippers are responsible to the CVW commander who, in turn, reports directly to the captain of the carrier to which his CVW is assigned.

The Pacific Fleet has a total of seven aircraft-carriers on charge, these comprising USS *Midway* (CV-41), *Ranger* (CV-61), *Kitty Hawk* (CV-63), *Constellation* (CV-64), *Enterprise* (CVN-65), *Nimitz* (CVN-68) and *Carl Vinson* (CVN-70). With the solitary exception of the *Midway* (home-ported at Yokosuka, Japan, and truly unique in being the only Navy carrier to be permanently stationed outside the USA), all of these are based on the west coast, deploying from there for periods of sea duty of varying length.

Short deployments are not uncommon and are generally conducted in support of the 3rd Fleet at Ford Island, Hawaii with responsibility for the Eastern Pacific (EastPac). Major deployments are much longer in duration, normally lasting around six months including transit time to and from the principal area of operations. In times of crisis, though, it is not unknown for carriers to spend considerably longer than six months away from the USA.

Broadly speaking the 7th Fleet's area of activity encompasses the Far East, and the fleet operates for most of the time under the direction of the specified Pacific Command (PaCom), an all-service organisation made up of elements drawn from the Air Force, Army, Marine Corps and Navy. Thus, while operational orders may be routed via normal naval channels, they may also originate from the National Command Authorities (NCA) in Washington, being passed via the joint chiefs of staff to PaCom and on to the 7th Fleet commander.

In addition to carrierborne forces, the 7th Fleet also controls other aviation-related assets, these being exemplified by Lockheed P-3 Orion-equipped patrol squadrons (VP). Once again, the operating system for these assets is based on deployment from US bases for extended periods of overseas duty – a typical tour lasting around six months. Bases which support VP units in the WestPac area are Kadena on Okinawa, Misawa in Japan, Agana on Guam (Naval Station Guam), and

Pacific Fleet: principal air bases

There are five principal West Coast US Navy air bases, each housing particular 'communities' of operational aircraft types and their associated operational infrastructures. In addition there are several secondary bases which provide front-line support such as training and maintenance.

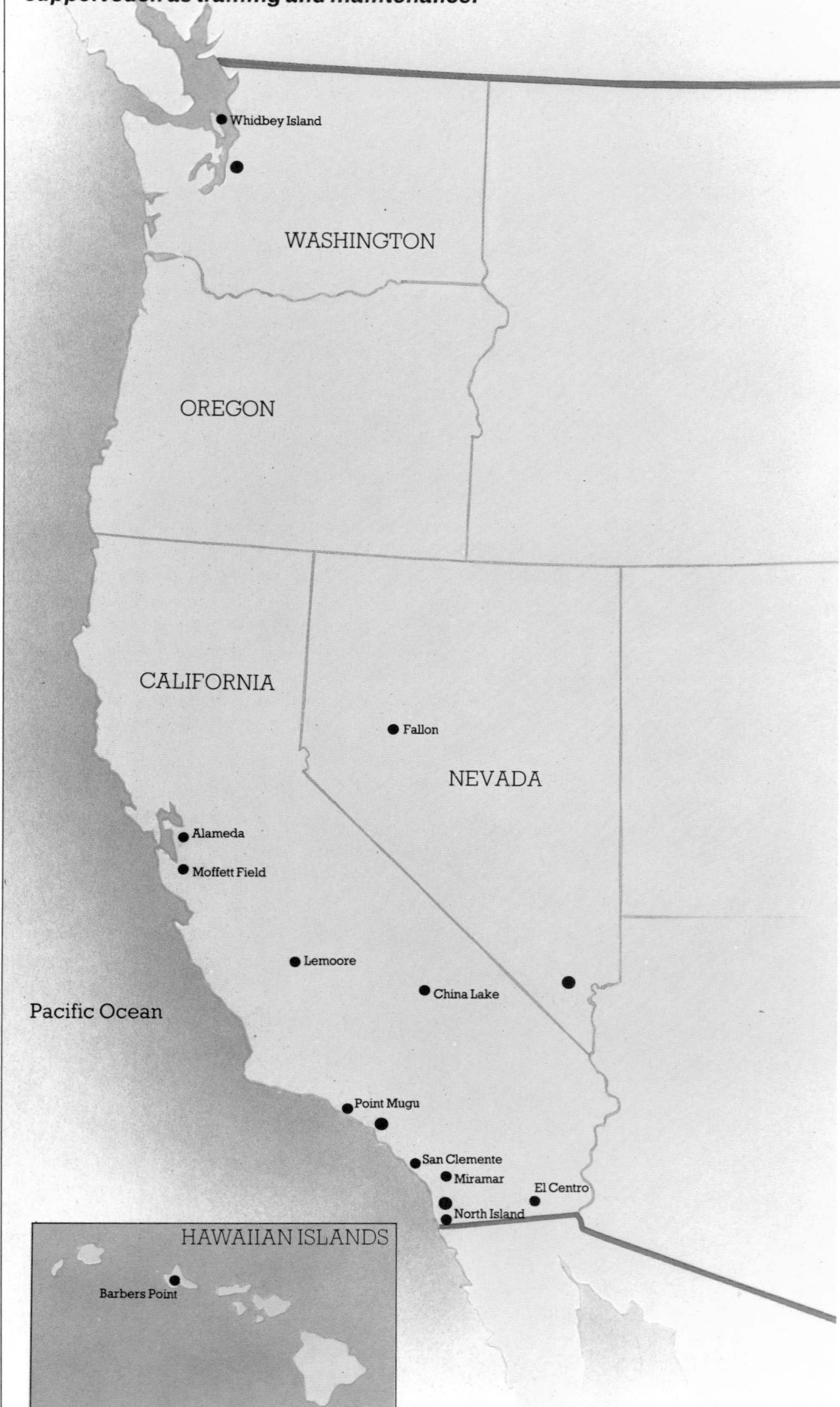

Thrown into the air by the steam catapult, a Vought A-7E Corsair II heads off for another mission in support of LAtWingPac operations with the Carrier Air Wing. For so long the backbone of the light attack force (invariably two squadrons per CVW), the venerable 'Fruit Fly' is quickly giving way to the F-18 Hornet within US Navy operations.

NAS Cubi Point in the Philippines.

Helicopter detachments

There is also a growing number of light helicopter ASW (HSL) squadrons which furnish LAMPS detachments to surface combatants like guided-missile cruisers, frigates and destroyers. A typical detachment will consist of a single helicopter (either a Kaman SH-2F Seasprite or Sikorsky SH-60B Seahawk) plus associated air and ground crew. Not surprisingly, the 'community' concept is pursued, most west coast HSL units being concentrated at North Island, also the home for some of the handful of helicopter combat support squadrons (HC) which are now active with the Pacific Fleet.

Pacific Fleet Aircraft Carriers

Carrier	Air Wing	Home Port
USS *Carl Vinson* (CVN-70)	CVW-15	Alameda
USS *Constellation* (CV-64)	CVW-14	San Diego
USS *Enterprise* (CVN-65)	CVW-11	Alameda
USS *Kitty Hawk* (CV-63)	CVW-9	San Diego
USS *Midway* (CV-41)	CVW-5	Yokosuka
USS *Ranger* (CV-61)	CVW-2	San Diego

Equipment assigned to and operated by HC units includes the Boeing UH-46 Sea Knight, Sikorsky HH-60H and the Sikorsky CH-53E Super Stallion, these generally being engaged on support duties varying from vertical replenishment while ships are under way at sea to more conventional resupply from fixed landing bases to ships at anchor offshore. Once again, extensive use is made of detachments, support vessels like combat store ships and ammunition ships featuring landing platforms and hangarage facilities for up to two UH-46s. Forward basing of a CH-53E squadron at NAS Cubi Point has, however, given a significant boost to helicopter support capability in the West-Pac area.

Resupply missions requiring both longer range and higher performance are undertaken by a couple of fixed-wing transport units (VR/VRC) operating a miscellany of types which includes examples of the McDonnell Douglas C-9B Skytrain II, the Rockwell CT-39 Sabreliner, the carrier-compatible Grumman C-2A Greyhound and Lockheed US-3A Viking and last, but by no means least, the Lockheed C-130F Hercules. Between them these types can generally meet immediate requirements, the fairly modest need for strategic airlift support normally being satisfied by Lockheed C-141B StarLifter and Lockheed C-5A/B Galaxys of the USAF's Military Airlift Command.

To return to the various 'communities', a more detailed look at their resources would seem to be appropriate and in view of the fact that the aircraft-carrier is by far the most powerful single-surface element of the Navy, carrierborne units would appear to be a good starting point.

With the exception of the McDonnell Douglas F/A-18 squadrons which are shore-based at Atsugi and routinely operate as part of CVW-5 aboard *Midway*, all Pacific Fleet fighter squadrons are concentrated at NAS Miramar, California, when not deployed. Universally equipped with the F-14A Tomcat, the 10 squadrons involved are all nominally attached to the Fighter and Airborne Early Warning Wing Pacific (FitAEWWingPac) – two squadrons being assigned to each of the five CVWs supported by US-based units (CVW-2, 9, 11, 14 and 15).

'Pairing' of units means that these always deploy together: thus, for instance, VF-1 and VF-2 have enjoyed an association which dates back to the time of their formation in the early 1970s, while VF-114 and VF-213 have even longer links, having operated together since 1964.

Other fighter units within the FitAEWWingPac organisation include a Tomcat-equipped training squadron (VF-124) and the much vaunted 'Top

The latest major helicopter type to enter service with the Pacific Air Fleet is the Sikorsky SH-60B Seahawk, primarily equipped for the Light Airborne Multi-Purpose System (LAMPS) role. The majority of the SH-60Bs deploy aboard the smaller ships within the Pacific Fleet such as 'Oliver Perry' class surface vessels, extending their operational capabilities in areas such as anti-ship surveillance.

The Carrier Air Wings in the Pacific Air Fleet are deployed aboard six aircraft-carriers, five of which are based on the west coast of the USA. In this shot, the USS Enterprise *shows off its fighting might in the form of Carrier Air Wing 11 (CVW-11). Up to 100 aircraft can be carried, and launches can be performed every 15 seconds when all four of the steam catapults are in operation.*

A Lockheed S-3 Viking gets the 'Go!' signal from the deck launch officer at the start of another anti-submarine sortie over Pacific waters. Viking operations are supplemented by the close-in surveillance task performed by the Sikorsky SH-3H helicopters.

Gun', more correctly known as the Fighter Weapons School, which operates General Dynamics F-16Ns, Northrop F-5 Tiger IIs and Skyhawks as 'aggressors' in the development of air combat skills.

As its title obviously implies, FitAEWWingPac also looks after the AEW elements of the Pacific Fleet, half-a-dozen squadrons flying the E-2 Hawkeye. Despite the fact that their missions may be said to be light years removed from one another, the combining of fighter- and AEW-dedicated aircraft within a single functional wing command does make good sense, for the Tomcat interceptors are in fact heavily dependent on the AEW skills of the Hawkeye for 'trade'. By putting both types on a single base, one is able to gain maximum benefit from 'cross-fertilisation'; liaison between those who fly these two disparate types actually being very close.

As already noted, the LAtWingPac is situated at NAS Lemoore, California, although, once again, two of the dozen front-line squadrons are forward-deployed at Atsugi. 'Teaming' is also a feature of the light attack force squadrons, these now being in the stages of a major re-equipment project which, ultimately, will witness the disappearance of the A-7E Corsair from the front-line inventory in favour of the rather more flexible F/A-18A Hornet.

Re-equipment has made good progress in the past couple of years, and the wider capability of the latter type has prompted a number of redesignations, former pure attack squadrons (VA) being known as strike fighter squadrons (VFA) upon conversion, a change which reflects the dual fighter and attack duties which the Hornet can perform with near equal facility. As is commonplace, LAtWingPac also features a number of permanently shore-based training units in its complement.

Northern base residents

Moving some considerable way north, NAS Whidbey Island in Washington serves as home for the Medium Attack/Electronic Warfare Wing Pacific (MAt/VAQWingPac) and controls the fortunes of a mixture of A-6E Intruder-equipped attack squadrons and EA-6B Prowler-equipped EW units, one example of each category being resident at Atsugi as part of CVW-5.

As far as the rest of the units are concerned, the five Intruder squadrons at NAS Whidbey Island permit assignment of one to each US-based CVW. But, in terms of squadron numbers, the Prowler force is somewhat larger with about a dozen members. The reason for this is quite simple, for Whidbey Island is the only Navy base with this type and, accordingly, it has to meet carrierborne EW requirements of both the Atlantic and Pacific Fleet CVWs. Training units are also in evidence at Whidbey Island; VA-128 fulfilling Pacific Fleet medium attack needs while VAQ-129 supports the Prowler force in its entirety.

Glossary

ASW Anti-Submarine Warfare
ASWWingPac Anti-Submarine Warfare Wing Pacific
ComNavForJapan Commander Naval Forces, Japan
CVW carrier air wing
EW Electronic Warfare
HC rotary-wing combat support squadron
HS rotary-wing anti-submarine squadron
HSL rotary-wing light anti-submarine squadron
LAMPS Light Airborne Multi-Purpose System
NAS Naval Air Station
VA attack squadron
VAQ electronic warfare squadron
VAW airborne early warning squadron
VC fleet composite squadron
VFA strike fighter squadron
VP patrol squadron
VQ fleet air reconnaissance squadron
VR fleet logistic support squadron
VRC fleet logistic support squadron, carrier capable
VS fixed-wing anti-submarine squadron
WestPac Western Pacific

The ability to operate a large number of aircraft in a variety of different but inter-related roles from aircraft-carriers offers the United States an excellent form of power projection. For the Pacific Air Fleet, operations are a round-the-clock affair.